HEIRLOOM FURNITURE

Living Room in the Author's Home

HEIRLOOM FURNITURE

FRANKLIN H. GOTTSHALL

BONANZA BOOKS · NEW YORK

To Mrs. I. Y. Stauffer, my Sister, who induced me to go to college to receive the type of training without which I could never have undertaken a work such as this.

ACKNOWLEDGMENTS

The author gratefully acknowledges the valuable assistance received from the following in the preparation of this book:

Mr. Daniel H. Unger, Boyertown, Pa., for permission to photograph and make measured drawings of the Unger corner cupboard and the Sheraton-type grandfather's clock.

Mr. and Mrs. I. Y. Stauffer, Boyertown, Pa., for permission to make measured drawings and take photographs of the Stauffer corner cupboard.

The Sherwin-Williams Co., of Cleveland, Ohio, for permission to quote a section of their brochure F-501 on furniture finishes.

Mr. William Moeller, Gilbertsville, Pa., for information and directions on how to apply a hard oil finish.

Mr. Guy Reinert, Boyertown, Pa., for his photograph of the Stauffer corner cupboard.

Mr. Harry H. Saunders, Bockport, Maine, for the photograph of the light Sheraton side chair which he adapted from plans in the author's book HOW TO DESIGN PERIOD FURNITURE.

Mr. Daniel L. Bush, upholsterer, Boyertown, Pa., for valuable technical help on methods of upholstering the chairs shown in this book.

To the firm of Ball and Ball, Whitford, Pa., manufacturers of fine period brasses, who gave invaluable help in selecting and providing hardware from which the sketches were prepared for the various pieces of furniture.

Popular Science monthly, for permission to include the following which first appeared as magazine articles: the Welsh dresser, the lowboy, the Colonial ladder-back armchair, the Colonial slat-back rocker, the Chippendale wing chair, and paneled cedar chest.

Popular Homecraft magazine, for permission to include the following which first appeared as magazine articles: the Hepplewhite side chair, the Hepplewhite sideboard, the child's ladder-back rocker, the Butterfly table, the child's Hepplewhite rocker, the Georgian slant-top desk, the Governor Winthrop secretary, and the spinet desk.

The Homecraftsman magazine, for permission to reproduce the following which first appeared as magazine articles: the Colonial ladder-back rocker, the roll-top Duncan Phyfe desk, and the William and Mary dressing table, stool, and mirror.

The Furniture Manufacturer magazine, for permission to reproduce the following which first appeared as a magazine article: the Jacobean chest of drawers.

Industrial Arts and Vocational Education magazine, for permission to reproduce the following which first appeared as magazine articles: the hanging wall shelf and the trestle table.

FOREWORD

The United States has been fortunate in its heritage of the fine furniture which has survived from colonial days. For most of the fine pieces designed by the pioneer furniture makers and their English contemporaries embody elements of design which make them acceptable to present-day homes in which gracious living is characterized by a quiet dignity and serenity that provide relief from the rush of occupational and community life. In such surroundings, it is possible to have and enjoy the beauty of carefully adapted furniture which has its inspiration in early American pieces and in the better work of English designers of the late eighteenth century.

In the present book, a lifelong student and teacher of American and English furniture design has collected the best pieces of work done in his own shops by himself and by a few of his gifted students. He has correctly held that beauty in furniture is never the result of accident. True beauty is rather the outcome of a combination of careful planning and of observation and study of the rules of design tested and handed down by the master of bygone generations; it is also a result of keen understanding of the surroundings into which given pieces are to fit. And finally, Mr. Gottshall has supplemented his careful observance of the historic principles of the several periods, his own touches of talent, touches which add immeasurably to the charm and quality of the pieces. Truly every piece in this book is heirloom furniture.

WILLIAM C. BRUCE

CONTENTS

1.

THE STAUFFER CORNER CUPBOARD

This corner cupboard is one of the finest the author has seen. It is wide and deep, and the paneling on both ends adds to the refinement of this extraordinary piece of furniture. The Stauffer cupboard is built of American black walnut, which is native to eastern Pennsylvania. In this part of the state, where a considerable portion of the population takes justifiable pride in the ownership of family heirlooms, corner cupboards are among the most cherished of heirlooms.

The author has arbitrarily named this "The Stauffer Corner Cupboard," because it belongs to Mr. Isaac Stauffer and his wife, who is the author's sister. Mr. Stauffer's father purchased it at a country auction for a trifling sum many years ago, when many such priceless pieces were being discarded and replaced by the more flashy Empire and Victorian styles. Needless to say, the value of this cupboard today would exceed the value of a houseful of the furniture which replaced it.

Some of the original hardware has been replaced, and, as is often the case when substitutions are made, the wrong style drawer pulls were substituted. The hinges, the latches on the upper doors, and the escutcheons on the lower doors are the original ones. Through the courtesy of Mr. William Ball, Jr., of Ball and Ball, manufacturers of authentic period hardware, the author is able to show the proper hardware for this and other pieces shown throughout this book. The drawings have been made from Ball and Ball's large stock of originals.

The feet on the Stauffer cupboard have probably been shortened to reduce the height so the cupboard would fit into a low-ceilinged room. The original shape of the feet was something like the shape shown in Figure 7. Any reproduction of this piece should have feet of the correct design.

Stauffer Corner Cupboard

1

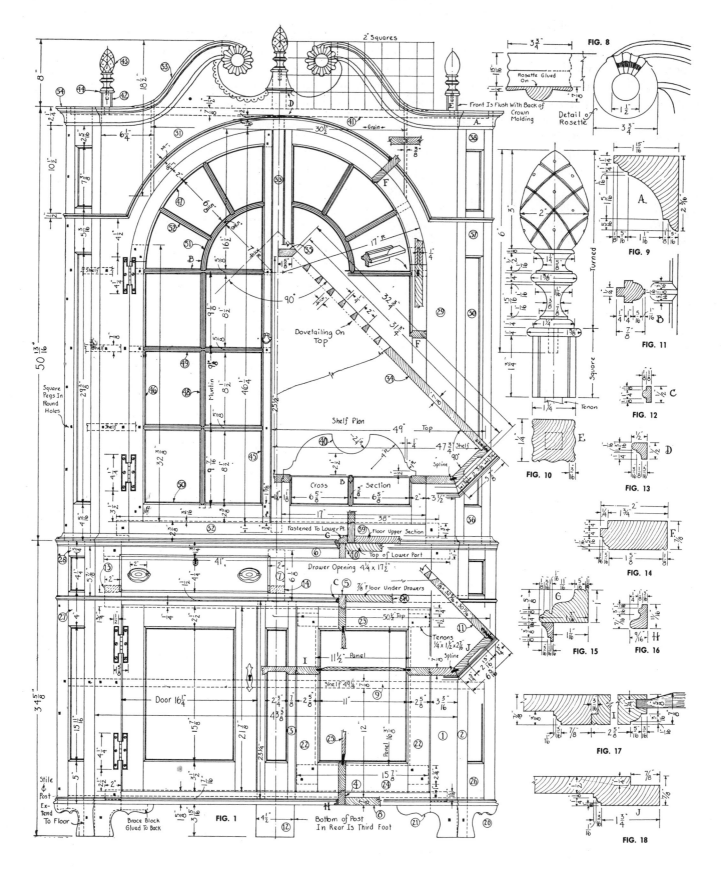

FIG. 1

FIG. 8

FIG. 9

FIG. 10

FIG. 11

FIG. 12

FIG. 13

FIG. 14

FIG. 15

FIG. 16

FIG. 17

FIG. 18

PROCEDURE

Corner cupboards of this type, with the exception of those which are built in and, therefore, an integral part of the architectural setting, are always built as two separate units which are placed one upon the other. Start by building the lower section first. This unit consists essentially of two wide boards for the back, *11*, a back post, *12*, two corner posts, *2*, two stiles, *1*, three rails, *4*, *5*, and *6*, and another stile, *3* (Fig. 1).

Glue up the stock for the wide backs. Since the inside of the upper section of the cupboard is to be painted white, ivory, or a pale yellow-green, the backs, floor, shelves, top, and back posts of both lower and upper sections should be made of wood suited to this purpose, such as white pine or poplar. There are other good reasons for using pine or poplar: (1) the completed corner cupboard will be lighter in weight, and (2) wider boards usually are available in pine or poplar. Wide boards are a mark of quality in old pieces of furniture and, therefore, should enhance the value of reproductions.

Next, make the corner posts. These posts are shown in Figures 3 and 4 exactly as they appear on the original piece. However, two alternate types of construction are suggested here which might simplify the job. The corner posts can be made up of two stiles, three rails, and two panels. If equipment for making molding is at hand, the stiles and rails should be molded on their edges. The construction will then be as shown in Figure 2. A still simpler method is to make the stiles and rails without molded edges, and then glue and brad the panel molding on afterward. The latter method would be the least expensive and easiest way, but the quality of the finished product also would be reduced accordingly.

BILL OF MATERIAL

LOWER SECTION (Italicized numbers correspond with encircled numbers in the drawings, Figures 1, 4, and 6.)

DESCRIPTION	PIECES	DIMENSIONS
1. Stiles	2	7/8 x 3 3/8 x 34 5/8
2. End posts	2	7/8 x 6 5/16 x 34 5/8
3. Stile	1	7/8 x 4 7/8 x 23 1/4
4. Rail	1	7/8 x 1 5/8 x 41
5. Rail	1	7/8 x 1 3/4 x 41
6. Rail	1	7/8 x 1 3/4 x 41
7. Stile	1	7/8 x 2 x 6 1/8
8. Floor	1	7/8 x 26 9/16 x 49 1/4
9. Shelf	1	7/8 x 26 9/16 x 49 1/4
9A. Floor under drawers	1	7/8 x 26 9/16 x 49 1/4
10. Top	1	7/8 x 26 9/16 x 50 1/2
11. Backs	2	7/8 x 32 9/16 x 30 11/16
12. Back post	1	7/8 x 4 1/2 x 34 5/8
13. Short drawer guides	2	7/8 x 2 x 9 7/8
14. Middle drawer guide	1	7/8 x 2 x 26 9/16
15. Drawer fronts	2	7/8 x 4 1/2 x 17 7/8
16. Drawer sides	2	9/16 x 4 1/2 x 16 5/16
17. Drawer sides	2	9/16 x 4 1/2 x 10 1/16
18. Drawer backs	2	9/16 x 3 1/2 x 17 1/2
19. Drawer bottoms	2	1/2 x 16 3/4 x 16 1/4
20. Foot facing	2	11/16 x 3 15/16 x 6 1/2
21. Foot facing	2	11/16 x 3 15/16 x 7 1/4
22. Door stiles	4	7/8 x 3 1/8 x 21 7/8
23. Door rails	2	7/8 x 3 x 15 7/8
24. Door rails	2	7/8 x 4 x 15 7/8
25. Door panels	2	1/2 x 11 1/2 x 16 3/8
26. Fill-in rails corner posts	2	3/8 x 6 x 2 13/16
27. Fill-in rails corner posts	2	3/8 x 4 1/2 x 2 13/16
28. Fill-in rails corner posts	2	3/8 x 2 x 2 13/16

DESCRIPTION	PIECES	DIMENSIONS
UPPER SECTION		
29. Stiles	2	7/8 x 6 1/4 x 51 13/16
30. End posts	2	7/8 x 5 7/8 x 50 13/16
31. Front of pediment	1	7/8 x 18 1/2 x 30 1/2
32. Rail under doors	1	7/8 x 2 3/8 x 38
33. Stile between doors	1	7/8 x 1 7/8 x 48 3/8
34. Backs	2	7/8 x 31 3/4 x 50 13/16
35. Rear post	1	7/8 x 4 1/2 x 50 13/16
36. Fill-in rails end posts	2	3/8 x 4 9/16 x 2 3/8
37. Fill-in rails end posts	2	3/8 x 5 11/16 x 2 3/8
38. Fill-in rails end posts	2	3/8 x 4 13/16 x 2 3/8
39. Floor upper section	1	7/8 x 25 1/2 x 47 3/4
40. Shelves	3	7/8 x 25 1/2 x 47 3/4
41. Top	1	7/8 x 26 x 49
42. Finial pedestals	2	1 1/4 x 1 1/4 x 2 5/8
43. Finials	3	2 diam. x 6
44. Pedestal caps	3	1/4 x 1 5/8 x 1 5/8
45. Door stiles	2	7/8 x 1 1/8 x 46 1/4
46. Door stiles	2	7/8 x 2 3/8 x 32 3/8
47. Arched rails (make from stock)	2	7/8 x 9 x 24
48. Muntins (makes 6)	2	7/8 x 5/8 x 28
49. Muntins	6	7/8 x 5/8 x 17
50. Rails for doors	2	7/8 x 2 3/8 x 17
51. Curved muntins (make from stock)	2	7/8 x 4 x 11 1/2
52. Short muntins	4	7/8 x 5/8 x 7 1/8
53. Ogee pediment molding	2	1 15/16 x 5 1/2 x 20
54. Crown molding on end posts	2	1 15/16 x 2 1/4 x 7

Sizes of stock used for other moldings is not given, but should be determined from drawing. The same is true of hardware, glass, etc.

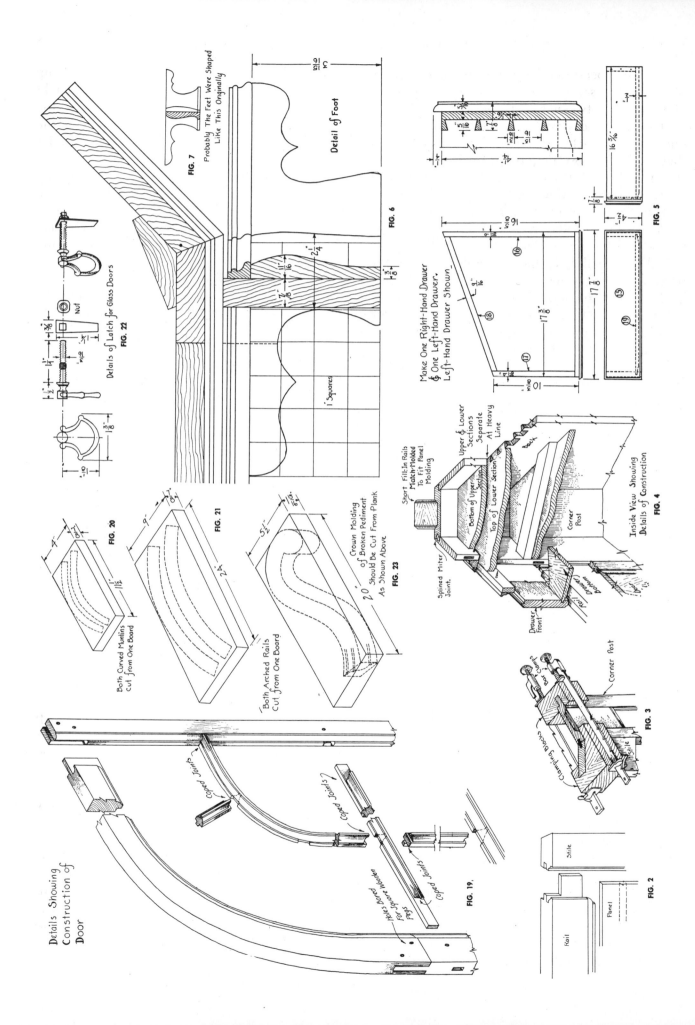

Details of Latch for Glass Doors
FIG. 22

Probably The Feet Were Shaped Like This Originally

Detail of Foot

FIG. 7

FIG. 6

Make One Right-Hand Drawer & One Left-Hand Drawer. Left-Hand Drawer Shown.

FIG. 5

1" Squares

Both Curved Muntins Cut from One Board

FIG. 20

Both Arched Rails Cut from One Board

FIG. 21

Crown Molding of Broken Pediment Should Be Cut From Plank As Shown Above

FIG. 23

Short Fill-In Rails Match-Molded To Fit Panel Molding

Upper & Lower Sections Separate At Heavy Line

Bottom of Upper Section

Top of Lower Section

Back

Corner Post

Drawer

Spined Miter Joint.

Drawer Front

Inside View Showing Details of Construction

FIG. 4

Corner Post

Clamping blocks

Stile

FIG. 3

Details Showing Construction of Door

Coped Joints

Coped Joints

Coped Joints

Coped Joints

Holes Bored For Square Wooden Pegs

FIG. 19.

Rail

Stile

Panel

FIG. 2

What has been said regarding the construction of the end posts also applies to the construction of the stile between the doors, 3.

Once the end posts have been made, rabbet one edge of each for the rabbet-and-butt joint that joins the post to the back (Fig. 18). Glue this joint and further reinforce it with walnut pegs, as shown in the plan view (Fig. 1). A few 2-in. brads, driven on a slight angle through the back into the posts, will also help strengthen this joint.

Make the stiles, 1, and the rails, 4, 5, and 6, next. Also make the short stile, 7, which goes between the drawers. Cut and fit the mortises and tenons on these pieces. Cut tenons on both ends of stile 3 and fit to the mortises in the rails. This stile is also rabbeted on both edges for a door stop. After the mortises have been cut on stiles 1, bevel the stiles and the corner posts to an angle of 67½ deg. on those edges on which they are to be joined together with a splined miter joint. Then cut the ¼-in. grooves for the spline.

Make the back post and bevel it on both edges to an angle of 45 deg. Next make the floor, 8, the shelf, 9, the floor under the drawers, 9A, and the top, 10. The dovetails on the top can be laid out more accurately after the frame has been assembled.

Now, assemble the frame of the lower section. To do this, first glue stiles 3 and 7 to the three rails, 4, 5, and 6. Then glue these rails to stile 1. Then, glue and assemble the splined miter joint, thus joining the corner posts to the assembled front frame. To make this joint tight, use clamps. For this purpose, first cut clamping blocks (Fig. 3). No fewer than three sets of these blocks should be used to glue a stile to a post.

Fasten the floor, 8, and the floor under the drawers, 9A, to the assembled parts. Do this by simply driving wooden pegs through holes bored into the stiles and end posts, as was done on the original cupboard. If this is done, glue blocks in back of the corner posts and stile 3 to help support the shelf. Nailing will give adequate support at the back. A better way is to use wood screws to fasten the shelf at the front, counterboring the screw holes to a depth of about ¼ in. and then plugging the holes with wooden pegs. The holes for the screws at the bottom of the frame need not be counterbored nor plugged, for the base molding will cover the screws. Apply glue to the edges of the backs, and fasten the

backs to the rabbets on the corner posts. Clamp these joints, glue, and peg them. Nail the backs to the shelf and floor. Then glue and nail the back post to these pieces. Before fastening the top in place, make and fasten drawer guides 13 and 14.

Trim the top so that it accurately fits the top of the assembled frame; then lay out the dovetails. Lay out and cut the tail members on the top first. Then, laying the top on the assembled frame, lay out the pin members with a scriber or sharp knife.

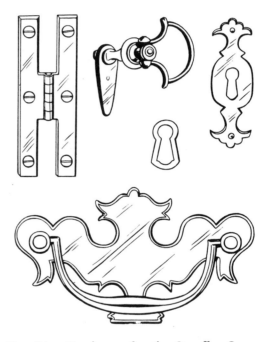

Fig. 24. Hardware for the Stauffer Corner Cupboard including the correct type of dawer pull

When the dovetails have been cut, fasten the top with glue on the dovetail joints and with screws at the front. These screw holes need not be plugged for the molding will hide them.

Make and attach the moldings C, D, H, and G. These should be glued fast, though a few small brads can be used to help hold them in place.

Now make the doors. Use Figures 1, 2, and 17 as a guide for making the joints, beveling the border of the door panels in the back. The doors are rabbeted on all edges to keep the cupboard dustfree. When locks have been installed, fasten the doors to the frame.

Next, make the drawers. Details are given in

Figure 5. Plywood, ⅜ in. thick, can be used for drawer bottoms in place of the solid stock found on the original cupboard.

Make the face boards for the scrolled bracket feet. It is best to cut a board long enough to make all four pieces, *20* and *21,* and to shape them as shown in Figure 6. Miter the corners to make the joint. Then, saw the scrolled brackets to shape on the band saw. Lay the feet on the stiles and corner posts where they are later to be fastened, and trace their shape on these members. Then remove the protruding parts of the stiles and corner posts with a coping saw so they will not show after the facings have been glued on.

The methods employed for making the lower section of the corner cupboard will also apply when making the upper section. The doors on the upper section are quite difficult and require equipment not ordinarily found in a home or school workshop. Most craftsmen will prefer to have them made in a planing mill. Construction details for making these doors are given in Figures 19, 20, 21; it is possible for a skilled craftsman with a shaper or molding planes to make the doors himself. This is true also of the other moldings needed for this cupboard. Large moldings, like those needed for the Ogee crown moldings and the molding *E* on the finial pedestal, are often carved entirely by hand with woodcarving chisels. The author has made many moldings in this manner.

Instructions for finishing this piece are found on page 149.

THE UNGER CORNER CUPBOARD

Curly maple is beautiful and its appearance improves with age. As a material for this unusually fine corner cupboard, it was a happy choice. Somewhat smaller and less roomy than the Stauffer corner cupboard, the Unger corner cupboard has characteristics which make it a very desirable piece of furniture to own.

The reason good curly maple pieces are so rare is that this distinctive type of marking is not found too frequently in maple lumber. The figure often is lost in the process of planing or turning. The masterful matching of grain on similar parts of this unusual corner cupboard, the beauty of other elements such as the lovely curvature of the swan-necked pediment and the bold, well-executed, carved brackets and finial — all bespeak the superb craftsmanship of a master. While the design would be worthy of reproduction in woods such as knotty pine, plain maple, cherry, or walnut, the choice of curly maple cannot be improved upon. Anyone who successfully reproduces this corner cupboard will have a replica of a masterpiece which museums would be proud to display.

It should be noted that plywood was not used on the original corner cupboard. Since its use for backs and drawer bottoms on a reproduction will be an improvement on the original construction, the substitution is justifiable. A superior grade of plywood should be used, such as panels faced with birch, maple, or white pine.

This corner cupboard and the Sheraton-type grandfather's clock (p. 111) are part of the fine antique collection belonging now to a close friend of the author, Mr. Daniel Unger. These unusual pieces had been gathered by Mr. Unger's father. It has been a privilege and a pleasure to reproduce two such fine designs in this book.

PROCEDURE

The Unger corner cupboard, like most corner cupboards, is built in two sections. Make the lower section first. Lay out stock for the corner posts, the back post, and the stiles back of the pilasters, cutting the mortises for rails 3, 4, and 5, Figure 1, on the inside edge of both stiles. Cut the rabbets on one edge of the corner posts for joining the backs.

The corner posts and stiles are joined together

Unger Corner Cupboard

7

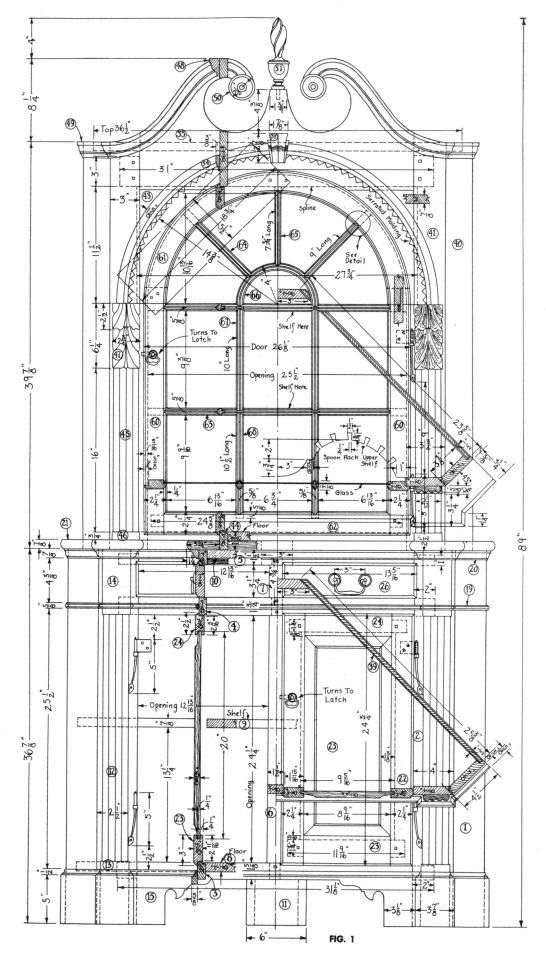

FIG. 1

with tongue-and-groove joints. The edge of the corner post should make an angle of 67½ deg. with the front of the post. Run the tongue-and-groove joints *after* the angles on these edges have been cut. The edge of the corner post can be angled for only half of its thickness before cutting the short tongue, unless the board is first made slightly wider than that called for on the bill of material. Glue these pieces together with extreme care to get the correct inside angle of 135 deg. (Fig. 10). (Angles for the lower-section corner posts and stiles will be the same as for those on the upper section.)

Next, make rails 3, 4, and 5, and lay out and

BILL OF MATERIAL

LOWER SECTION (Italicized numbers correspond with the encircled numbers in drawings, Figures 1, 2, and 9.)

DESCRIPTION	PIECES	DIMENSIONS
1. End posts	2	⅞ x 4½ x 36⅞
2. Stiles	2	⅞ x 4 x 36⅞
3. Lower rail	1	⅞ x 1⅝ x 31⅛
4. Rail under drawers	1	⅞ x 1¾ x 31⅛
5. Rail above drawers	1	⅞ x 1½ x 31⅛
6. Stile between doors	1	⅞ x 1½ x 26⅝
7. Stile between drawers	1	⅞ x 1½ x 4¾
8. Bottom of lower part	1	⅞ x 19⅜ x 39½
9. Shelf in lower part	1	⅞ x 19⅜ x 39½
10. Top of lower section	1	⅞ x 19⅜ x 39½
11. Back post in lower section	1	⅞ x 6 x 36⅞
12. Pilasters on lower section	2	¾ x 2½ x 24¼
13. Bases of pilasters	2	¾ x 2⅝ x 6¼
14. Capitals of pilasters	2	¾ x 2⅝ x 5⅞
15. Feet, scroll-sawed part below doors	1	⅝ x 5 x 28⅞
16. Short returns on sides of capital bases	4	⅝ x 5 x 1⅜
17. Ends of feet	2	⅝ x 5 x 4¾
18. Molding above feet		approx. 48
19. Molding between drawers and doors		approx. 48
20. Molding above drawers		approx. 48
21. Shelf, or table board, with half-round front edge, at top of lower section	1	⅞ x 6¾ x 43¼
22. Stiles in doors	4	⅞ x 2¼ x 24¾
23. Lower rails in doors	2	⅞ x 3 x 11⁹⁄₁₆
24. Upper rails in doors	2	⅞ x 2½ x 11⁹⁄₁₆
25. Panels	2	⅝ x 9⁹⁄₁₆ x 20
26. Drawer fronts	2	⅞ x 3½ x 13⁵⁄₁₆
27. Short drawer sides	2	⁹⁄₁₆ x 3³⁄₁₆ x 9½
28. Long drawer sides	2	⁹⁄₁₆ x 3³⁄₁₆ x 14½
29. Angled drawer sides	2	⁹⁄₁₆ x 3³⁄₁₆ x 8¼
30. Drawer backs	2	⁹⁄₁₆ x 3³⁄₁₆ x 8⅜
31. Drawer bottoms (plywood)	2	¼ x 12¹⁄₁₆ x 13⅞
32. Strip above drawers	1	⅝ x 3 x 19⅜
33. Long drawer run	1	⅞ x 3½ x 19⅜
34. Long drawer guide	1	⅞ x 1½ x 19⅜
35. Short drawer runs	2	⅞ x 7⅛ x 9⅝
36. Short drawer guides	2	⅞ x 6⅛ x 8⅜
37. Long support for drawer runs	1	⅞ x ⅞ x 36

DESCRIPTION	PIECES	DIMENSIONS
38. Short support for drawer runs	1	⅞ x ⅞ x 6
39. Backs (plywood)	2	½ x 25⅝ x 31½

UPPER SECTION

DESCRIPTION	PIECES	DIMENSIONS
40. End posts	2	⅞ x 3⅞ x 39⅞
41. Stiles	2	⅞ x 3¾ x 40⅞
42. Pediment board	1	⅞ x 13⅛ x 31
43. Corner pieces below pediment board	2	⅞ x 11½ x 8½
44. Rail below door	1	⅞ x 1⅝ x 31
45. Pilasters	2	⅝ x 2½ x 16
46. Base of pilasters	2	¾ x ¾ x 2⅝
47. Carved brackets	2	1⅜ x 2¾ x 6¼
48. Curved molding at top of pediment	2	⅞ x 4¼ x 16½
49. Molding at ends of top	2	⅞ x 1½ x 4¾
50. Rosettes	2	1 x 2½ diam.
51. Carved finial	1	2¼ diam. x 8¹⁄₁₆
52. Block under finial	1	⅞ x 1¾ x 5¼
53. Keystone block	1	¾ x 1⅞ x 2⅞
54. Serrated molding	2	⅜ x 5½ x 22
55. Top of upper part	1	⅞ x 17½ x 36¾
56. Shelves in upper section	2	⅝ x 17½ x 36¾
57. Floor of upper section	1	⅞ x 17½ x 36¾
58. Strip of wood at center, under floor	1	¾ x 3 x 17½
59. Back post	1	⅞ x 6 x 39⅞
60. Door stiles	2	⅞ x 2¼ x 23¹⁵⁄₁₆
61. Arched rail at top of door	2	⅞ x 5½ x 18¾
62. Bottom rail of door	1	⅞ x 2¼ x 24⅝
63. Horizontal muntins	2	⅝ x ⅞ x 25½
64. Slanted muntins at top of door	2	⅝ x ⅞ x 9
65. Vertical muntin at top of door	1	⅝ x ⅞ x 7¾
66. Arched muntin	1	⅞ x 4⁵⁄₁₆ x 8
67. Vertical muntins on middle of door	2	⅝ x ⅞ x 10
68. Vertical muntins on bottom of door	2	⅝ x ⅞ x 10½
69. Backs (plywood)	2	½ x 23⅝ x 39⅞

Hardware:

3 latches
3 pair rat-tail hinges
2 drawer pulls

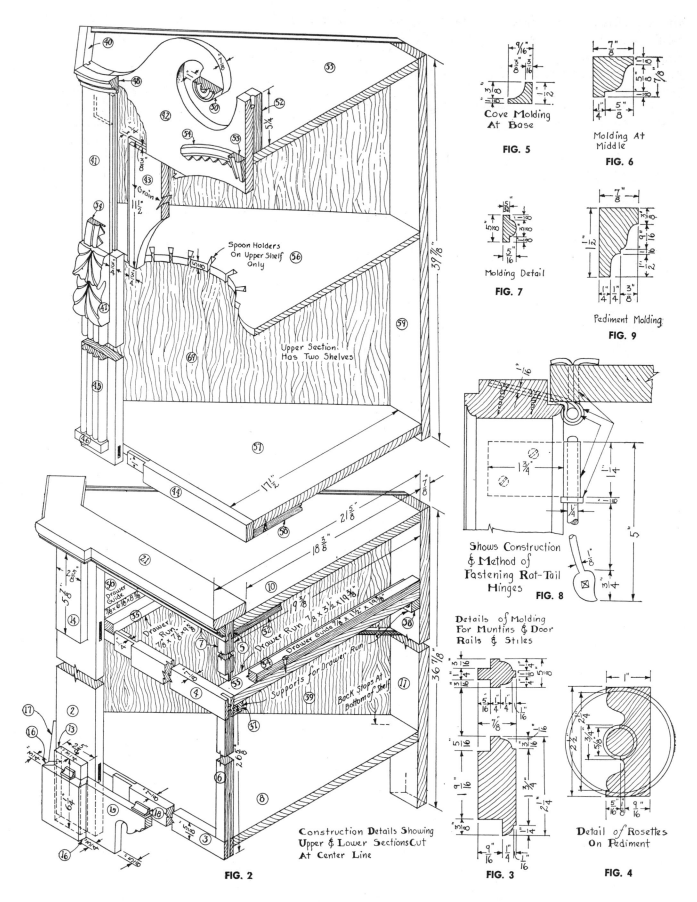

Cove Molding At Base
FIG. 5

Molding At Middle
FIG. 6

Molding Detail
FIG. 7

Pediment Molding
FIG. 9

Spoon Holders On Upper Shelf Only

Upper Section Has Two Shelves

Grain

Shows Construction & Method of Fastening Rat-Tail Hinges
FIG. 8

Details of Molding For Muntins & Door Rails & Stiles

Back Stops At Bottom of Shelf

Supports for Drawer Run

Drawer Guide
Drawer Run

Construction Details Showing Upper & Lower Sections Cut At Center Line
FIG. 2

FIG. 3

Detail of Rosettes On Pediment
FIG. 4

cut all mortises and tenons on these three pieces. Make stiles 6 and 7. Assemble pieces 3, 4, 5, 6, and 7, gluing and pegging the joints as shown in Figure 1. Carefully square the angles of all joints in this assembly. Join the assembled pieces to the assembled stiles and corner posts.

Now make the floor, 8, the shelf, 9, and the top, 10. Cut out the plywood backs and nail them to the back post. After properly placing the floor, the shelf, and the top, nail or screw them fast to the backs and backpost. In the front of the cabinet, nail the floor, shelves, and top where the pilasters will hide the nails after they have been glued to the stiles.

Make the drawer runs, 33 and 35, the drawer guides, 34 and 36, and the drawer run supports 37 and 38. Also, make the strip, 32, which keeps the drawers from dropping down when pulled out. Fasten all of these pieces in their proper places (Fig. 2).

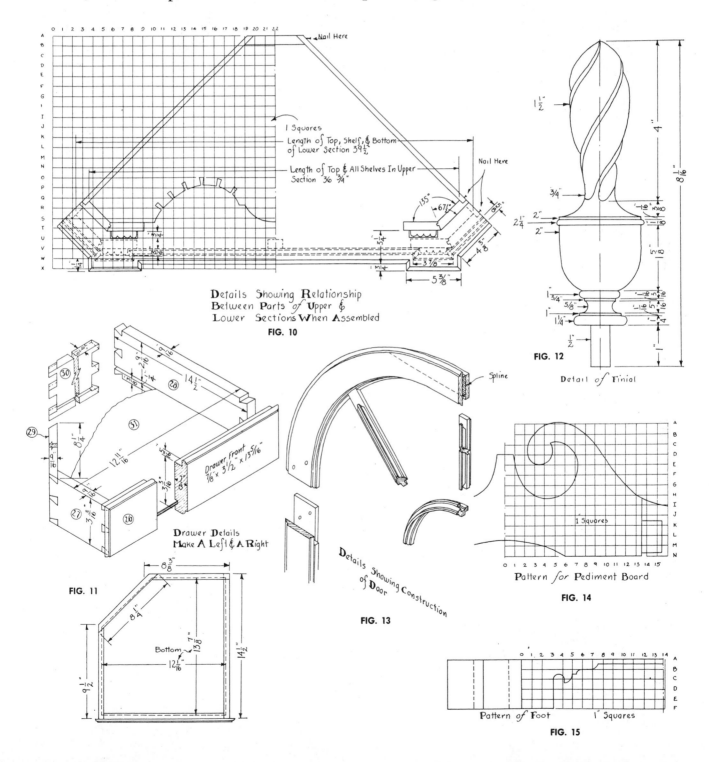

Details Showing Relationship Between Parts of Upper & Lower Sections When Assembled
FIG. 10

Detail of Finial
FIG. 12

Drawer Details
Make A Left & A Right
FIG. 11

Details Showing Construction of Door
FIG. 13

Pattern for Pediment Board
FIG. 14

Pattern of Foot
1" Squares
FIG. 15

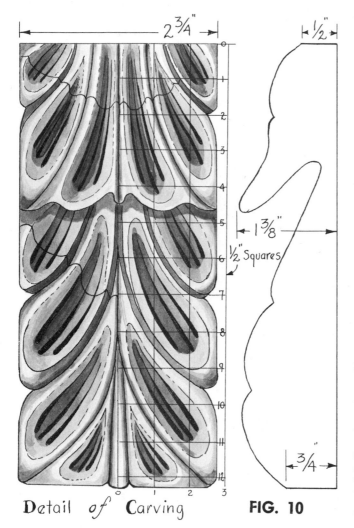

2 3/4"   1/2"

1 3/8"

1/2" Squares

3/4"

Detail of Carving   **FIG. 10**

Construct the drawers. The front, *26*, the sides, *27* and *28*, and the back, *30*, are dovetailed together (Fig. 11). As indicated in Figure 11, a right- and a left-hand drawer must be made.

On the upper section, as on the lower section, construction begins with the preparation of the corner posts, *40*, the stiles, *41*, and the back post, *59*. The stiles for the upper section are partly cut away at the upper end where the pediment face board, *42*, and the triangular-shaped pieces, *43*, are joined to them. The grooves and the mortises for the rail, *44*, and for joining the stiles and the pediment board should be cut first on the inside edges of the stiles. Then, cut the grooves on the opposite edges where the stiles are joined to the posts.

Cut the rabbets on one edge of the posts; then, glue the posts to the stiles, observing the same precautions recommended for assembling the frame for the lower section. Suggestions for making jigs with which to clamp such joints are shown in Figure 3 for the Stauffer corner cupboard.

Make the corner pieces, *43*, and the pediment board, *42*. A pattern for laying out the latter is shown in Figure 14. Glue the corner pieces and pediment board together; then glue this piece and the bottom rail, *44*, to the mortises and grooves in the stiles.

Prepare the backs, *69*, and nail them to the back post. Make the shelves, *56*, the floor, *57*, and the top, *55*. Nail these pieces to the stiles; then nail the assembled backs and post to the shelves and corner posts.

Make strip *58* and screw it fast to the bottom of the floor. Short pieces similar to this also can be fastened to each corner, below the floor, to strengthen these parts and to facilitate sliding the upper section into place upon the lower section.

Cut out the shelf, *21*, for the lower section at this time and fasten it with wood screws from below to the top of the lower section.

Lay out the pilasters, *45*, the bases, *46*, and the brackets, *47*, sawing them to shape as indicated in the side view of Figure 16. Carve the brackets. The details given in Figures 2 and 16 are sufficiently clear to indicate how the carving is to be done. Glue these members, *45, 46* and *47*, to the stiles. Make the arched molding, *54*, and the keystone, *53;* carve the keystone, and glue and brad both pieces fast. Shape or carve the curved molding and the short return mold-

After the upper section has been made, make the shelf, *21*, which fits around the upper section and holds it in place. The angles on the back edges of the shelf can then be marked accurately by placing the upper section on it and marking around it with a sharp pencil.

Next, cut out the pilasters, *12,* the bases of the pilasters, *13,* and the capitals of the pilasters, *14.* Glue these parts to the stiles.

Make the parts to be used for the feet, or base, next. Cut the miters carefully, as shown in Figure 2. Lay out a pattern for the scroll-sawed part from the detail in Figure 15. Cut out the small cove molding (Fig. 5) and fasten it to the top of this base. Make the moldings shown in Figures 6 and 7, and fasten these to their respective places.

Next, prepare the paneled doors. Figure 8 shows in detail how the rat-tail hinges are constructed and installed.

ing for the top; fasten these with glue and wood screws to the pediment board. Turn the rosettes as shown in Figure 4, and glue these fast. Turn the finial and carve it as shown in Figure 12.

The door remains to be made and assembled. As indicated in the chapter on the Stauffer cupboard, many craftsmen prefer to have this work done in a planing mill where better facilities are available. With details like those shown in Figures 1, 3, and 13, there is no reason why the door cannot be made in a home workshop of more limited facilities if the builder has the necessary skill. First, make the stiles, lower rail, and arched rails. Mortise these pieces after shaping the edges. Cut the muntin rails as long as the door is wide. Consult Figure 13 to make the joints. Note also that the two arched rails are joined to the stiles with a lapped joint, later glued and pinned with wooden pegs, and joined at the top with a spline. The spline necessitates cutting short the tenon of the vertical muntin at the top of the door.

After all the pieces are made, assemble them in the following order: First, join together the horizontal muntin rails, 63, and the 10-in. vertical muntins, 67. Join vertical muntins, 68, to lower horizontal muntins, 63; then glue these to the bottom door rail, 62. Glue these assembled pieces to the door stiles, 60. Then glue fast the arched

Fig. 17. Wrought iron rat-tail hinge for Unger Corner Cupboard.

muntin, 66. Fasten the slanted muntins, 64, and vertical muntins, 65, to the arched rails at the top, after they have first been joined together. Then fasten these assembled pieces to the lower part to complete the door.

Fasten the door to the upper section in the way the doors to the lower section were attached. Put on the latches. Except for putting glass in the door and giving the cupboard its finish, the Unger corner cupboard is completed.

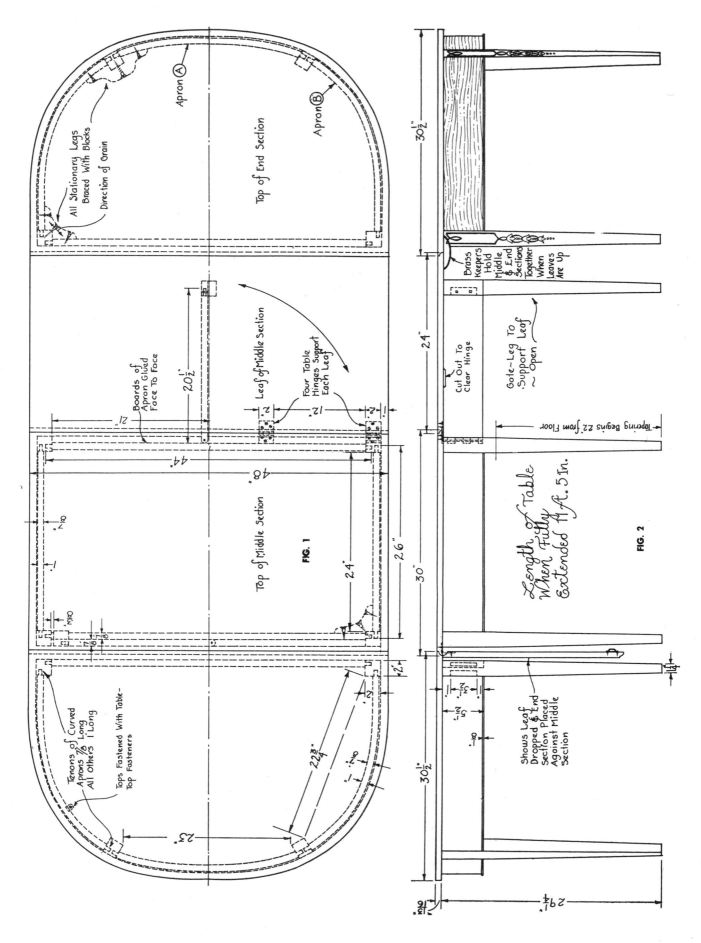

3.

HEPPLEWHITE DINING ROOM SUITE—DINING TABLE

We read, in historical novels and in history, of the elegance of eighteenth-century living among the gentry — the polished mahogany table, the snowy damask cloth, the gleaming silver, and the fine china. In show places like Mount Vernon, Monticello, and the "Palace" in Williamsburg, erected during furniture's golden age and preserved for posterity in their original or near-original state, we are given a glimpse of the grandeur of those bygone days.

These great houses contributed much to graceful living. The elegantly furnished dining rooms, for example, were an important part of the gay and colorful social life of the times. Some of this past glory deserves to be recaptured in homes of the present day. Perhaps no better start could be made than to build this dining-room suite. The suite was designed in the Hepplewhite style by the author and built by students at the Berry Schools, Rome, Ga., under the author's supervision. Hepplewhite was one of the greatest master craftsmen of the eighteenth century.

The building of such a suite should begin with the table, the most useful of the pieces. This table has many fine features. It has the beauty of fine materials: enduring mahogany, beautifully figured veneers, and exquisite marquetry. It has generous proportions. It has versatility, for its parts are adaptable to different uses. With the leaves raised, the central section seats ten people. Fully extended and with the end sections in place, the table will seat twelve and can seat more.

Mahogany used for this table and for all pieces of this suite should be of a top-grade Cuban or Honduras mahogany.

PROCEDURE

Square the 14 legs to the size given in the bill of material. Lay out and cut all the mortises (Figs. 1, 2, and 5). Make the layouts for tapering two opposite sides of each leg, then saw and plane them. Now taper, saw, and plane the two remaining sides of each leg.

Hepplewhite Dining Table

15

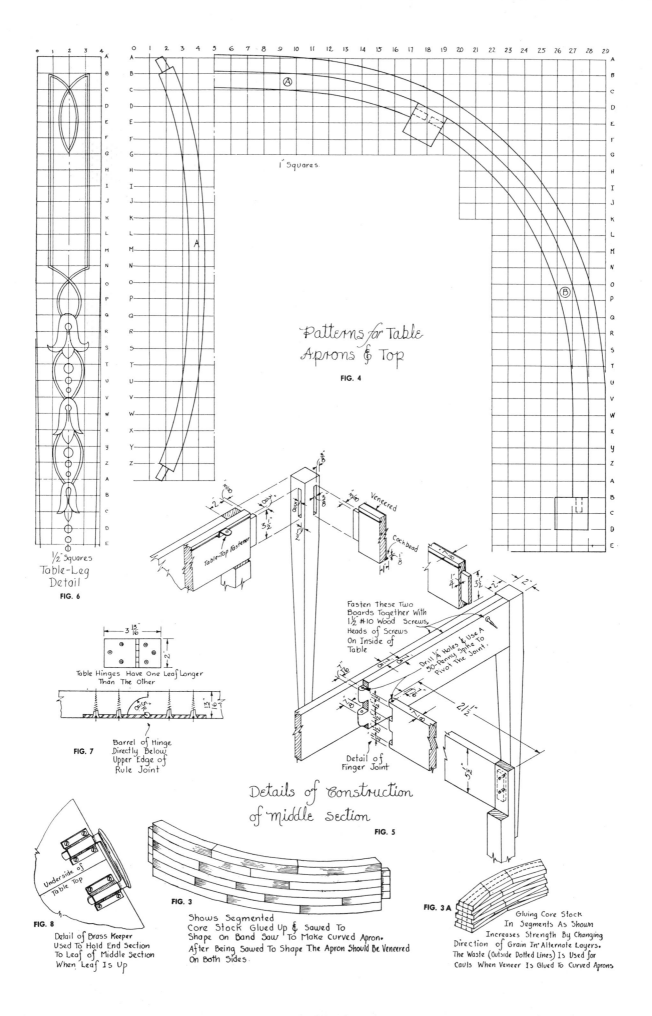

1" Squares

Ⓐ

Ⓑ

Patterns for Table Aprons & Top

FIG. 4

½" Squares
Table-Leg Detail
FIG. 6

3 13/16
2
Table Hinges Have One Leaf Longer Than The Other

5R
1 5/16

FIG. 7
Barrel of Hinge Directly Below Upper Edge of Rule Joint

Table-Top Fastener

Veneered

Cock bead
⅛

Fasten These Two Boards Together With 1½ #10 Wood Screws, Heads of Screws On Inside of Table

Drill ¼ Holes & Use A 50-Penny Spike To Pivot The Joint.

2½"
2"
2"
5½"

Detail of Finger Joint

Details of Construction of Middle Section

FIG. 5

Underside of Table Top

FIG. 8
Detail of Brass Keeper Used To Hold End Section To Leaf of Middle Section When Leaf Is Up

FIG. 3
Shows Segmented Core Stock Glued Up & Sawed To Shape On Band Saw To Make Curved Apron. After Being Sawed To Shape The Apron Should Be Veneered On Both Sides.

FIG. 3A
Gluing Core Stock In Segments As Shown Increases Strength By Changing Direction Of Grain In Alternate Layers. The Waste (Outside Dotted Lines) Is Used For Cauls When Veneer Is Glued To Curved Aprons

Marquetry is veneer with an inlaid design of contrasting colored woods that stand out boldly. Because mahogany is dark, the contrasting woods are usually white, yellow, or cream-colored, such as holly, satinwood, or tulipwood. These inlays frequently are shaded by singeing parts of them in hot sand, or dying them in various colors. The making of marquetry and inlays is a highly specialized art; it is advisable, therefore, to purchase marquetry from firms who specialize in their manufacture. The cost is reasonable.

Marquetry comes from the manufacturer with brown wrapping paper glued to one side. Glue the wood side of the marquetry to the face of the leg (Fig. 2), using a cold-water casein glue or a good grade of hot glue such as pure hide glue. If hot glue is used, both the veneer or marquetry and the stock should be warmed, over steam pipes or in some other manner, so that the glue will not chill before the clamps are made fast. A strip of ⅜-in. plywood clamped to the leg over the marquetry will insure a good bond, provided enough clamps are used.

After the glue has hardened and the clamps have been removed, sponge off the paper backing. When the surface has dried, clean it with fine

Hepplewhite Dining Table End Section

sandpaper. Care must be taken not to scratch or sand through the surface.

Next, glue up the stock for the curved aprons. Use well-seasoned or kiln-dried stock. Yellow pine and Honduras mahogany make the best core stock because they shrink less than most other woods and hold glue well. Figures 3 and

BILL OF MATERIAL

DESCRIPTION	PIECES	DIMENSIONS
Legs	14	2 x 2 x 29¼
Long aprons for end sections	2	⅞ x 5½ x 44
Long aprons for middle section	2	⅞ x 5½ x 44
Short aprons for ends of middle section[1]	2	⅞ x 5½ x 26
Stationary aprons with finger joints	2	⅞ x 5½ x 22
Movable aprons with finger joints	2	⅞ x 5½ x 20½
Curved aprons (A)[2]	2	
Curved aprons (B)[2]	4	
Veneer for curved aprons (A)[3]	4[4] 2[5]	5½ x 26

DESCRIPTION	PIECES	DIMENSIONS
Veneer for curved aprons (B)[3]	4[4] 4[5]	5½ x 26
Marquetry for legs	14	2 x 30
Table top for end sections	2	1¾₁₆ x 30½ x 48
Table top for middle section	1	1¾₁₆ x 30 x 48
Table leaves	2	1¾₁₆ x 24 x 48
Brace blocks	12	1¾
Cock beading		18 ft., ⅛ x ¼
Table hinges	4 pr.	2 x 3¹³⁄₁₆
F.h. wood screws for hinges	36	No. 8 x ¾
Brass keepers and screws in antique color	4	
Table-top fasteners		
50-penny nails or	2	(To pivot finger joints)
¼-in. hickory dowels		
Wood screws		(To fasten brace blocks)

[1] Mahogany or core stock.
[2] Glue up segments cut from kiln-dried core stock such as yellow pine (Fig. 4). The width and length of the stock will be determined by the number of segments in each layer, while the number of layers will be determined by the required thickness of the stock from which the aprons are to be cut. No accurate estimate of the amount of stock needed for these aprons is practical. Have an ample supply of material on hand.

Cauls will be needed to clamp the veneer to the core stock. Make the glued-up stock for one section of aprons A and B sufficiently wide so that the waste from the band-sawed pieces can be used for cauls.

[3] It is good practice to veneer both sides of core stock such as the curved aprons. This prevents unequal drying or seasoning, which might result in unequal strains and stresses and damage to the member. Veneering which is not visible need not be of the same high quality as the mahogany veneer. It should, however, be the same thickness. Plain veneers for the inside surfaces of aprons A and B should be provided.

[4] Mahogany.   [5] Plain veneer.

3A show how the stock should be glued up and sawed to shape to make the aprons. Core stock, which has been bent by steaming and clamping the wood over forms until dry, can also be used. Because of the special facilities required to bend wood, it is advisable to buy this stock from a reliable manufacturer.

To make the patterns for the curved aprons, see Figure 4. Patterns A and B should be laid out full size on plywood or some other suitable material and then used to determine the length and width of the glued-up stock. The patterns will again be used to lay out the apron on the glued-up stock (Fig. 3A).

After the curved aprons have been band-sawed to shape, cut the apron veneer to size. If hot glue is to be used, heat the cauls, the core stock, and the veneer. Have brown wrapping paper and pieces of felt at hand. While the application of

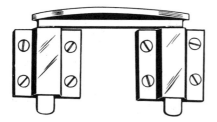

Fig. 9.   Hepplewhite dining table keeper

glue should not be too thick, the surface of the wood should be well covered. Place the veneer over the glued apron, a piece of brown wrapping paper over the veneer, a piece of felt over the paper, and, finally, the cauls over the felt. Use enough clamps to insure a good bond between the veneer and the core stock.

Plane and square up the straight aprons. Lay out and cut the tenons, fitting them to their respective mortises. When all mortises and tenons have been fitted, cut the rabbets for the cock beading on the lower edge of the curved and straight aprons. The cock bead protects the veneer at the lower edge where it might easily be damaged. Cut the rabbets for the cock beading on a shaper or by using a dado head on a variety saw. Carefully glue the cock beading to the rabbeted edge (Fig. 5).

Now, glue the table frames together. To join the curved aprons firmly to the legs of the end sections, use special clamps with steel bands. Pull the band on each clamp tightly around the curved section to join the leg and apron together. If such clamps are not available, tighten the joints

by gluing or screwing blocks to the inside and near the end of each apron, pull the joints tight with the clamps and these blocks. Then tie a rope or piece of strong webbing around the outside of the frame and tighten it in tourniquet fashion by twisting it with a stick. When clamping the frames, the marquetry and the veneer must at all times be protected from clamp marks with smooth blocks of wood or by other means, since the thin veneer permits very little sanding.

Next, make the finger-jointed aprons for the middle section. The details for laying out the finger joints are given in Figure 5. These joints should not be loose, but should be carefully laid out and snugly fitted together. The member which is fastened to the long apron should be glued on as well as screwed fast from the inside, though the screws alone will hold it if enough are used.

Now make the top (Fig. 1). It was a matter of pride with famous cabinetmakers of the past to use a single wide board for the table top on a fine piece of furniture. Since it is sometimes difficult to obtain boards of such generous width, it may be necessary to carefully match narrower boards for figure and color and glue them together. Fasten the finished top to the frame with table-top fasteners, as shown in Figures 1 and 5.

Rule joints are used to join the leaves to the middle section (Fig. 7). The curved part of the molding for this joint should be in the form of an exact quarter circle, so that the leaf may be raised or lowered without creaking or binding.

The arrangement for joining the end sections to the middle section or to the leaves of the middle section is ingenious. The rule joint is used (Fig. 2). Brass keepers (Figs. 8 and 9) hold the members together. Note that the member of the keeper which is fastened under the top of the end section must be mortised into the top of the leg. That is, the top of the leg must be hollowed out to make place for the keeper. While this could be avoided by making the tops of the end sections a little wider than they now are, the additional overhang on the straight side might warp and result in an improperly fitting joint when the pieces are mated. This danger is lessened if genuine Honduras or Cuban mahogany, properly seasoned, is used. These woods warp very little if properly fitted.

The finish for this table should be the same as that used for the other pieces in this suite.

4.

HEPPLEWHITE DINING ROOM SUITE— SIDEBOARD

Sideboards in their present form are thought to have been invented by Thomas Shearer, an English cabinetmaker and a contemporary of Sheraton and Hepplewhite. Earlier sideboards were, for the most part, high and long narrow tables devoid of drawers and compartments. Sheraton is credited with perfecting the sideboard. In comparison with Shearer's sideboards, Sheraton's were better proportioned and more graceful. George Hepplewhite, too, designed and built many beautiful sideboards, some of which appear in a book published after his death by his wife. Various elements on Hepplewhite and Sheraton furniture, and particularly on the sideboards, are so similar that it is difficult to attribute them definitely to either style. Most Sheraton sideboards have turned legs, while the square, tapered legs, often with spade feet, are typical of Hepplewhite. However, because of the interchange of characteristic elements, it cannot be said that the square leg absolutely denotes a Hepplewhite design or the turned leg a Sheraton design.

The sideboards of the eighteenth century are beautifully ornamented. The practice, then coming into fashion, of veneering plain surfaces to bring out the full beauty of the richly figured grain of mahogany and rare woods, did much to lighten the structure and reduce the scale of earlier and heavier styles.

The sideboard for the Hepplewhite dining-room suite is comparatively light and graceful, although built of solid stock. The drawer fronts are inlaid with 1/16-in. white boxwood banding. The face of each front leg is veneered with marquetry, an inlaid veneer. The motif is the classical cornflower.

PROCEDURE

To make the sideboard, first cut the six legs to the size given in the bill of material and Figures 1 and 2. Taper the legs by setting the marking gauge to 5/16 in., and drawing gauge lines that distance in from each side on the bottom of each leg. Then, with a pencil and try square, draw a line around each leg 22 in. from the floor. Using a straightedge, draw the taper lines on two

Hepplewhite Sideboard

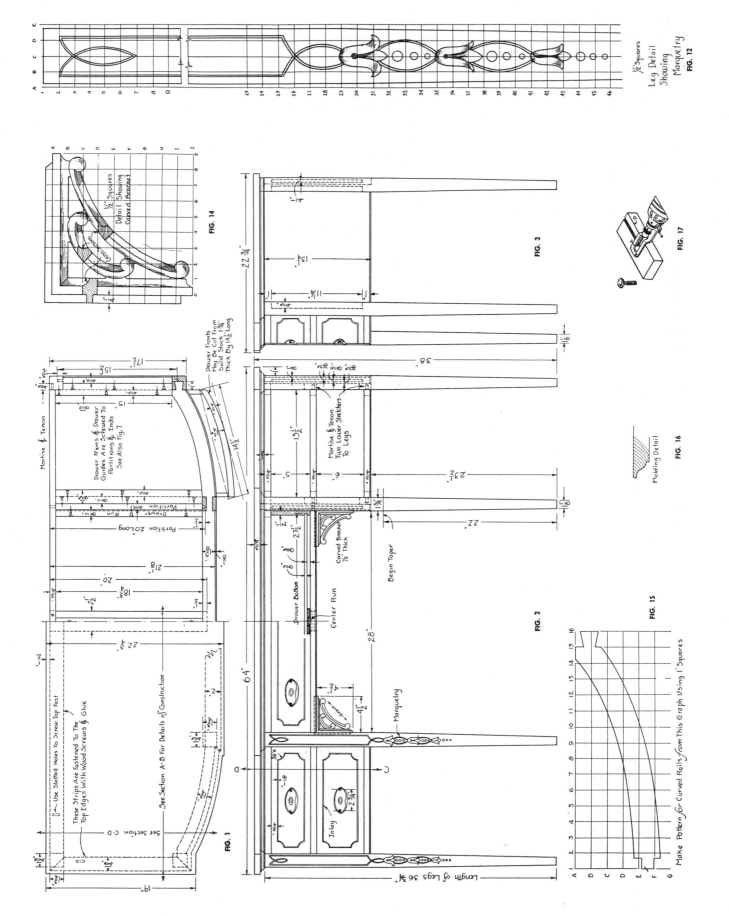

½ Squares
Leg Detail
Showing
Marquetry
FIG. 12

½ Squares Showing
Detail
Carved Bracket
FIG. 14

FIG. 3

FIG. 17

Molding Detail
FIG. 16

FIG. 15

Make Pattern for Curved Rails From This Graph Using 1" Squares

Drawer Fronts
May Be Cut From
Solid Stock 1¾
Thick By 14½ Long

Mortise & Tenon

Drawer Runs & Drawer
Guides Are Screwed To
Partitions & Ends
See Also Fig.7

Partition Run

Partition 20 Long

Drawer Run

See Section A-B For Details of Construction

These Strips Are Fastened To The
Top Edges With Wood Screws & Glue.

Use Slotted Holes To Screw Top Fast

See Section C-D

FIG. 1

Mortise & Tenon
Two Lower Stretchers
To Legs

Drawer Bottom

Center Run

Carved Bracket
½ Thick

Begin Taper

Marquetry

Inlay

Grain

Length of Legs 36¾"

FIG. 2

opposite sides of each leg. Saw the taper on the band saw and plane the legs to these exact lines. Proceed in the same manner to taper the third and fourth sides of each leg.

Next, glue the marquetry to the face of each front leg. It would be better to buy the marquetry than try to make it, unless you have developed considerable skill in the art (Fig. 12). The cost of the marquetry will be nominal since only four pieces are needed. Before gluing the marquetry to the legs, saw four pieces of ⅜-in. plywood at least 1¾ in. wide and 36¾ in. long. The plywood will serve as cauls when clamping the marquetry to the legs. Several strips of heavy wrapping paper should be at hand to go between the marquetry and the cauls to prevent their sticking together. With the point of a sharp knife or the corner of a chisel, scratch crisscrossed lines on the face of the leg to which the marquetry is to be glued. In shops where veneering is done regularly, a toothing plane is used to prepare the surface to hold more glue and make a better joint with the veneer. A toothing plane has teeth filed into the cutting edge of the blade, which is set upright in the plane.

Warm the leg and the marquetry over a radiator or steam pipes. Then apply a good grade of hide glue to the leg. Place the underside of the marquetry upon the glued surface. Lay strips of wrapping paper over the marquetry. Then clamp on the cauls, and apply enough pressure with the clamps to make a good joint. After the joints have dried, and the cauls have been removed, sponge and sandpaper off the paper covering the surface of the marquetry.

After the marquetry has been applied, lay out and cut the mortises on the legs. The bridle joints and the dovetailing at the top of the front legs are not to be cut until the upper front rail has been made. Use the pattern in Figure 15 to lay out the curves at both ends of the upper front rail. Trace the outlines for these joints on the tops of the legs by marking around the rail with the sharp point of a knife or a scratch awl.

Saw the short rails to shape from the pattern used for the long rail (Fig. 15). Next, make the

BILL OF MATERIAL

DESCRIPTION	PIECES	DIMENSIONS
Mahogany:		
Legs	6	1¾ x 1¾ x 36¾
Marquetry for front legs	4	1¾ x 36¾
Ends	2	¾ x 13¼ x 15½
Top	1	¾ x 22¾ x 64
Partitions	2	¾ x 13⅝ x 20
Middle drawer front	1	¾ x 5 x 28
Upper small drawer fronts	2	1¾ x 5 x 14½
Lower small drawer fronts	2	1¾ x 6 x 14½
Upper rail	1	¾ x 5½ x 60½
Front molding strip	1	½ x 5½ x 63
End molding strips	2	½ x 1¾ x 18
Brackets	2	½ x 4¾ x 4¾
Rail below long drawer	1	¾ x 1¾ x 29½
Rails between small drawers	2	¾ x 2¾ x 16
Rails below small drawers	2	¾ x 2⅞ x 16
Cock-bead strips below partitions	2	⅛ x ⅞ x 19½
Cock-bead strips below ends	2	⅛ x ⅞ x 14
Poplar:		
Sideboard back	1	¾ x 13¼ x 60
Sides for long drawer	2	½ x 5 x 20⅛
Long sides for upper small drawers	2	½ x 5 x 20⅛
Short sides for upper small drawers	2	½ x 5 x 16⅝
Long sides for lower small drawers	2	½ x 6 x 20⅛
Short sides for lower small drawers	2	½ x 6 x 16⅝
Maple, Birch, or Oak:		
Middle drawer runs	4	¾ x ⅞ x 18¾
Center-run strip, middle drawer	1	5⁄16 x 1 x 18¾
Center-run strips, middle drawer	2	5⁄16 x 1 x 19⅝
Supporting strip for center run	1	¾ x 2½ x 20
Long small drawer runs	4	¾ x ¾ x 18¾
Short small drawer runs	4	¾ x ¾ x 15
Long runs above upper small drawers	2	¾ x 1⅝ x 18¾
Short runs above upper small drawers	2	¾ x 1⅝ x 15
Long guides, small drawers	4	⅞ x 1½ x 18¾
Short guides, small drawers	4	⅞ x 1½ x 14
Plywood:		
Back for long drawer	1	⅜ x 4¼ x 27½
Backs for upper small drawers	2	⅜ x 4¼ x 13
Backs for lower small drawers	2	⅜ x 5¼ x 13
Bottom, long drawer	1	⅜ x 19⅞ x 27½
Bottoms, small drawers	4	⅜ x 13 x 19⅞
Oval, antique-finished brass drawer pulls	6	2¾-in. boring

ends (Fig. 3), the partitions (Fig. 1), and the back (Figs. 1 and 6). Join the partitions to the back as shown in Figure 6. Make a trial assembly of the whole frame when all the joints have been made and fitted together. Saw the two brackets on a jig saw and carve them according to the pattern shown in Figure 14. First glue the brackets to the grooves which have been cut

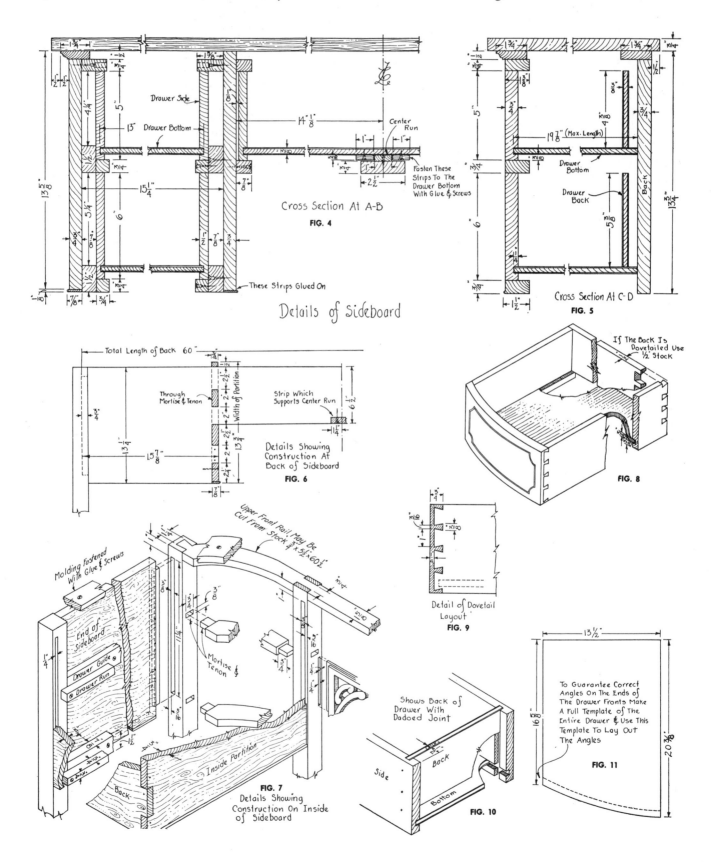

Cross Section At A-B

FIG. 4

Details of Sideboard

Cross Section At C-D

FIG. 5

Details Showing Construction At Back of Sideboard

FIG. 6

If The Back Is Dovetailed Use ½" Stock

FIG. 8

Detail of Dovetail Layout

FIG. 9

FIG. 7
Details Showing Construction On Inside of Sideboard

Shows Back of Drawer With Dadoed Joint

FIG. 10

To Guarantee Correct Angles On The Ends of The Drawer Fronts Make A Full Template of The Entire Drawer & Use This Template To Lay Out The Angles

FIG. 11

into the rail under the long drawer. This rail, with the brackets attached, can be glued to the legs when assembling the frame.

Be certain to square the frame when gluing it up. Nothing will cause more trouble when drawers are being fitted than a frame which is not square.

The drawer guides and drawer runs should be made next. Figures 4 and 7 give the sizes and show how to attach them to the frame.

Now, make the drawers. Figures 8 and 10 show two types of construction. For a piece as fine as this, only construction with dovetailed joints should be considered, at least for fastening the sides to the front of the drawer. The best construction uses dovetail joints at both front and back, though in the bill of material, as well as in Figure 14, the dadoed joint has been designated. If a dovetailed joint is used to fasten the backs and the sides of the drawers, substitute solid stock for the plywood, and make the solid wood backs as long as the drawer fronts.

Cut the grooves for the inlay on the drawer fronts with a $\frac{1}{16}$-in. router bit in a high-speed hand router or rotary tool. Figure 17 shows an attachment in which the routing is done with the tool held horizontally. With a shoelike attachment similar to the shoe or foot of a sewing machine, it is possible to rout the curved corners with a $\frac{1}{16}$-in. router bit.

When cutting drawer fronts to the shape used for the end drawers, make a template like the one in Figure 11. Experience has shown that a template of the drawer front alone is not sufficiently accurate to get the exact angles. Cut the drawer fronts to the proper curvature on a band saw and plane them smooth with a curved-bottom plane or sharp scraper blades.

When the drawers have been made and fitted into the proper places, prepare the molded strips which are to be fastened just under the top of the sideboard. The molding can be cut on the shaper or on a drill press, if the proper attachments are available. Finish the corners where the offsets appear by hand with wood-carving chisels. Fasten the top to these molded strips with wood screws. Slotted holes (Fig. 1) are drilled into the strips for that purpose. The holes are slotted because a top as wide as this tends

Fig. 13. Marquetry detail for Hepplewhite Dining-Room Suite

to swell or shrink during different seasons of the year, and some provision should be made to prevent strains which might split the top. At the ends of the sideboard, the screws that fasten the top go through both the runs placed above the drawers and the molded strip. Use washers under the heads of the screws.

To finish the sideboard, apply quicklime dissolved in water. This will color the mahogany a rich red without changing the color of the inlay. When dry, the surface will look as if it had been whitewashed. Carefully clean off the surface with burlap or rags dipped in a mixture of boiled linseed oil and turpentine. When all traces of the lime have been removed, apply a natural-colored

Fig. 18. Hepplewhite sideboard pull

filler and rub it well into the pores of the wood. Follow with a wash coat of shellac and several coats of the best floor varnish. Each coat of finish, beginning with the shellac coat, should be rubbed down until smooth with No. 00 steel wool. The final coat of varnish should also be rubbed down with pumice stone and rubbing oil.

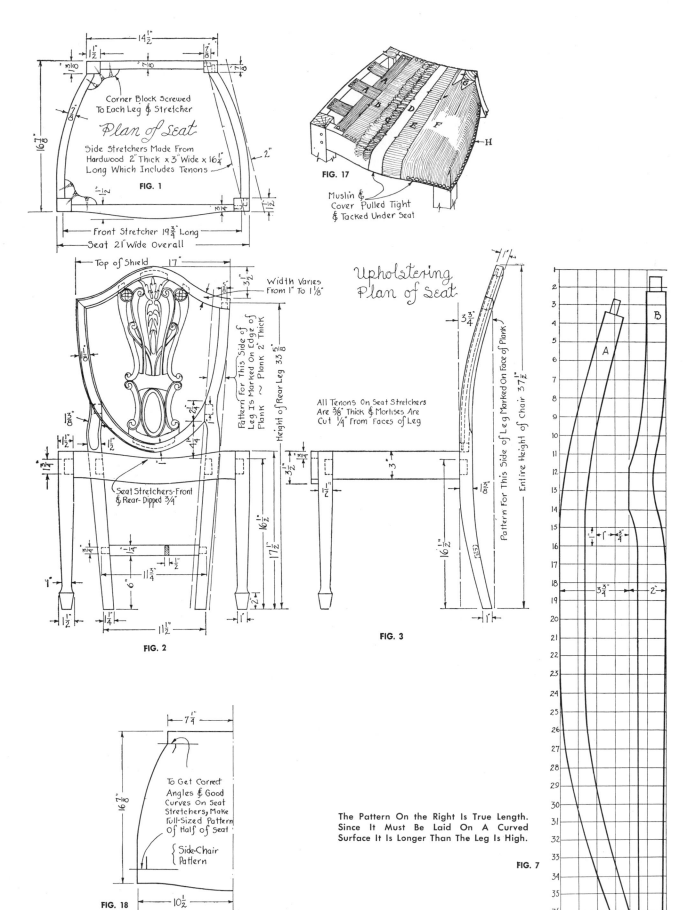

FIG. 1

Corner Block Screwed To Each Leg & Stretcher

Plan of Seat

Side Stretchers Made From Hardwood 2" Thick x 3" Wide x 16¼" Long Which Includes Tenons

14½"

16⅞"

2"

Front Stretcher 19¾" Long

Seat 21" Wide Overall

FIG. 17

Muslin & Cover Pulled Tight & Tacked Under Seat

FIG. 2

Top of Shield   17"

Width Varies From 1" To 1⅛"

Pattern For This Side of Leg Is Marked On Edge of Plank ~ Plank 2" Thick

Height of Rear Leg 33⅝"

Seat Stretchers-Front & Rear-Dipped ¾"

16½"

17½"

11¾"

6"

11½"

FIG. 3

Upholstering Plan of Seat

All Tenons On Seat Stretchers Are ⅜" Thick & Mortises Are Cut ¼" From Faces of Leg

Pattern For This Side of Leg Marked On Face of Plank

Entire Height of Chair 37½"

3¾"

3"

16½"

FIG. 18

7¼"

16⅞"

To Get Correct Angles & Good Curves On Seat Stretchers, Make Full-Sized Pattern Of Half of Seat

Side-Chair Pattern

10½"

FIG. 7

The Pattern On the Right Is True Length. Since It Must Be Laid On A Curved Surface It Is Longer Than The Leg Is High.

A B

3¾"   2"

5.

HEPPLEWHITE DINING-ROOM SUITE— SIDE CHAIR AND ARMCHAIR

The most distinctive of the furniture designed by Hepplewhite is the shield-back chair which he developed and perfected. The lines of a good shield-back chair are simple and clean cut and suggest refinement. A good Hepplewhite chair is comparatively expensive to build, requiring thick pieces of mahogany from which to cut the gracefully curved members. Considerable skill in the cabinetmaker's and wood carver's craft is essential to make these chairs. Factory-made substitutes of the finer models are turned out in considerable quantity at greatly reduced cost, but at the loss of much of their character and beauty. A good design requires a great deal of painstaking handwork and careful attention during its conception and construction. Given these, the finished product will be a worth-while object.

The design of both the side chair and the armchair is in the finest Hepplewhite tradition. Their construction is based on sound principles of comfort, beauty, and enduring worth.

Hepplewhite Side Chair

Hepplewhite Armchair

BILL OF MATERIAL

DESCRIPTION	PIECES	DIMENSIONS
SIDE CHAIR		
Back legs (makes both)	1	2 x 5½ x 33⅝
Front legs	2	1½ x 1½ x 17½
Splat	1	1½ x 8¼ x 19¾
Top shield stretcher	1	1 x 4½ x 17½[1]
Bottom shield stretcher	1	1 x 6 x 13¼[2]
Lower back stretcher	1	½ x 1¼ x 11¾
Front seat stretcher	1	1½ x 3½ x 19¾
Rear seat stretcher	1	⅞ x 3½ x 13¼
Side seat stretchers	2	2 x 3 x 16¼
Corner bracing blocks	4	(See Fig. 1.)
ARMCHAIR		
Back legs (makes both)	1	2 x 5½ x 33⅝
Front legs	2	1½ x 1½ x 17½
Splat	1	1½ x 8¼ x 19¾
Top shield stretcher	1	1 x 4½ x 19½[1]

DESCRIPTION	PIECES	DIMENSIONS
Bottom shield stretcher	1	1 x 6 x 15½[2]
Lower back stretcher	1	½ x 1¼ x 13¼
Front seat stretcher	1	1½ x 3½ x 20
Rear seat stretcher	1	⅞ x 3½ x 14⅝
Side seat stretchers	2	2 x 3 x 16¼
Arms	2	1 x 3 x 12
Arm supports	2	1⅜ x 4⅜ x 11
Corner bracing blocks	4	

Seat springs, burlap, twine, webbing, curled hair, muslin, cotton batting, upholstering tacks and nails, upholstering material, etc.

[1] An extra ¼ in. is left on each end for trimming after the back has been glued up.

[2] Extra wood is left on each end until the chair back has been glued up (Fig. 6).

PROCEDURE

The best obtainable grade of hard mahogany should be used in the construction of these chairs. Cuban mahogany, because of its hardness and fine texture, is recommended. If Cuban mahogany is not obtainable, genuine Honduras mahogany is a good substitute.

Cut out the front legs first, squaring them to the size given in the bill of material, and shape them roughly on a band saw. Then dress the legs with a spokeshave, a chisel, and a half-round cabinetmaker's file. The taper on the legs begins about 13 in. above the floor. Do not taper the legs clear to the top but allow 4½ in. to provide square joints with the seat stretchers.

Make cardboard patterns (Fig. 7) for the rear legs. Two legs can be cut from a single plank as indicated in the bill of material. Care must be taken to form graceful curves. It is very important to true up the curves so that they are beautifully shaped. Band-saw the legs to the shape shown at A, Figure 7. Then lay out the pattern for the front of the leg (Fig. 7, B) on the edge of the partly sawed plank and saw out the shape, as shown in the front elevations, Figures 2 and 9. Dress the legs to squared sections, from top to bottom, and to the dimensions given in the drawings. Round the back of the shield and carve the splat and front of the shield after the chair back has been assembled and glued.

Make the layouts for all mortises on the chair legs. The mortises can be cut on a mortising machine, drilled out on a drill press as shown on page 61, in Figure 7, and chiseled by hand, or bored with a brace and bit and chiseled. It depends upon the type of equipment available. In mass-producing chairs, jigs are devised to hold the shaped members for mortising. This device assures boring or mortising at the correct angles. However, when only a few chairs are to be built, it is usually not worth the trouble to build jigs. With care, the mortises can be made in the time required to build the jigs. If the boring angles are laid out on the face of the piece with reasonable care, the mortises can be cut with sufficient accuracy to insure good joints.

To make the joints, first draw a vertical center line on a piece of wallboard or on a clean floor, then mark the distances between the legs at the top and bottom (Fig. 6), taking half the distance on each side of the center line. Once the stretcher has been sawed to shape, mark the shoulder angles in the manner shown in Figure 6, by clamping it to the legs. Work from a vertical center line at all times in squaring chair layouts. Lay out the shoulder angles for the tenons on the seat stretchers in the same way. It is now possible to mark the lines across the adjacent edges with a try square, completing the layout for the shoulder of the tenon with absolute accuracy. The joints for fitting the rail at the top of the shield should be laid out and made *after* the joints of the other three rails have been made and fitted properly. Glue none of the joints until the splat has been made and fitted to its place.

To make the splat, first draw the pattern for the curve of the splat on the edge of the board (Fig. 5). Cut this curve on a large band saw. Mark the mortise and tenon joints as shown in Figure 6A, then cut and fit the splat to the back before making the cutouts shown in Figure 4. Cut out the splat design on a jig saw and true it up with files and sandpaper.

Now glue up the chair back. When the glue has dried and the clamps have been removed, round and shape the upper rail and the back legs above the seat as shown in the cross sections in Figure 4. The back of the lower rail in the shield is not rounded. Now carve the front of the shield and the splat. Make a full-sized pattern for this carving with cross sections showing the contour from Figure 4 or 11, depending upon which of the two chairs is being built. Carve that part of the shield to which the arm is fastened after the arm is in place. Much of the beauty of the completed chair will depend upon the quality of the carving. The modeling is not deep, seldom more than ⅛ in. and in many places less.

When the back has been carved, assemble and glue the rest of the chair. Glue and screw bracing blocks securely into each corner. The braces should be at least 1½ in. thick, since they add considerably to the strength and durability of the chair.

When the armchair is being built, the arms and arm supports should now be made and fitted to the chair. Make patterns for the arms from Figures 12 and 13; lay and cut out the arms — one right and one left. Carve the arms before fastening them to the chair. The arm's back end is gained into the shield about ⅛ in., just enough to hold it securely once it has been glued and screwed fast (Fig. 8). The screw hole is counterbored and the hole plugged with wood.

To finish these chairs, follow the directions given for finishing the sideboard.

To upholster the chair seat, one of two methods may be used. Both have been employed by the author with good results. These dining-room chairs were upholstered by using coiled springs in the seats. The placing of the springs and the method of tying them is the same as that shown and described in the chapter on the light Sheraton side chair (Fig. 6 and 6A). The second method, and the one preferred by the author for this chair, is shown in Figure 17. The saddle-shaped seat is not only comfortable to sit on, but it also is the simpler of the two upholstery methods.

To upholster the chair shown in Figure 17, first stretch a good grade of webbing from the front to the back of the chair, tacking it to the top

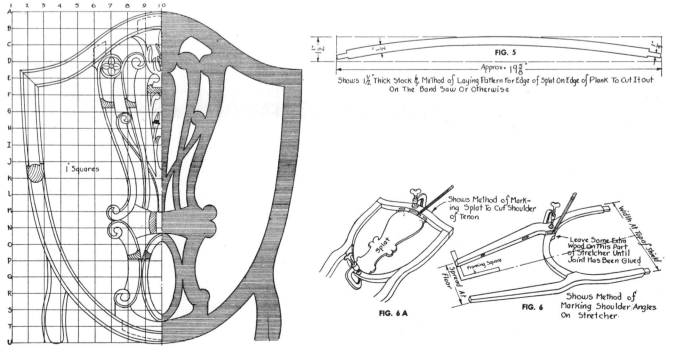

FIG. 4

1" Squares

FIG. 5

Shows 1½ Thick Stock & Method of Laying Pattern For Edge of Splat On Edge of Plank To Cut It out On The Band Saw Or Otherwise

Approx. 19⅝

Shows Method of Marking Splat To Cut Shoulder of Tenon

FIG. 6 A

Leave Some Extra Wood On This Part of Stretcher Until Joint Has Been Glued

Width At Top of Shield

Framing Square

Spread At Floor

FIG. 6

Shows Method of Marking Shoulder Angles On Stretcher

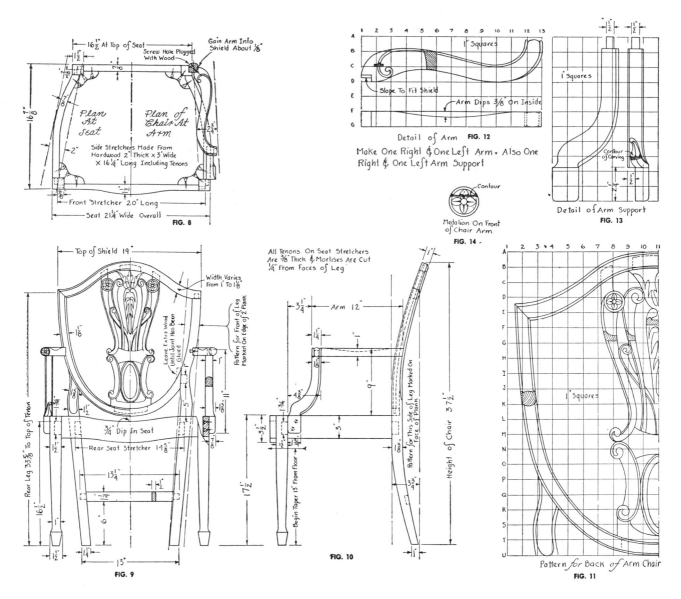

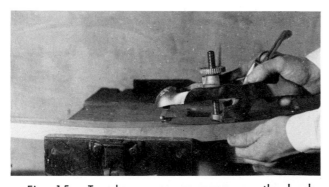

Fig. 15. To plane concave curves on the back legs, use a special plane on which the bottom can be adjusted.

of the frame. Use three strips of 3½-in. webbing. This wide webbing will give the proper dipped, or saddle, shape to the seat. Weave three strips of webbing crosswise, but do not stretch the webbing too tightly so as to preserve the saddle

shape. Tack it to the side stretchers. This webbing is shown at A in Figure 17. On top of the webbing tack a sheet of good burlap. This forms the base for the filling. The burlap is shown at B in Figure 17. Sew the burlap to the webbing with a thin, strong twine. The seat may be filled with curled hair, the best and most expensive filling material. If a less expensive filling material is desired, substitute a good grade of moss. The filling material must be evenly distributed over the whole seat and should be allowed to hang over the edges to pad the sharp corners at the top of the seat (C, Fig. 17). Over this is stretched a piece of first-quality muslin, D. The muslin is slip-tacked. Begin at the centers of the seat rails and tack toward the ends. After properly fitting and stretching the muslin, hammer the tacks. The muslin, as well as the cloth, should be fitted carefully at the corners. There will be a pleat at the front corners, the cloth being folded under to prevent a raw edge. A layer of cotton felt is then laid over the muslin, *E*. This helps to make the surface smoother. Now place the upholstery material over the cotton. Pleat and blind-stitch the front corners. The manner of cutting the cloth to fit it around the rear legs is shown at *G* (Fig. 17). The cloth also is folded under at the back to form a finished edge. Proper care in fitting the muslin cover will give practice for fitting the final cover. Several stitches will serve to hold the center of the seat to the proper dipped shape. If there are any lumps or places not properly filled, adjust them with a regulator before putting on the upholstering material.

Fig. 16. Detail of the carving of the shield and splat

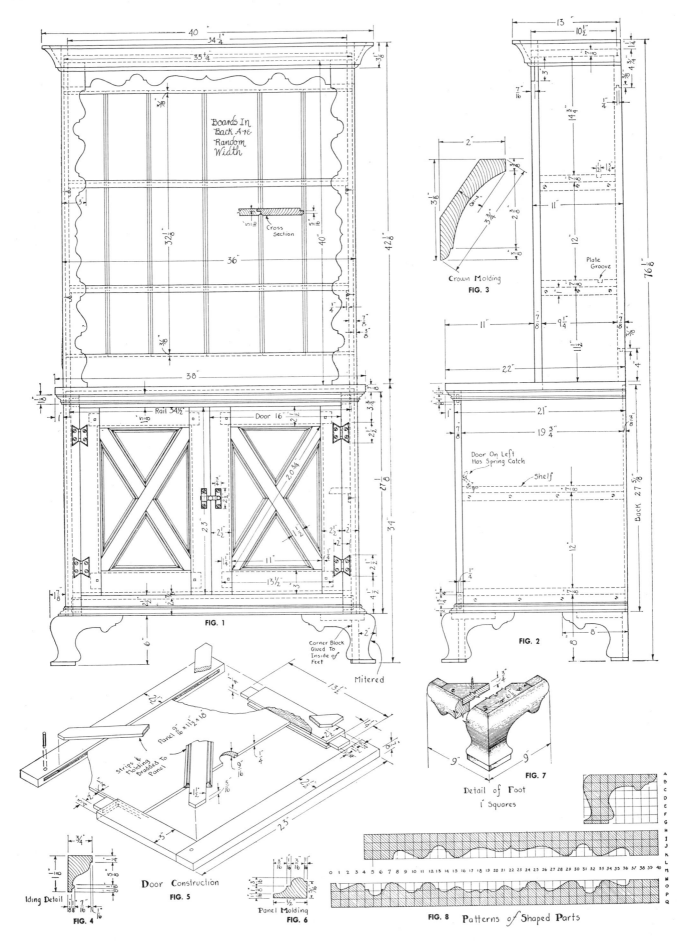

Boards In Back Are Random Width

Cross Section

Crown Molding
FIG. 3

Plate Groove

Rail 34½

Door 16"

Door On Left Has Spring Catch

Shelf

Back 27⅝

FIG. 1

FIG. 2

Corner Block Glued To Inside of Feet

Mitered

Detail of Foot
1" Squares

FIG. 7

Panel 9/16 x 11½ x 16

Strips & Molding Bradded To Panel

Door Construction
FIG. 5

Iding Detail
FIG. 4

Panel Molding
FIG. 6

0 1 2 3 4 5 6 7 8 9 10 11 12 13 14 15 16 17 18 19 20 21 22 23 24 25 26 27 28 29 30 31 32 33 34 35 36 37 38 39 40

FIG. 8   Patterns of Shaped Parts

6.

WELSH DRESSER

Welsh dressers are so called because they resemble a type commonly found in Wales. The term has been applied rather loosely to all dressers having open shelves in the upper part and a cupboard, with or without drawers, below. Early Welsh dressers often were made of oak, although pine, poplar and other domestic softwoods replaced oak in most early American cupboards.

The dresser shown here, with its decorative scrollwork, is a Pennsylvania type. It can be used as an attractive bookcase or for the display of china, pewter, or bric-a-brac. The random-width boards in the back are knotty pine; in fact, all the wood used in the dresser is white pine with the exception of the feet, for which maple was used to provide greater strength.

PROCEDURE

First, glue up the sides as shown on the left in Figure 10. Rabbet the *inside* back edge of each side to make a pair. These rabbets are not the same size from the bottom to the top because of the difference in the thicknesses of the upper and lower backs.

Next, glue up the table board, and cut it to shape, as shown on the right in Figure 10. Rabbet the bottom rear edge so that the table board and plywood back can be joined later (Fig. 11). Make the floor and the top. Fasten cleats B, E, F, and G to the inside of each side (Figs. 1, 2, and 11). Then nail, glue, and screw fast the top, table board, and floor. Square everything properly.

Make the upper back next. Cut the two horizontal pieces and make a ¼-in. groove, ⅜ in. deep, in one edge of each board (Figs. 2 and 11). Prepare the vertical boards by cutting rabbets along their edges and beveling the edges as shown in the cross section of Figure 1. This rabbeted, beveled joint is necessary to provide for the swelling and shrinking of the boards

which will occur during different seasons of the year, even though kiln-dried stock is used. Cut ¼-in. tenons, ⅜ in. high, on both ends of each board to join to the horizontal pieces. Assemble the back without glue, and nail it from the rear to the sides above the table board. The lower back can be made of a single piece of ⅜-in. panel stock. Nail the lower back to the rabbeted edges of the table board and sides.

Welsh Dresser

Fig. 9.   Shaping the feet on a
circular saw.

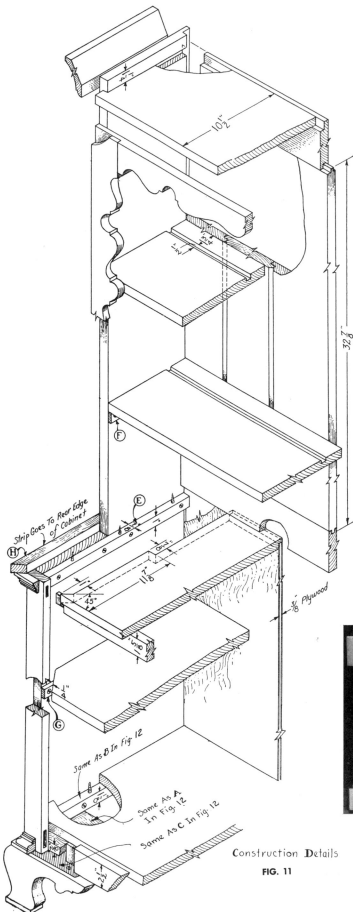

Strip Goes To Rear Edge
of Cabinet

H

F

E

B

3/8 Plywood

G

45°

11 7/8"

7"

1"

Same As B In Fig. 12

Same As A
In Fig. 12

Same As C In Fig. 12

10 1/2"

32 7/8"

4 1/4"

Construction Details

FIG. 11

Fig. 10.   Left: A glued-up side; right:
the glued-up table board.

Fig. 12.   Assembling and bracing the feet.

BILL OF MATERIAL

DESCRIPTION	PIECES	DIMENSIONS
Sides	2	⅞ x 10⅛ x 70⅛
	2	⅞ x 10 x 27⅛
Table board	1	⅞ x 11⅞ x 38
	1	⅞ x 10⅛ x 34¼
Floor	1	⅞ x 19¾ x 34¼
Cupboard shelf	1	⅞ x 19¾ x 34¼
Top	1	⅞ x 10½ x 35¼
Upper shelves	2	⅞ x 9¼ x 34¼
Upper back	1	⅞ x 4¾ x 35¼
	1	⅞ x 4 x 35¼
Plus required number of random width boards		⅞ x 35¼ x 32⅞
Lower back (plywood)	1	⅜ x 27⅝ x 35¼
Scrolled rail	1	⅞ x 3 x 36
Scrolled stiles	2	⅞ x 3 x 40
Door frames	1	⅞ x 1⅝ x 34½
	1	⅞ x 2½ x 34½
	2	⅞ x 2 x 27⅛
Door stiles	4	⅞ x 2½ x 23
Upper door rails	2	⅞ x 2½ x 13½
Lower door rails	2	⅞ x 3 x 13½
Door panels	2	9⁄16 x 11½ x 18
X rails	4	5⁄16 x 1½ x 20¾
Braces (Fig. 12A)	2	⅞ x 4 x 34¼
(B)	2	⅞ x 1⅛ x 19¾
(C)	4	⅞ x 5⅜ x 9¼
(D)	1	⅞ x 6 x 37½
Cleats (Fig. 11E)	2	⅞ x 1 x 19¾
(F)	4	¼ x 1 x 9¼
(G)	2	¼ x 1 x 19¾
(H)	2	⅞ x 1 x 22
Crown molding	1	⅞ x 3¾ x 70
6 feet	1	2 x 6 x 60
Molding (Fig. 4)		14 ft.
Panel molding (Fig. 6)		22 ft.
Wrought-iron butterfly hinges	2 pr.	
Wrought-iron latch	1	
Spring elbow catch	1	

Place the shelf in the lower cupboard either before the back or before the frame is nailed to the cabinet. Four pieces are required for the frame to which the doors will be fastened. Mortise and tenon the pieces together and nail the frame to the front edges of the sides with 6-penny finish nails.

Fit and place the upper shelves in the dresser after cutting a plate groove into both shelves as shown in Figure 2. Lay out the patterns for and cut out the scrolled pieces for the top section (Fig. 8). The pieces are joined together at the top with end-lap joints and then nailed to the sides (Fig. 11). Fill all nail holes with plastic wood and sand smooth and clean.

Make the feet from a plank of hardwood 2 in. thick. Figure 9 shows saw cuts being made on a circular saw to begin the shaping of the feet. When enough saw cuts have been made to rough out the shape, use a wide gouge to smooth up and form the curves. Cut the six pieces needed for the feet from this shaped board. Miter the corners of the four front feet (Fig. 1). Rabbet the top of the front feet for the bracing members (Figs. 7, 11C, and 12C). The back feet are rabbeted at the top and the back (Fig. 2) for bracing members C and D (Fig. 12). Cut the two pieces shown as A in Figure 12 and attach to strips B. To fasten the feet to the cabinet,

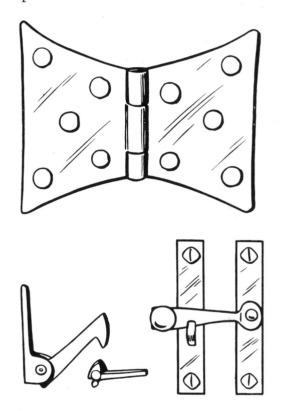

screw the triangular-shaped braces of the feet to the strips A.

Make the small moldings on a shaper or buy similar moldings. Make the crown molding by the same method used to make the feet; that is, first rough out the cove on a circular saw. To cut the miters, place the molding in a miter box with the vertical side (Fig. 3) against the back and the horizontal side resting on the bottom. Set the saw at an angle of 45 deg.

To make the doors, follow the directions given in Figure 5. The crossed strips and the panel molding are bradded to the panel after the door has been assembled.

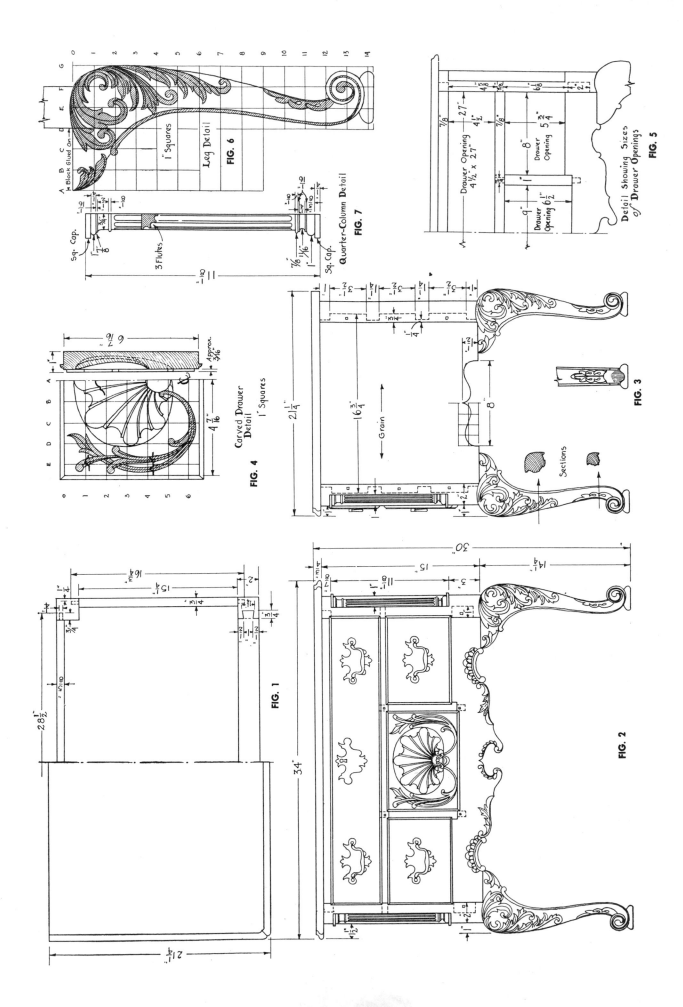

FIG. 6

1" Squares

Leg Detail

0 1 2 3 4 5 6 7 8 9 10 11 12 13 14

A B C — M Block Glued On

FIG. 7

Sq. Cap.

3 Flutes

Sq. Cap.

Quarter-Column Detail

11"

FIG. 5

Detail Showing Sizes of Drawer Openings

Drawer Opening 4½" x 27"

Drawer Opening 6½"

8" Drawer Opening

27"

4½"

5¾"

8"

9"

FIG. 4

Carved Drawer Detail

1" Squares

6½"

4 7/16"

Approx. 3/16"

A B C D E

0 1 2 3 4 5 6

FIG. 3

Sections

21¼"

16¾"

Grain

8"

FIG. 1

16½"

15¼"

3¾"

3/4"

2"

1¼"

28½"

21¼"

FIG. 2

30"

15"

14¼"

34"

11¼"

7.

CHIPPENDALE LOWBOY

The beautiful, very decorative lowboys built by Chippendale, and by those who imitated his designs, are numbered among the finest examples of eighteenth-century cabinet-work. The lowboys built in or around Philadelphia in the latter half of the eighteenth century are among the best of these designs.

Students of furniture design are not altogether sure about the use to which these lowboys were put. If they served as dressing tables, as did earlier lowboys, they were not particularly well suited to this purpose because of the low skirt. This may explain in part why lowboys were not included among the pieces created by designers who followed Chippendale. While unsuitable as a dressing table, the lowboy is adapted easily to other uses. It can be placed in the hallway under a large mirror or in the dining room as a serving table which holds silver and table linen. It will also be useful in the living room or bedroom.

This beautiful Chippendale lowboy will grace the finest home, and if properly constructed according to this design, may someday be a museum piece. It should be built of the best Cuban or Honduras mahogany.

PROCEDURE

Thick mahogany is required for the cabriole legs of the lowboy. The usual practice of gluing on extra pieces for the curve at the knee and the flare at the front of the foot is not recommended for furniture of this quality. It will be necessary, however, to glue on blocks at the top of the leg, as shown in Figure 6; this usually is done without impairing the quality of workmanship. The method used to saw out cabriole legs has been thoroughly explained in the chapters dealing with the Chippendale wing chair and the Queen Anne highboy, and will not be repeated here. After the curved parts of the leg have been shaped and before they are carved, cut out the outside cor-

Chippendale Lowboy

35

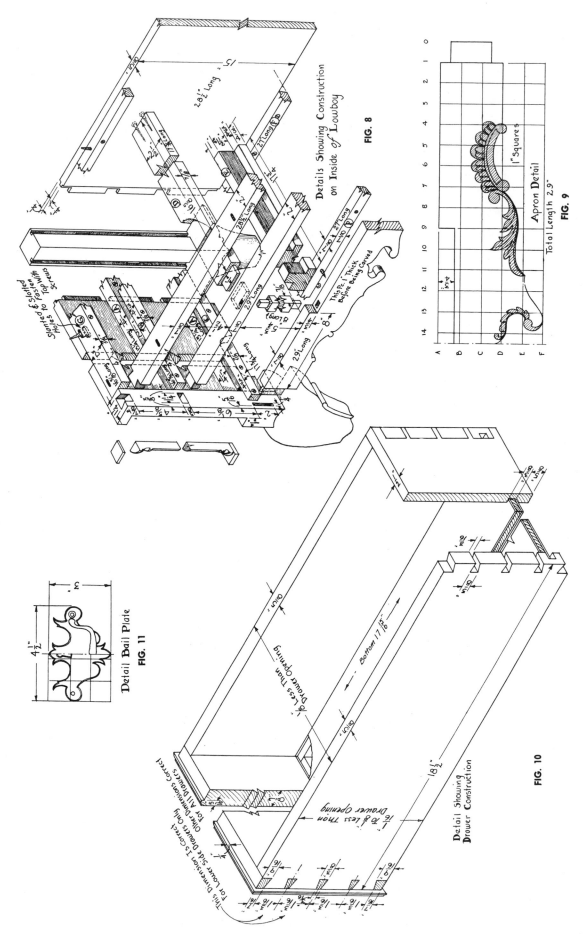

Details Showing Construction on Inside of Lowboy

FIG. 8

Apron Detail

Total Length 2.9"

1" Squares

FIG. 9

Detail Bail Plate

FIG. 11

Detail Showing Drawer Construction

FIG. 10

ners of the front legs on a mortising machine to make room for the fluted quarter columns.

The making of quarter columns has been thoroughly explained and diagramed in the chapter dealing with the making of the Jacobean chest of drawers (see Fig. 7 for design details).

Lay out and cut mortises into the legs for joining the ends, back, and stretchers (Figs. 1 and 8). Cut the dovetails at the tops of the front legs after the frame has been assembled. When the top stretcher has been made, lay it on the two front legs and accurately mark the shape of the dovetails on each leg with a knife (Figs. 1 and 8).

When the legs have been made and mortised, carve them (Fig. 6). It will not be necessary to carve the rear face of the back legs since it is seldom seen. All carved parts stand from ⅛ in. to 3/16 in. above the surface.

Next, make the ends, the back, all rails and stretchers, and the two short stiles which go between the small drawers. Cut all mortises and tenons on these pieces. Drill or bore slotted screw holes into the upper rails where the top will be screwed to the frame (Fig. 8). The use of slotted instead of round holes permits the expansion and contraction of the wide top at different seasons of the year, preventing warping or splitting, and practically eliminating pressures on the joints of the frame which might cause the joints to open up or come apart.

Saw out and carve the lower rail or skirt (Figs. 8 and 9). The carving on this piece is not glued to the rail, but is carved on the solid piece. This requires careful scraping and sanding of the lowered background before assembling the frame.

First, assemble the lower rail, the middle rail, and the two stiles separating the small drawers (Fig. 8). Then assemble the legs, front rails, and the back. Peg the joints at the back and where the lower stretcher joins the front legs. Use pegs also to strengthen the joints at both ends of the lowboy. These pegs should be about 3/16 in., roughly octagoned, and driven into drilled holes in which they will fit tightly. Put glue into the holes before driving in the pegs.

Next make and fasten stretchers *D*, Figure 8, to the middle front stretcher. These stretchers, which keep the small drawers from dropping when they are pulled out, are fastened to the back with long wood screws. The stretchers can be fastened with machine screws or stove bolts if holes are bored into the back of the stretcher for the nuts. Screw supporting battens, *F*, to the inside of the skirt and to the inside of the back (Fig. 8). Now assemble the front, back, and ends, squaring the frame carefully.

Make all drawer runs and drawer guides next,

BILL OF MATERIAL

DESCRIPTION	PIECES	DIMENSIONS
Legs	4	3 x 3 x 29¼
Bracket-blocks (for upper part of legs)	8	3 x 3 x 3
Ends	2	¾ x 15 x 16¾
Back	1	⅝ x 15 x 28½
Upper front rail	1	⅞ x 2 x 28½
Rail below long drawer	1	⅞ x 2 x 29
Carved skirt	1	1 x 5 x 29
Stiles between small drawers	2	⅞ x 1 x 8
Top	1	¾ x 21¼ x 34
Quarter columns	1	2 diam. 10⅝
Caps and bases of quarter columns	4	¼ x 1⅛ x 1⅛
Large drawer front	1	⅞ x 5 x 27½
Carved drawer front	1	1 x 7 x 9½
Small drawer fronts	2	⅞ x 6¼ x 8½
Oak or Maple:		
Drawer guides (*A*)	4	1⅜ x 1¼ x 15¼
Drawer runs (*B*)	2	¾ x ⅞ x 16⅝
Drawer runs (*C*)	2	¾ x ⅞ x 17¾

DESCRIPTION	PIECES	DIMENSIONS
Upper supports for small drawers (*D*)	2	⅞ x 2½ x 17⅝
Drawer runs and guides (*E*)	2	2¼ x 2½ x 17¾
Supports for drawer runs (*F*)	2	⅞ x ⅞ x 27
Strips for fastening top (*G*)	2	⅞ x 2 x 16⅝
Yellow Poplar:		
Large drawer sides	2	⅝ x 4 7/16 x 18½
Carved drawer sides	2	⅝ x 6 7/16 x 18½
Small drawer sides	4	⅝ x 5 11/16 x 18½
Upper drawer back	1	½ x 4 7/16 x 26⅞
Carved drawer back	1	½ x 6 7/16 x 8⅞
Small drawer backs	2	½ x 5 11/16 x 7⅞
Plywood:		
Large drawer bottom	1	⅜ x 17 15/16 x 26¼
Carved drawer bottom	1	⅜ x 17 15/16 x 8¼
Small drawer bottoms	2	⅜ x 17 15/16 x 7¼
Bail handles	4	
Escutcheon plate	1	
Drop pull	1	

Fig. 12.   Chippendale lowboy hardware

and fasten them to the assembled frame (Fig. 8). Make the upper front stretcher and glue it to the tops of the front legs.

Turn the column from a piece of glued-up wood and split it into quarters. Glue the quarter columns into the niches provided for them (Fig. 8).

The construction of the drawers is clearly shown in Figure 10. Carve the middle drawer front from solid stock (Fig. 4); no part of the decoration should be glued on. Observance of the above rule and hand cutting the dovetailing as shown will result in a piece of furniture which will rank with the finest.

Make and fasten the top to complete the piece. Finish the lowboy and apply the hardware (Fig. 11).

8.

COLONIAL LADDER-BACK CHAIRS

Ladder-back chairs were very popular in early Colonial days. They are sturdy, yet light and graceful. When designed with slanted backs, as are these four, ladder-back chairs are very comfortable.

Most people like to sit in a rocking chair because it is so conducive to complete relaxation. During the past several years, rockers have regained much of their early popularity. Their unpopularity a few years back was due largely to the fact that rocking chairs were not in style during the era in which the better period furniture was developed. If Duncan Phyfe, the last great cabinetmaker to develop an important period of style, ever designed a rocking chair, it has escaped attention; and Phyfe's era came to a close early in the nineteenth century.

Though the origin of the rocking chair is un-certain, it is possible that there were rocking chairs before the Duncan Phyfe era. Benjamin Franklin has been credited by some authorities with inventing the rocking chair, although there is no substantial proof. Possibly the rockers on the cradle gave someone the idea. Most authorities on furniture agree that rocking chairs were created at a comparatively recent date and, unfortunately, during a period when good furniture design had been almost cast aside in the cabinet-making trade. Consequently, rocking chairs are synonymous with mediocre design. This is unfortunate, for the rocker can be as beautifully designed as any chair.

The child's ladder-back rocker and the Colonial ladder-back rocker are made of black walnut, while the Colonial slat-back rocker and the

Child's Ladder-Back Rocker

Colonial Ladder-Back Rocker

ladder-back armchair are made of maple, birch, and sycamore. The legs, arms, and rockers are maple; the slats are sycamore, and the rungs are birch, with the exception of the seat rungs, which are oak for greater strength. The seat rungs of the walnut chairs also are made of oak.

PROCEDURE

Since all the chairs are similar, the method used in their construction will be described as though they were one chair, with the few differences being noted in each step.

The first step consists of turning the legs and rungs on a lathe. The front and back legs, or posts, are turned first and, in some cases, the location of the slats and rungs is marked with the point of a skew chisel while the leg is still in the lathe. The back posts of the slat-back rocker (so named to distinguish it from the other two rockers) are turned to a diameter of 1⅝ in. and then are formed with a spokeshave, a scraper blade, and a wood file (Figs. 2 and 3). A lathe bed which will accommodate stock 46 in. long is required for the back legs of the armchair.

The holes for the rungs on chairs of this kind always are bored so that the side holes do not meet those on the front or back of the chair,

Colonial Ladder-Back Armchair

Colonial Slat-Back Rocker

although they can come close together.

Slats are made by band-sawing several out of one thick plank of the proper length. Several slats can be sawed from a plank 2 in. thick, while as many as five can be cut from a 4 by 4-in. plank. The forming and smoothing of the slats, with the exception of the tenons, can be done on a sanding machine (Fig. 29).

The back and front of the chair are assembled first. Draw center lines from the top to the bottom of each post on which to locate the holes for the front and back rungs and the mortises for the slats. Turn dowels on both ends of all rungs to make shoulders (Figs. 7 and 8). Correctly determine the shoulder measure of each slat so that the shoulders of each member will fit tightly against the legs before gluing and final assembly. Since the back posts are tapered on all four chairs, the shoulders of each slat will be slightly angled. This angle, as well as the exact length from shoulder to shoulder, can be properly arrived at only by carefully fitting each member as shown in Figures 7 and 8. Note that the shoulder of each slat is curved to conform to the curve of the leg (*A*, Fig. 26).

If hand tools are used to bore the rung holes in the front and back legs, place the leg in a level position in a vise with the center line on top. Then, by lining up the bit with a try square (Fig. 6), each hole can be bored perfectly straight. Mortise holes are drilled, or bored, in the same manner. If this work is done with machinery, clamp the legs to the mortising machine or drill press so that the center of the leg lies level during the cutting. This is especially important when drilling or mortising the tapered legs.

After the pieces for the front and back of the chair have been properly fitted, glue them together. With the clamps still in place, drill 3/16-in. holes through the joints and drive in roughly octagoned pegs, dipped in glue (Fig. 16).

With the front and back of the chair assembled, draw center lines on the posts to locate the places in which to bore the holes for the side rungs and the arms. The center lines of the holes for the side stretchers are not placed an exact quarter turn around the post from the holes already made, but slightly *more* than a quarter turn on the back posts, and *less* than a quarter turn on the front posts. Determine the proper position for this second center line on both front and back posts from the angles given in the plan views: Figures 1, 9, 14, and 22. Lay out these angles on the lower ends of the posts. Then draw the center lines. The bit to bore the holes will be started where the center line intersects with the rings drawn or scribed around the posts.

Figure 27 shows how to bore holes for the side rungs into the front legs. The sliding T bevel

BILL OF MATERIAL

DESCRIPTION	PIECES	DIMENSIONS
Colonial Slat-Back Rocker		
Back posts	2	1⅝ diam. x 37⅜
Front posts	2	1⅝ diam. x 15
Front seat rung	1	1 diam. x 16
Lower front rungs	2	¾ diam. x 16
Side seat rungs	2	1 diam. x 13 11/16
Middle side rungs	2	¾ diam. x 13⅜
Lower side rungs	2	¾ diam. x 13⅛
Rear seat rung	1	1 diam. x 13¼
Lower rear rung	1	¾ diam. x 13¼
Rockers	2	1¼ x 4½ x 32
Upper slat	1	1¼ x 3¼ x 13½
Second slat	1	1¼ x 2⅞ x 13⅜
Third slat	1	1¼ x 2½ x 13 5/16
Lower slat	1	1¼ x 2¼ x 13¼
Multicolored art fiber	1¼ lb.	3/16 in.
Colonial Ladder-Back Rocker		
Back posts	2	1¾ diam. x 38
Front posts	2	1¾ diam. x 19⅜
Front seat rung	1	1 diam. x 18
Lower front rung	1	⅞ diam. x 18
Side seat rungs	2	1 diam. x 15
Lower side rungs	2	⅞ diam. x 14¼
Rear seat rung	1	1 diam. x 14
Lower rear rung	1	⅞ diam. x 13⅞
Upper slat	1	1 x 4 x 14
Second slat	1	1 x 3¾ x 13⅞
Third slat	1	1 x 3½ x 13¾
Lower slat	1	1 x 3 x 13⅝
Rockers	2	⅝ x 6 x 31
Arms	2	¾ x 4 x 22½
Arm pieces to be glued to front	2	¼ x 3 x 1

DESCRIPTION	PIECES	DIMENSIONS
Multicolored art fiber	1½ lb.	3/16 in.
Child's Ladder-Back Rocking Chair		
Back posts	2	1¾ diam. x 34½
Front posts	2	1¾ diam. x 21¾
Front rungs	2	⅞ diam. x 16½
Side seat rungs	2	⅞ diam. x 13½
Lower side rungs	2	⅞ diam. x 13
Arm spindles	2	1¼ diam. x 14¼
Rear seat rung	1	⅞ diam. x 12⅛
Lower rear rung	1	⅞ diam. x 12
Upper slat	1	1 x 4 x 12
Middle slat	1	1 x 3½ x 12
Lower slat	1	1 x 3 x 12
Rockers	2	⅝ x 7 x 30
Multicolored art fiber	1¼ lb.	3/16 in.
Ladder-Back Armchair		
Back posts	2	1¾ diam. x 45
Front posts	2	1¾ diam. x 25¼
Front seat rung	1	1 diam. x 19¼
Lower front rungs	2	⅞ diam. x 19¼
Side seat rungs	2	1 diam. x 16⅜
Middle side rungs	2	⅞ diam. x 15¾
Lower side rungs	2	⅞ diam. x 15¼
Rear seat rung	1	1 diam. x 15¼
Lower rear rung	1	⅞ diam. x 15⅛
Upper slat	1	1¼ x 4 x 15⅜
Second slat	1	1¼ x 3½ x 15¼
Third slat	1	1¼ x 3 x 15⅛
Lower slat	1	1¼ x 3 x 15
Arms	2	1 x 4 x 19
Multicolored art fiber	1¾ lb.	3/16 in.

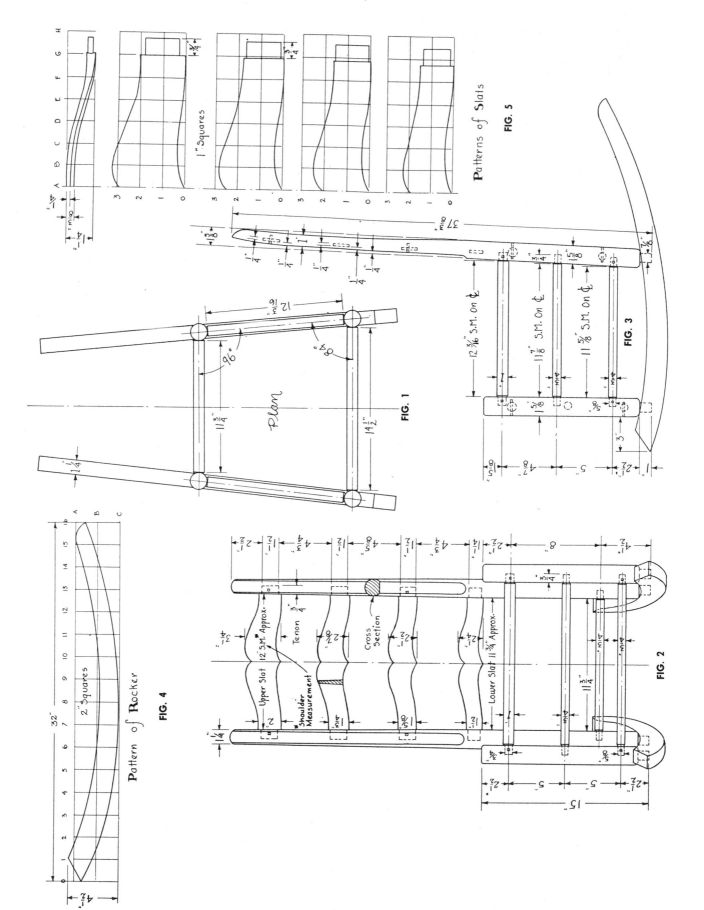

Patterns of Slats

FIG. 5

Plan

FIG. 1

FIG. 3

Pattern of Rocker

FIG. 4

FIG. 2

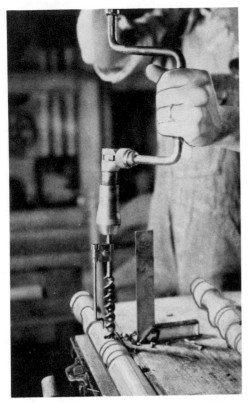

Fig. 6. To bore rung holes in the legs, place the leg in a level position in a vise, with the center line on top, and line up the bit with a try square.

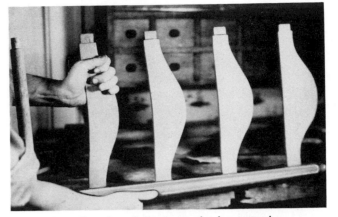

Fig. 7. Carefully fit each slat into the mortises on the back leg.

is set to the angle given in the plan view. In Figure 22, for example, this angle will be 82 deg. By lining up the bit with the blade of the sliding T bevel, the holes can be bored accurately.

Figure 28 shows how to bore holes for the side rungs into the back posts. First, lean the back against the wall at the angle in which it will be placed in the assembled chair. According to Figure 24, the bottoms of the posts will have to be fastened to the floor 3⅜ in. from the wall against which the back rests. Draw a center line on the floor and place the center of the chair back exactly over the center line. Draw lines on the floor to show the angles between the back and the sides as given in the seat plan. This angle, for example, would be 98 deg. for the armchair (Fig. 22). With the bit held level with the floor and in line with these 98-deg. lines, bore the holes in both posts for the side rungs.

When more than one chair is to be made and machinery is available, make jigs with which to bore the rung holes. Figure 30 shows such a jig in use. The slope on the side of the jig toward the worker is at the correct angle for boring holes into the back for the side rungs. The bit used

for this is a special type with a round shank and no threads on the spur. Tilt the drill-press table at the proper angle to give the back the correct slant. If the drill-press table cannot be tilted, then raise one end of the jig high enough to provide the same result. The drill-press table is not tilted when a jig is used for boring holes into the chair front for the side rungs because the front of the chair remains in a vertical position. Such a jig is shown in Figure 31. Once such jigs have been made, they provide a quick and accurate method for boring holes on an angle.

When the side rungs have been made and fitted properly, glue the side rungs and the assembled fronts and backs together. Take proper care to keep the angles alike on both sides of the chair when tightening the clamps. By adjusting the clamps as they are being tightened, this can be done easily.

Where arms are called for, they should be made

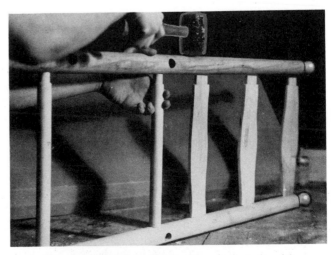

Fig. 8. The shoulders of each slat should fit tightly against the legs.

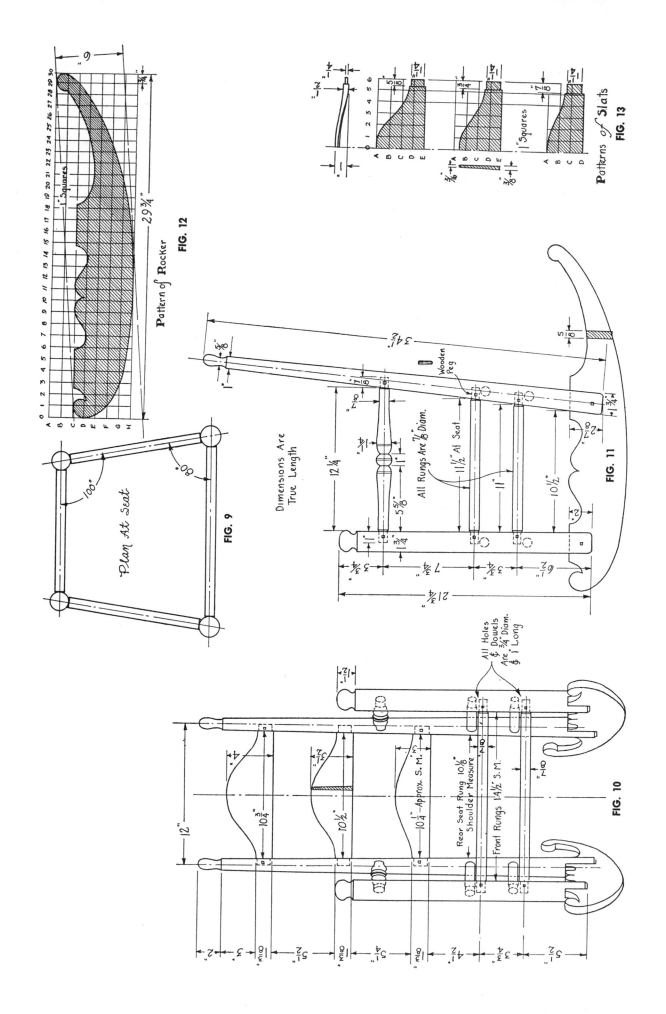

Pattern of Rocker

FIG. 12

Patterns of Slats

FIG. 13

Plan At Seat

FIG. 9

Dimensions Are True Length

All Rungs Are 7/8 Diam.

11½ At Seat

Wooden Peg

FIG. 11

All Holes & Dowels Are ¾ Diam. & 1 Long

Rear Seat Rung 10⅝ Shoulder Measure

Front Rungs 14½ S.M.

Approx. S.M.

FIG. 10

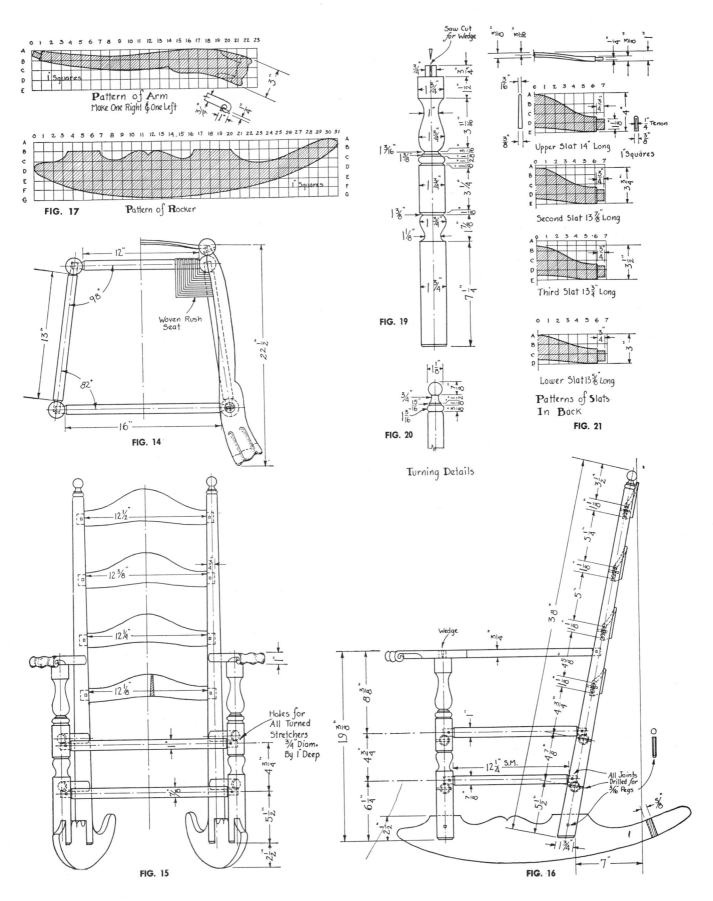

FIG. 17 Pattern of Arm — Make One Right & One Left

Pattern of Rocker

1" Squares

FIG. 14

98°

82°

12"

13"

22½"

16"

Woven Rush Seat

FIG. 15

12½"

12⅜"

12¼"

12⅛"

Holes for All Turned Stretchers ¾" Diam. By 1" Deep

FIG. 19

Saw Cut for Wedge

FIG. 20

Turning Details

Upper Slat 14" Long

Second Slat 13⅞" Long

Third Slat 13¾" Long

Lower Slat 13⅝" Long

1" Squares

1" Tenon

Patterns of Slats In Back

FIG. 21

FIG. 16

Wedge

38"

8⅛"

19⅜"

12¼" S.M.

6¼"

All Joints Drilled for 3/16 Pegs

7"

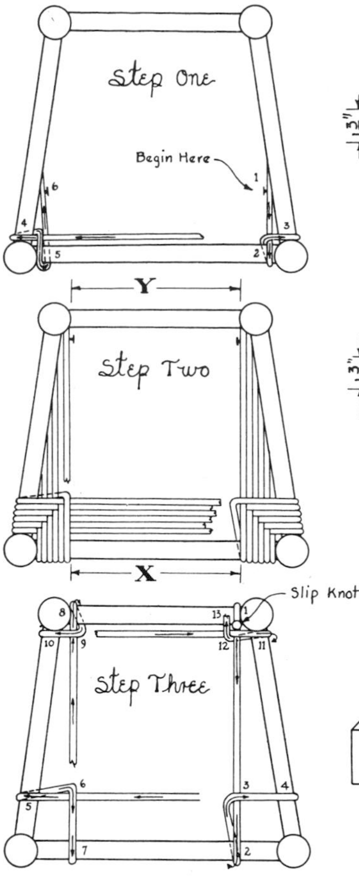
Step One
Begin Here
Y
Step Two
X
Slip Knot
Step Three

FIG. 33 Steps In Weaving A Chair Seat

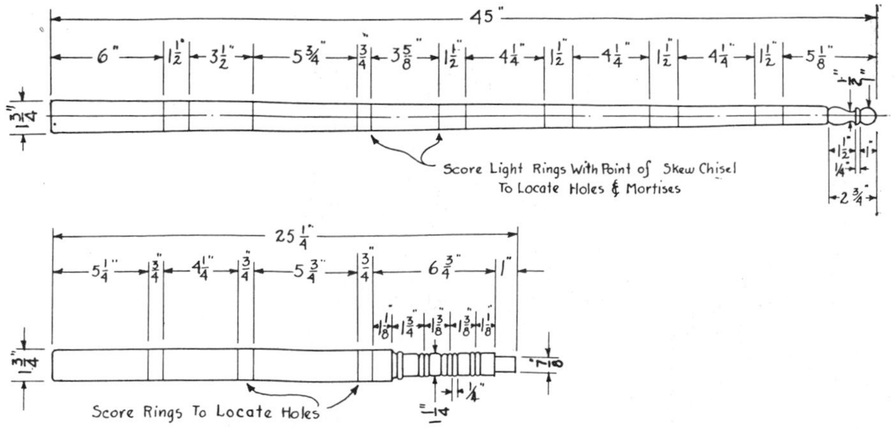
45"
Score Light Rings With Point of Skew Chisel To Locate Holes & Mortises
25 1/4"
Score Rings To Locate Holes

FIG. 25 - Turning Details for Legs

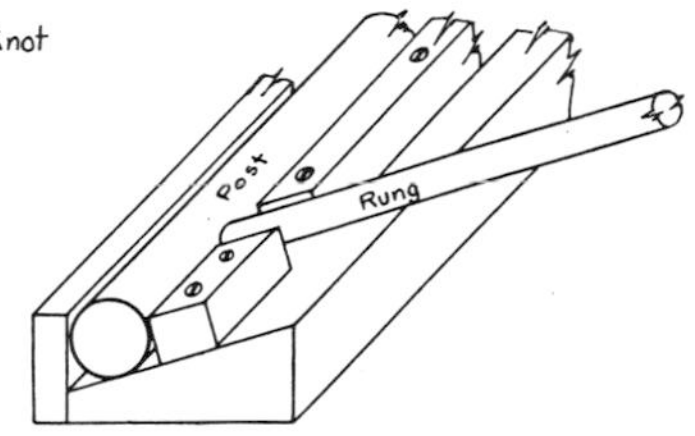
Post
Rung

FIG. 31

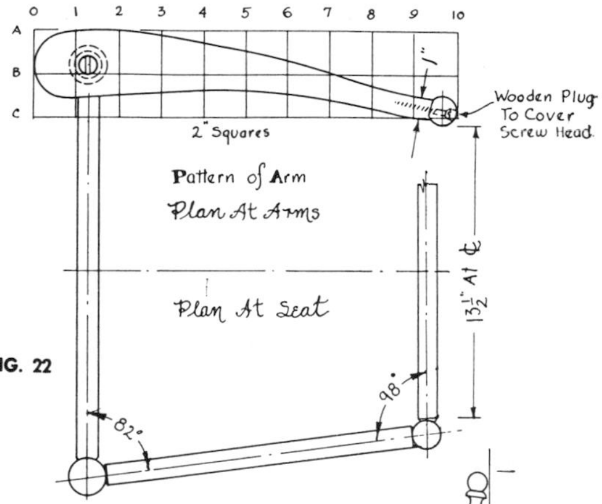
Wooden Plug To Cover Screw Head
2" Squares
Pattern of Arm
Plan At Arms
Plan At Seat
13 1/2" At ℄
98°
82°

FIG. 22

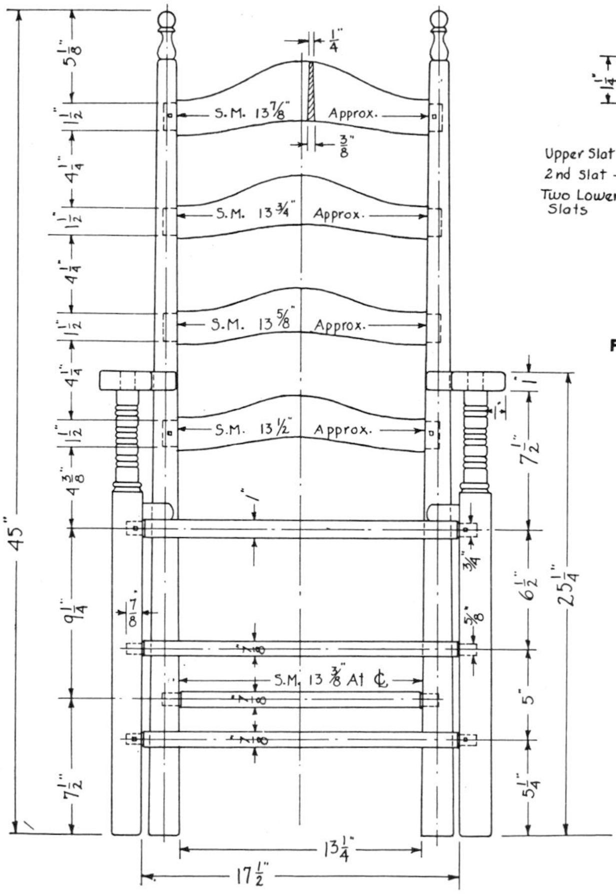
S.M. 13 7/8" Approx.
S.M. 13 3/4" Approx.
S.M. 13 5/8" Approx.
S.M. 13 1/2" Approx.
S.M. 13 3/8" At ℄
45"
25 1/4"
13 1/4"
17 1/2"

FIG. 23

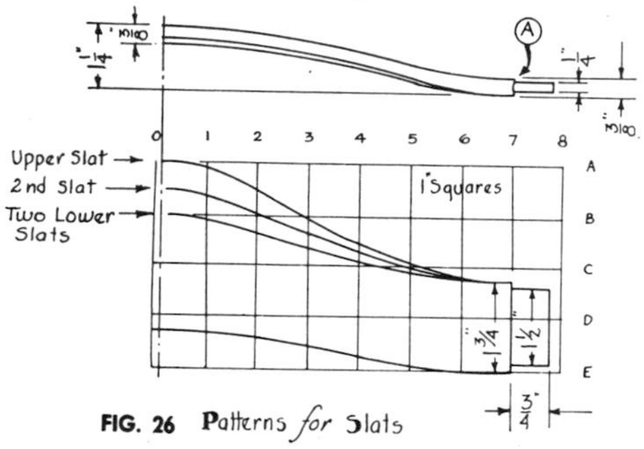
Upper Slat
2nd Slat
Two Lower Slats
1" Squares

FIG. 26 Patterns for Slats

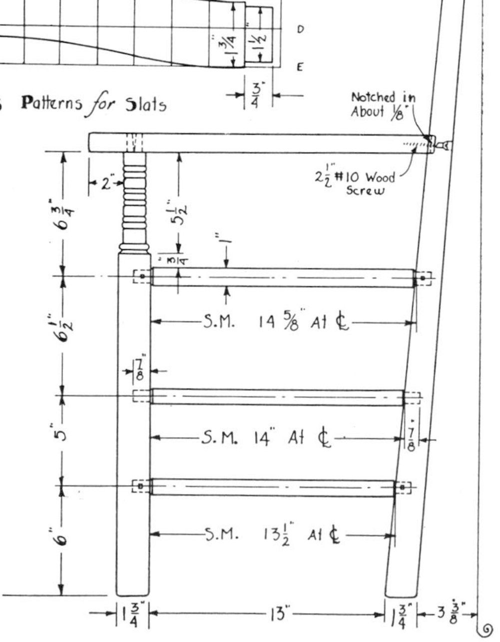
Notched in About 1/8"
2 1/2" #10 Wood Screw
S.M. 14 5/8" At ℄
S.M. 14" At ℄
S.M. 13 1/2" At ℄
13"

FIG. 24

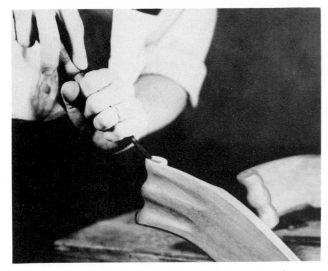

Fig. 18. Hand carve the front ends of the arms for the Colonial rocker.

Fig. 27. To bore holes for the side rungs into the front legs, set a sliding T bevel to the correct angle and line up the bit with the T bevel.

next. On the child's rocking chair, the extra rung which serves as an arm will be fastened to the chair with the other side rungs. On the armchair, the arms require little forming other than band-sawing and smoothing. When they have been mortised, fitted, and glued to the chair, the chair is ready to have the finishing coats applied. Only the seat needs to be woven to complete the chair. The arms of the Colonial rocker are first cut to shape on a band saw and then the front ends are hand carved, as shown in Figures 14, 15, 16, 17, and 18. These arms have a striking appearance and are well worth the trouble of carving them.

After the arms have been made and fastened to the chair, make the rockers. On the slat-back chair, the rockers are of the conventional type and fastened in the usual way. On the other two rockers, however, notches are sawed into the bottoms of the posts. The rockers are carefully fitted into these notches, glued, and further secured with wooden pegs. This style rocker lends an air of quaint charm to these two chairs.

When the rockers have been fastened into place, apply all the necessary finishing coats to the chairs, rub them down, and weave the seats.

The process of weaving these seats is illus-

Fig. 28. To bore holes for the side rungs in the back post, hold the bit level with the floor and in line with the 98-deg. lines.

Fig. 29. Forming and smoothing the slats on a sanding machine.

trated in Figures 32 and 33. Genuine rush (cat-tail leaves) can be used, although weaving with this material is work even for an experienced person. A seat almost equally durable and which, if properly done, will be difficult to distinguish from a genuine rush-bottomed seat, can be woven with ³⁄₁₆-in. multicolored art fiber. Furthermore, a good job can be done by amateurs and the inexperienced if they follow directions.

Start to weave the seat by tacking a piece of art fiber to the side rung on the right side of the chair. This place is found at *1*, step 1, Figure 33. Maintaining the proper twist on the strand being used, proceed from *1*, go over the top of the front rung, *2*, and then from the bottom of the front rung over and around the side rung, *3*. From there go to the top and around the other side rung, *4*, then over and around the front rung, *5*, and finally to *6*, on the left rung, where the strand is tacked fast and cut off.

Starting once more in back of *1*, tack a second strand and proceed as before to the left side of the chair. Keep repeating this process until the

Fig. 32.　Weaving a rush-bottomed seat.

distance X equals the distance Y, as shown in step 2, Figure 33. Then, with a slip knot, tie one end of a long strand to the right end of the rear stretcher, as at *1*, step 3, Figure 33. Proceed from *1* to *2*, from *2* to *3*, from *3* to *4*, and so on to *13*. Figure 32 shows the weaving of the Colonial rocker seat at this stage.

Repeat step 3, Figure 33, until the entire seat has been woven. Keep all strands parallel to the adjacent strand. If the strands tend to angle, push them together on the rung with the end of a wooden stick, or adjust them on the bias lines where they overlap with the end of a small screw driver. When the end of a long strand is reached, tie another strand to it underneath the seat where the knot will not show. If the strands close together on two sides before they close together on the other two sides, as they often do, continue back and forth on the last two rungs until the seat is entirely closed. Remember that the strand always comes from the *bottom* of one rung and goes to the *top* of the next rung and a mistake cannot be made unless the strand is wound around a rung once too often.

When the seat has been woven completely, the three layers of strong fiber make a sturdy and comfortable seat. Stuff narrow, folded strips of newspaper between the two bottom layers with a flat wooden paddle. This evens up and tightens the strands in the upper layer. Shellac the seat and the chair is ready for use.

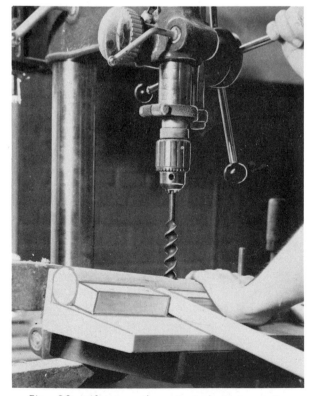

Fig. 30.　If more than one chair is to be made and machinery is available, make jigs with which to bore the rung holes.

9.

TURNED TRESTLE TABLE AND COLONIAL HANGING WALL SHELF

The trestle table and the hanging wall shelf form a nice set, although they need not be used together, for each is useful and beautiful by itself.

TURNED TRESTLE TABLE

The trestle table appears light for its size, because the members of the supporting framework are turned. The design is adapted from early Colonial models. The table may be made of maple, walnut, or any other domestic hardwood.

PROCEDURE

First, dress the stock to the sizes given in the bill of materials. Then turn the posts and stretchers on the lathe, following the dimensions given in Figure 3. Beautiful turnings have several characteristics which the craftsman should be aware of when starting a project of this kind. First, the curves are well rounded, full, and vigorous. A right angle is invariably formed where a properly turned curve and a fillet join each other. Where sharp edges are called for, they should be sharp not softened, as are turnings made on an automatic lathe. There is life in a curve which sweeps forward smoothly with a constant change of direction that neither falters nor appears erratic. U-shaped curves should be deep and should drop away sharply at the side, as shown in Figure 3.

BILL OF MATERIAL

DESCRIPTION	PIECES	DIMENSIONS
Posts	2	3 x 3 x 27¾
Stretchers	2	3 x 3 x 28⅜
Feet	2	3 x 3 x 30
Top	1	⅞ x 30 x 48
Cleats to support top	2	1¾ x 3 x 26

When the posts and stretchers have been turned, make the feet and the cleats which support the table top (Fig. 2). Next, lay out and cut all the mortises. Then lay out and cut the tenons.

To assemble the frame, first fasten the posts, feet, and cleats together (Fig. 2). Drill holes through each joint, and drive roughly octagoned hardwood pegs, which have been dipped in glue, into these holes to strengthen the joints (Fig. 4).

Turned Trestle Table and Colonial Hanging Wall Shelf

49

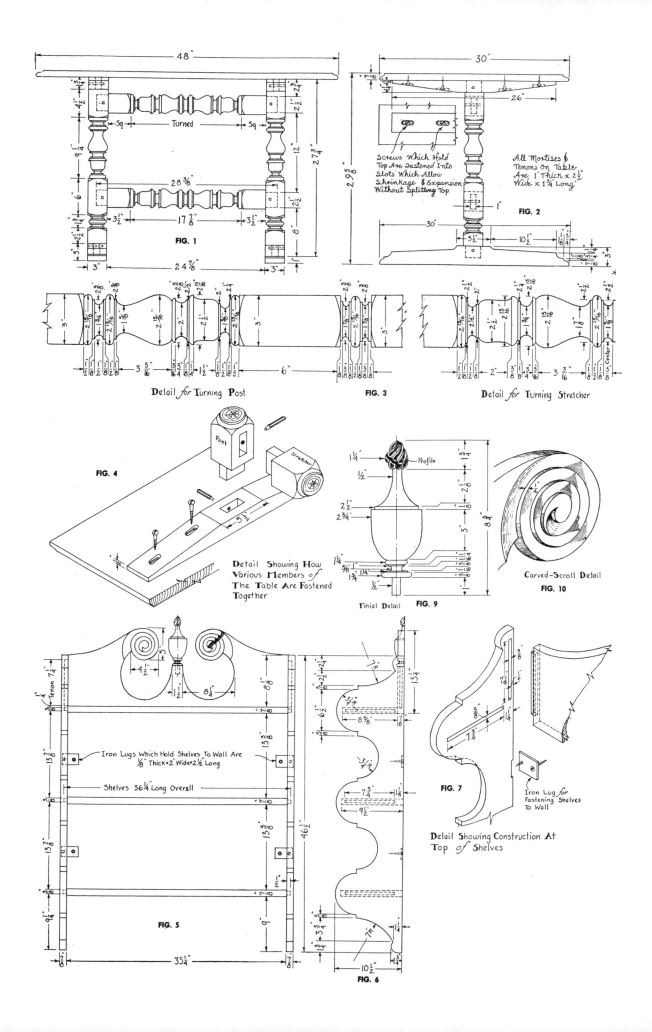

FIG. 1

FIG. 2

Screws Which Hold Top Are Fastened Into Slots Which Allow Shrinkage & Expansion Without Splitting Top

All Mortises & Tenons On Table Are 1" Thick x 2½" Wide x 1¾ Long

Detail for Turning Post

FIG. 3

Detail for Turning Stretcher

FIG. 4

Detail Showing How Various Members of The Table Are Fastened Together

Profile

Finial Detail   FIG. 9

Carved-Scroll Detail
FIG. 10

Iron Lugs Which Hold Shelves To Wall Are ⅛" Thick x 2" Wide x 2½ Long

Shelves 36¼" Long Overall

FIG. 5

FIG. 6

FIG. 7

Iron Lug for Fastening Shelves To Wall

Detail Showing Construction At Top of Shelves

This should be done while the mortise-and-tenon joints are being glued and the clamps which pull them tightly together are still in place. Such joints, if properly made, are very sturdy. Glue the two T-shaped table legs to the turned stretchers, pegging these joints also (Fig. 2).

Glue up the top and fasten it to the table frame (Fig. 4). To prevent splitting or warping of such a large top, provide for its expansion and contraction by cutting slots instead of drilling holes for the screws which fasten the top to the frame. Small washers are sometimes used under the screwheads.

COLONIAL HANGING WALL SHELF

The Colonial hanging wall shelf has ample space on which to display large books and art objects. The shelf is not only a piece of considerable distinction, but it is also a very useful and practical piece of furniture. Because its design was inspired by very early Colonial types, it is a fitting companion to the table with which it is shown.

PROCEDURE

Dress all stock to the sizes given in the bill of material. Lay out the places where the mortises are to be cut, as shown in Figures 5 and 6. Cut the mortises; then cut the tenons on the ends of the shelves. See that they fit together snugly.

Next, lay out the patterns for the sides and the top. The side pattern may be laid out directly

BILL OF MATERIAL

DESCRIPTION	PIECES	DIMENSIONS
Sides	2	⅞ x 10½ x 46½
Lower shelves	2	⅞ x 9½ x 36¼
Top shelf	1	⅞ x 8⅝ x 36¼
Back	1	⅞ x 13¼ x 36¼
Finial	1	2¾ diam. x 8¾
Iron lugs	4	⅛ x 2 x 2½

Use No. 14 wood screws to fasten the shelf to wooden walls or studs. Use toggle bolts to fasten it to hollow plastered walls.

on the wood, or a paper or cardboard pattern may be made first according to the dimensions given in Figure 6. A full-size pattern of the scroll top may be made on 1-in. graph squares (Fig. 8). This will also serve as a pattern for carving the scroll, a detail of which is shown in Figure 10.

Shape the sides and the top on a band saw; then file and sandpaper the curves until they are smooth. Carve the scroll. The shelf parts are now assembled and glued together. When clamping the shelves and sides together, square them properly.

The finial, after being turned and carved (Fig. 9), is planed flat at the back (see Fig. 6) so that the shelf will hang flat against the wall.

Iron lugs are screwed to the back to fasten the shelves to the wall (Fig. 7). Where screws cannot be driven into the studs in the wall, it is advisable to use toggle bolts. The lugs are spaced so that holes 32 in. apart may hit studs placed 16 in. apart.

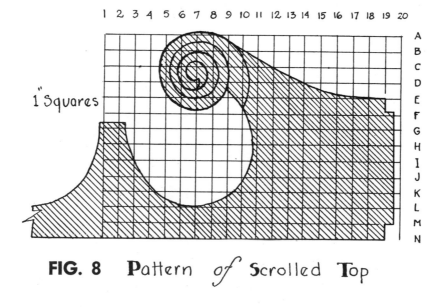

1 2 3 4 5 6 7 8 9 10 11 12 13 14 15 16 17 18 19 20

1" Squares

A B C D E F G H I J K L M N

FIG. 8 Pattern of Scrolled Top

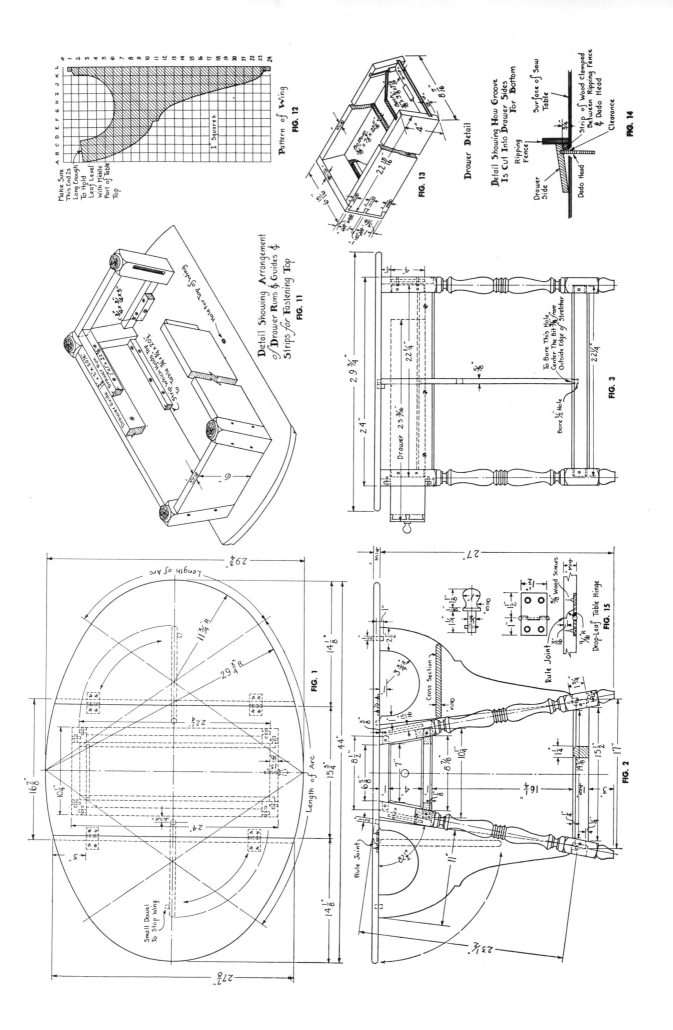

Pattern of Wing
FIG. 12

1" Squares

Make Sure This End Is Long Enough To Hold Leaf Level With Middle Part of Table Top

Drawer Detail
FIG. 13

Detail Showing How Groove Is Cut Into Drawer Sides For Bottom

Surface of Saw Table
Strip of Wood Clamped Between Ripping Fence & Dado Head
Ripping Fence
Clearance
Drawer Side
Dado Head
FIG. 14

Detail Showing Arrangement of Drawer Runs & Guides & Strips for Fastening Top
FIG. 11

Hole for top of wing

FIG. 3

To Bore This Hole Center The Bit ⅜" From Outside Edge of Stretcher
Bore ½ Hole

FIG. 1

Length of Arc
11¾" R
29¾" R
Length of Arc
Small Dowel To Stop Wing

FIG. 2

Rule Joint
Cross Section
Rule Joint
Drop-Leaf Table Hinge
FIG. 15
⅝ Wood Screws

10.

BUTTERFLY TABLE

There's much that's intriguing about a butterfly table. It has a quaint charm and a simple beauty seldom surpassed by other tables which serve the same purpose.

This small table may be placed next to a lounging chair or along a wall to hold lamps and decorative or useful objects. It may serve as a card table. No matter how it is used, this table, with raked legs and uniquely shaped wings, commands attention.

PROCEDURE

First square and turn the legs, then lay out the mortises. It is best to turn the legs before cutting the mortises and the angles at the ends. The details for doing the turning are found in Figure 5. Figure 4 shows the layout for cutting the mortises in the right front leg. With this layout as a guide, it will not be difficult to lay out the mortises on the other three legs. The angled mortises may be cut by fastening the leg to a mortising machine so that the leg is tilted at an 11-deg. angle. Cut the mortises on the adjacent side of the leg in the usual manner.

If the shoulder angles on the aprons and stretchers (Figs. 6 to 10) are cut properly, and the mortising also has been done properly, the rake, or angle, of the legs will automatically be correct. To guarantee correct angles for the front and back of this table, make a full-sized layout of the legs and stretchers (Fig. 2) on a large plywood panel or even on a clean shop floor. By placing each member in its proper position on this layout, the joints may be fitted together correctly.

When all parts of the frame have been fitted properly, they can be assembled and glued. Make the drawer guides and drawer runs next, and fasten them to the inside of the frame with wood screws (Fig. 11).

Fig. 13 shows the necessary details for mak-ing the drawer and the dovetail joint. With the sides of the drawer pitched at an angle, the details given in Figure 14 will aid in grooving the drawer sides. After the drawer is finished, make a knob (Fig. 15) and attach it (Fig. 2).

After the drawer has been fitted to the table, make the top. In all properly made table tops of this kind, the leaves are joined to the central part of the table top with rule joints (Fig. 15). For the table leaves to work properly when they are being raised or lowered, the curve must be an exact quadrant (90-deg. arc). The hinge used on rule joints has one leaf longer than the other. The center of the hinge joint must be placed directly below the dividing line on the upper surface of the two boards, as shown in Figure 15. Furthermore, the central section of the table top must be wide enough to allow the leaf to hang vertically when lowered, without interference from either the legs or the folded-back wing.

After the rule joints have been cut on the shaper, fasten the hinges before laying out the elliptical leaves. If the ellipse is sawed out with the hinges in place, good joining at the edges

Butterfly Table

With leaf dropped, table may be placed
with furniture.

BILL OF MATERIAL

DESCRIPTION	PIECES	DIMENSIONS
Legs	4	1¾ x 1¾ x 27¾
Upper side aprons	2	1¹³⁄₁₆ x 6⅛ x 22¼
Stretcher below drawer	1	1¹³⁄₁₆ x 1 x 10¼
Stretcher above drawer	1	1¹³⁄₁₆ x 1 x 8½
Rear apron	1	1¹³⁄₁₆ x 6 x 10¼
Front and rear stretchers at bottom of table	2	1¼ x 1¾ x 17
Side stretchers at bottom of table	2	1¼ x 1¾ x 22¼
Wings	2	⅝ x 11 x 23½
Table top (middle section)	1	¾ x 16⅞ x 29¾
Table-top leaves	2	¾ x 14⅛ x 27⅞
Drawer front	1	1¹³⁄₁₆ x 4 x 8⁷⁄₁₆
Drawer sides	2	⅝ x 4 x 22¹⁵⁄₁₆
Drawer bottom (plywood)	1	⅜ x 7⅞ x 22¹¹⁄₁₆
Drawer back (plywood)	1	⅜ x 3⅜ x 7¹³⁄₁₆
Drawer guides	2	¹⁵⁄₁₆ x 2 x 20½
Drawer runs	2	1 x 1 x 22⅜
Strips to hold top to table frame	2	¾ x ¾ x 20½
Short end strips to hold top to table	2	¾ x ¾ x 5
Short dowels to stop wings	2	½ diam. x 1
Drawer pull	1	1 diam. x 2½
Table-leaf hinges	4	1½ x 2½

will result (Fig. 1). To lay out the ellipse, first lay off two center lines at right angles. As shown in Figure 1, measure off distances of 44 in. on the major axis, and 29¾ in. on the minor axis. Next, measure off distances of 11¾ in. from both ends of the major axis. Then draw straight lines from both ends of the minor axis through the points located on the major axis, extending the lines to the arcs which are now to be drawn with the given radii. All four of the arcs composing the ellipse begin, end, and meet on these extended lines.

From the pattern given in Figure 12, draw a full-sized pattern, and with it lay out and cut two wings. Round the edges as shown in Figure 2. Bore holes for the wings into the table top

and into the bottom stretchers, locating them as shown in Figures 1, 2, and 3. With the table top laid bottom side up, place the table frame on it and, with the wings in place, fasten the frame to the top with wood screws (Fig. 11). To complete the table, bore holes in the leaves for the short dowel stops and glue these in place (Figs. 1 and 2).

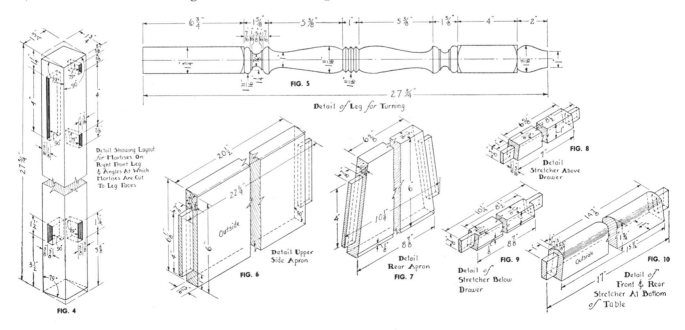

FIG. 5   Detail of Leg for Turning

FIG. 4   Detail Showing Layout for Mortises On Right Front Leg & Angles At Which Mortises Are Cut To Leg Faces

FIG. 6   Detail Upper Side Apron

FIG. 7   Detail Rear Apron

FIG. 8   Detail Stretcher Above Drawer

FIG. 9   Detail of Stretcher Below Drawer

FIG. 10   Detail of Front & Rear Stretcher At Bottom of Table

11.

LIGHT SHERATON SIDE CHAIR

Although the author prefers the Chippendale style, it is his firm conviction that Thomas Sheraton was the greatest eighteenth-century furniture designer. The author places Sheraton first for three reasons. First, he had a highly developed sense of good proportion — superior, we think, to that shown by his distinguished contemporaries. Second, he had a talent for invention unmatched by any cabinetmaker of his day, and by very few since. Third, his designs are practical and sound from the standpoint of good construction. This is not always true of the designs of his contemporaries. Chippendale, for example, was not averse to sacrificing orderly structure to achieve ostentation. The Brothers Adam were more concerned about striking architectural effects than sound construction, and did not always adhere to accepted standards of logical structure. Many Hepplewhite and Chippendale designs incline toward ponderosity. Sheraton's designs are methodically well proportioned, gracefully light, yet structurally sound. By consistently using straight lines structurally, he was able to reduce size without sacrificing essential strength.

Those qualities enumerated above have been embodied in the design of the light Sheraton side chair shown here. It is literally a cabinetmaker's gem.

PROCEDURE

Select a good grade of Honduras or Cuban mahogany for the back legs, front legs, and all members of the chair back. The seat stretchers may be made of close-grained domestic woods, such as birch, gum, or sycamore. The wood should be neither too hard nor too soft to hold tacks.

On a mahogany plank about 5½ in. wide and 1⅜ in. thick, trace the shape of the two back legs, using a pattern made from *B* in Figure 4. Band-saw these legs to shape; then plane all surfaces smooth and round the upper part of the

back legs with a spokeshave. The legs must be paired, one left and one right, by shaping them as shown in Figure 4, *A*. Make the layouts for the mortises and tenons, and cut these.

Make and fit the stretchers which go into the back, including the seat stretcher. Then lay out and cut the mortises on the mahogany stretchers into which the carved back is to be fitted.

Make a pattern for sawing out the carved chair back from Figure 5. This should be cut out on the jig saw, after which the tenons at each end may be made and fitted into their respective mortises. Once the mortises and tenons have been properly joined, the back may be carved (Fig. 5). This may be done either before or after gluing up the chair back.

The carving on the back stretchers, and on the front of the back legs above the chair seat should

Light Sheraton Side Chair

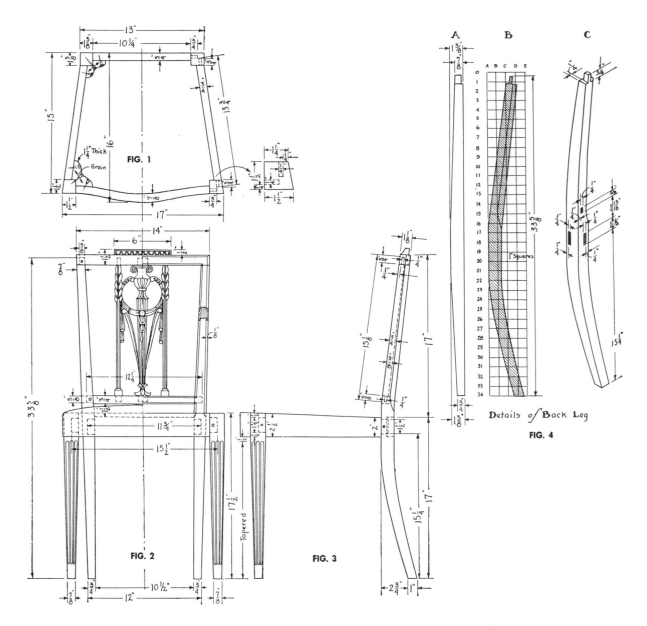

Details of Back Leg
FIG. 4

BILL OF MATERIAL

DESCRIPTION	PIECES	DIMENSIONS		DESCRIPTION	PIECES
Front legs	2	1½ x 1½ x 17½		No. 2 springs	9
Back legs	1	1⅜ x 5½ x 33⅝[1]		Spring twine	
Front seat rail	1	1⅞ x 2½ x 15½		10-oz. burlap	
Side seat rails	2	¾ x 2½ x 13¾		Curled hair or moss for filling	
Back seat rail	1	¾ x 2 x 11¾		material	
Top rail in back	1	1⅛ x 1½ x 14		Upholsterer's cotton felt	
Lower rail in back	1	¾ x ¾ x 12¼		Muslin	
Carved back	1	9/16 x 6 x 15⅛		Upholstering material (striped	
Front brace blocks in seat	2	1¼ x 1⅝ x 3½		damask has been used on	
Rear brace blocks in seat	2	1¼ x 1⅝ x 3		this chair)	
2½-in. webbing		10 ft.		Tacks	
				Stitching twine	
				Cambric for bottom of seat	

[1] This is large enough to make both legs.

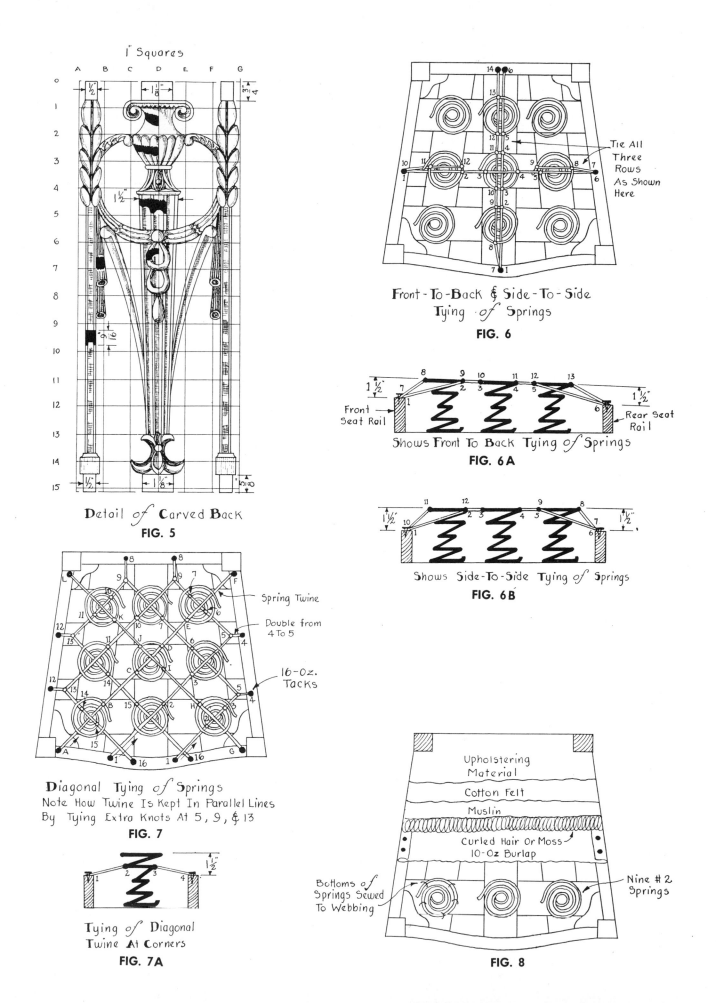

1" Squares

Detail of Carved Back
FIG. 5

Front-To-Back & Side-To-Side
Tying of Springs
FIG. 6

Tie All
Three
Rows
As Shown
Here

Front
Seat Rail

Rear Seat
Rail

Shows Front To Back Tying of Springs
FIG. 6A

Shows Side-To-Side Tying of Springs
FIG. 6B

Spring Twine

Double from
4 To 5

16-Oz.
Tacks

Diagonal Tying of Springs
Note How Twine Is Kept In Parallel Lines
By Tying Extra Knots At 5, 9, & 13
FIG. 7

Tying of Diagonal
Twine At Corners
FIG. 7A

Upholstering
Material

Cotton Felt

Muslin

Curled Hair Or Moss
10-Oz Burlap

Bottoms of
Springs Sewed
To Webbing

Nine #2
Springs

FIG. 8

be done after the assembling of the back has been completed.

Make the front legs next. Lay out and carve the fluting on the two outside faces of the legs (Figs. 2 and 3). Cut the mortises; make the seat rails and rail tenons; and complete the assembling of the chair. Fasten the bracing blocks to the inside of the seat with screws and wood glue, as shown in Figure 1. Roughly octagoned ³⁄₁₆-in. pegs are used in addition to glue, to hold all joints together.

Upholstering. To upholster the chair, stretch and tack the webbing on the bottom of the seat. Place nine No. 2 coiled seat springs on the webbing as shown in Figure 6, so that the twine may be tied in straight parallel lines in all directions. Sew the springs to the webbing (Fig. 8). The proper method of tying the springs is shown in great detail to guide the craftsman in upholstering this and similar chairs.

Tie the springs from front to back (Fig. 6A), then from side to side (Fig. 6B), and, finally, diagonally (Fig. 7). Drive a 16-oz. tack part way into the top of the front seat stretcher at *1* (Fig. 6). To this tack, tie the middle of a long piece of twine and tie the springs as shown in Figures 6 and 6A. Taking one of the ends of twine, proceed from *1* to *2*, from *2* to *3*, and so on to point *6*, tying the springs down to the required height at each point with a weaver's knot. Tack the end of the twine to the rear seat stretcher at point *6* (Fig. 6). Pick up the other end at *7*, tie it to the springs at points *8* to *13*, and then tack it at point *14*.

Follow the same procedure in tying from side to side, and diagonally. Note how the twine is kept parallel in the diagonal tying by making extra knots (Fig. 7). Few tacks are needed, and a good job is done by using long single pieces of twine from points *1* to *16*. Shorter pieces going from *A* to *F*, and from *G* to *L*, will complete the tying.

Figure 8 shows the steps in stuffing and covering the chair. First, tack a piece of 10-oz. burlap to the top of the rails over the springs. Then sew the first layer of filling material to the burlap at regular intervals with Italian stitching twine, using a running stitch. This will prevent sliding about, or "creeping," after the upholstering has been completed. Curled hair is best for stuffing the chair seat, although moss, a cheaper material, will make a durable seat. The filling material should be "picked," that is, pulled apart, until it is loose and springy. Build up the first layer with hair or moss spread evenly over the entire surface until it is thick enough to make a smooth and comfortable seat. Place muslin over the filling material, tacking it to the sides of the seat frame with 3-oz. tacks. Over the muslin place a layer of cotton felt (which need not be tacked) to smooth and soften the surface and prevent the filling and dust from coming through the surface material. The upholstering material is then cut, tacked, and sewed on; use gimp tacks where the tacks will show, and 3-oz. tacks underneath the seat frame.

Complete the upholstering by tacking a piece of cambric to the bottom of the seat.

12.

HEPPLEWHITE ROCKER FOR A SMALL CHILD

Furniture made for children becomes a treasured heirloom because of its association with the loved ones. This is all the more true if such pieces are designed to be beautiful and serviceable, as is this small mahogany rocking chair in the style of Hepplewhite.

PROCEDURE

The first step is to make full-sized patterns of the individual parts, especially the curved members, according to the details given in Figure 4. In several instances, two patterns of a single member will be needed, as, for example, a pattern for the front of the back leg, and another for the side of the same leg. Moreover, both a right and a left leg must be made by reversing the pattern when it is being laid out on the wood.

The patterns shown are accurate for the chair which the author built. Because slight variations are bound to occur when another person makes these pieces, constant checking and adjustment will be necessary during the process of construction. The author found this to be the case even when making two chairs of the same kind. It is particularly true of chair building, because even

BILL OF MATERIAL

DESCRIPTION	PIECES	DIMENSIONS
Back legs	2	2 x 2 x 24¼[1]
Front legs	2	1½ x 1½ x 10½
Rockers	2	1¼ x 3½ x 26¼
Side stretchers for seat	2	1½ x 2¼ x 13
Back stretcher for seat	1	¾ x 2¼ x 12
Front stretcher for seat	1	1⅝ x 2¼ x 15¼
Stretcher below seat on rear legs	1	½ x 1 x 11
Bottom of shield	1	¾ x 3½ x 12
Top of shield	1	⅞ x 3½ x 16
Arm supports	2	1 x 2⁹⁄₁₆ x 8¾
Arms	2	1 x 2¾ x 10¾
Wheat-sheaf splat	1	⁷⁄₁₆ x 8 x 15
Corner blocks	4	
Plywood (for seat)	1	⅜ x 14⅜ x 16¼
Cotton batting		
Muslin		
Upholstering material		
Tacks		

[1] This is the size of stock from which a single leg may be cut. Two legs may be cut from a single plank slightly wider than 3 in. Considerable material can be saved by carefully laying out patterns on wide pieces of stock, instead of first cutting the stock to the approximate sizes of single members.

Hepplewhite Child's Rocker

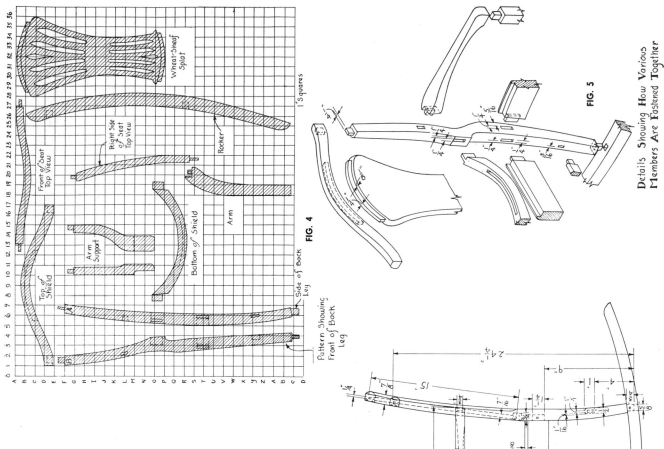

FIG. 4

1" squares

Wheat-Sheaf Splat

Front of Seat Top View

Right Side of Seat Top View

Rocker

Top of Shield

Arm Support

Bottom of Shield

Arm

Side of Back Leg

Pattern Showing Front of Back Leg

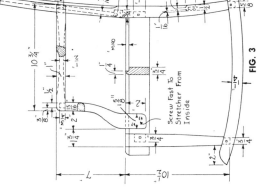

FIG. 3

Screw Fast To Stretcher From Inside

FIG. 5

Details Showing How Various Members Are Fastened Together

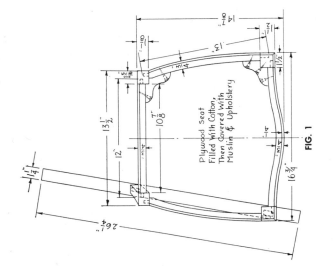

FIG. 1

Plywood Seat Filled With Cotton, Then Covered With Muslin & Upholstery

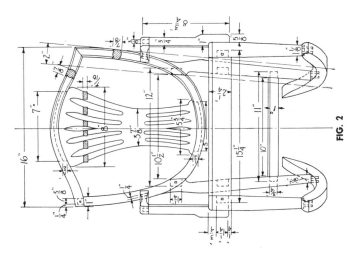

FIG. 2

Fig. 6. Planing the concave curves
on the back leg.

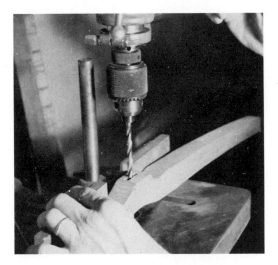

Fig. 7. A drill press facilitates
the cutting of mortises.

the slight variation of a curve on one member may make necessary a compensating change on an adjoining part. The wheat-sheaf splat should be cut out after the other members of the back have been joined and fitted together properly, for only by sheer luck could the exact length and shape of the curved joints be determined before this has been done.

Begin with the back legs. The pattern for the side of the leg, labeled *A* (Fig. 4), should be laid out and sawed on the band saw first. Do not cut the tenons at this time, but wait until the mortises into which they are to be fitted have been cut. Plane the front and back of the leg to the exact lines of the pattern before band-sawing the remaining two sides to shape. In this way, the front and back may be squared to the two sides of the leg which have not been sawed as yet. The two sides, in turn, may be squared with the front and back after the sides have been shaped.

To plane the concave curves on the back legs, use a special plane on which the bottom can be adjusted to any curve (see Fig. 6). The convex curve on the opposite side may be planed more easily with a jack plane or trimmed to the line with a sharp chisel.

After the front and back have been planed, tack the waste pieces back on the leg, carefully placing the nails in waste parts where the saw will not pass through them when the two sides are cut. Now lay out and cut pattern *B* (Fig. 4). With chisel, plane, spokeshave, files, scrapers, etc., dress the four sides of the leg to the exact size and shape (Figs. 2 and 3). Be careful to keep adjacent sides square to each other.

Now make the top and bottom rails of the shield, the rear seat rail, and the rail below the seat (Figs. 1, 2, 3, and 4). Do not cut the tenons

for these parts until the mortises into which they are to be fitted have been cut. The lower rail in the shield is flat in back and only ¾ in. thick, while the upper parts of the leg and the top rail are rounded in back and ⅞ in. thick.

Lay out and cut all mortises in the back legs and in the top rail of the shield. The drill press will come in handy for making these mortises, as shown in Figure 7. Now cut and fit the tenon at the top of each leg to the mortises in the top rail (Fig. 5).

To properly fit the shield rails to the back legs, clamp both legs to a table or workbench so that each leg lies at the correct distance and at the correct angle to the vertical center line of the chair back (Figs. 1 and 2). While the legs are in this position, lay out the shoulder angles of all tenons on the shield rails, as well as those at the top of the legs (Fig. 5).

When all these joints have been fitted, lay out the pierced splat which is the central member of the shield. Cut the mortises for the splat in both rails; then cut the tenons (Fig. 5). Fit the splat to the lower rail first. Mark the shoulder line of the upper tenon slightly higher than it should go, and first cut to this line. You probably will have to trim this shoulder several times. If, during a trial assembly of this joint, a flexible steel rule or a piece of cardboard is bent to fit the rail curvature and placed under it, the exact curve of the rail may be marked on the shoulder of the tenon. The operation may have to be repeated several times before the joint is perfect. When the splat joints

Fig. 8.   The assembled rocker
without the seat.

have been fitted, cut out the open places on the jig saw (Fig. 4).

Then make the back seat rail and the bottom rail for the chair back. Note that the top of the seat rail must be rabbeted (Figs. 1 and 2). When this has been done, glue up the chair back.

Now carve the front of the shield. The shape of the carving is shown in the cross-section views in Figure 2. Do that carving, where the arms join the back, after the arms have been attached.

Next make and assemble the front legs, the side rails, and the front seat rail. Rabbet the seat rails. Join this part to the back and glue all the joints (Fig. 5). Make the rockers and cut the mortises. Clamp the rockers to the sides of the legs, then mark the shoulders of the leg tenons. Determine the angles at which the tenons are to be cut, and mark them on the bottoms of the legs. The sides of the tenons are not parallel with the sides of the leg. Cut the tenons and fit the joints. Then glue the rockers to the legs.

Lay out the arms and arm supports; cut them out on the band saw. The dotted lines in Figure 3 show how the insides of the arms are sloped on the top and bottom. Cut and fit all joints, then glue them to the chair. Glue the arm supports to the seat rails and secure each with two wood screws.

Make the four corner blocks to brace the seat (Fig. 1). Fasten the blocks with glue and wood screws.

Outline the shape of the seat (Fig. 1) on a piece of ⅜-in. plywood. Saw out the seat, allowing about ⅛-in. clearance around each edge for the upholstering materials. To upholster the seat, first cover the plywood with a thick layer of cotton batting. Then draw muslin down over the batting and tack underneath. Always start tacking at the middle of each side and work toward the corners, drawing the material taught. Finally tack on the upholstering material. Place the seat on the rocker.

13.

COLONIAL MIRROR

The unusual feature of this Colonial mirror is the metal silhouette fastened over the glass at the upper part of the frame. The silhouette was cut out of 18-ga. copper, then polished and lacquered. The author has colored some copper silhouettes with liver of sulphur dissolved in water. Various colors can be obtained, depending upon the amount of liver of sulphur put into the solution and the length of time the copper is allowed to remain in the solution. Apply a coat of lacquer to the colored copper as soon as it is dry.

Other sheet metals, such as brass, pewter, or aluminum, also may be used. The metal should not be too thin or it will not stay tight against the mirror and will result in a fuzzy outline around parts of the design.

This particular silhouette is suitable for a Colonial-type mirror, showing, as it does, two Colonial girls, one spinning flax, and the other spinning wool or cotton. The hand-carved volute scrolls also add to the beauty of this maple mirror.

PROCEDURE

First make the molding for the frame (Fig. 1). The pieces can be cut from a rabbeted strip of wood about 9 ft. long. After mitering the corners, drill holes for bradding the joints. The joints should be glued as they are nailed. Figure 5 shows the proper way to assemble the frame.

The parts of the frame at the top and bottom, to which the pieces are attached, are not cut until the frame has been assembled. To do this without sawing into the nails, drill the nail holes so that none of the brads will protrude into the ⅜-in. spaces which are to be removed (Fig. 2). If solid wood of this width were not fastened through slotted holes as shown, the boards would split when expansion or contraction

BILL OF MATERIAL

DESCRIPTION	PIECES	DIMENSIONS
Sides	2	⅞ x 2⅝ x 31
Top and bottom	2	⅞ x 2⅝ x 22¼
Mirror separation piece	1	⅞ x 1 x 19½
Scrolled top	1	⅜ x 30 x 15¼
Scrolled bottom	1	⅜ x 28 x 8¼
Plate-glass mirror	1	¼ x 17½ x 19
	1	¼ x 6¾ x 17½
18-ga. sheet metal (copper, brass, or pewter)	1	6¾ x 17½
No. 8 roundhead screws	14	¾ in.
Washers	14	

Colonial Mirror

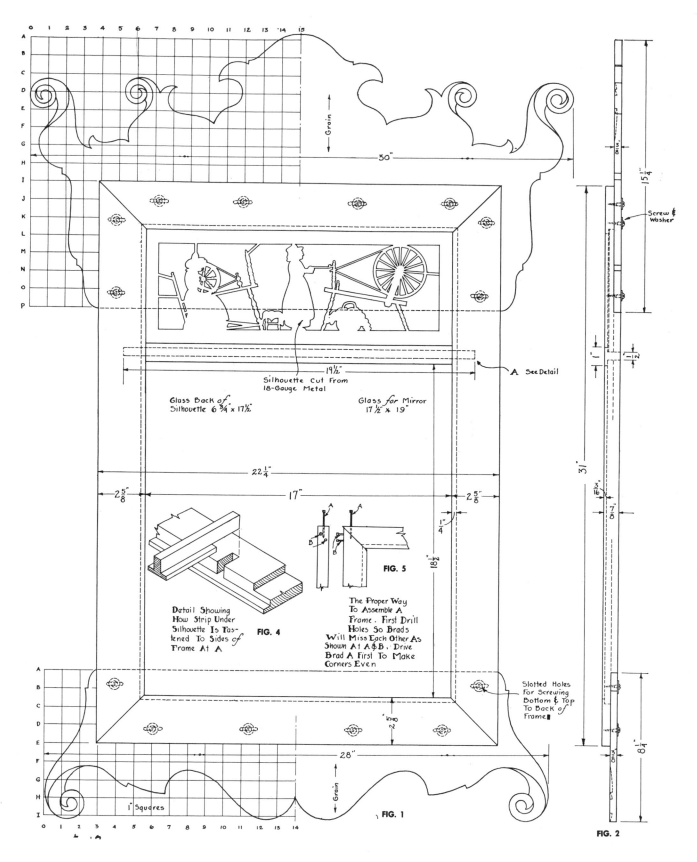

Grain

30"

Grain

A See Detail

Silhouette Cut From
18-Gauge Metal

19½"

Glass Back of
Silhouette 6¾" x 17½"

Glass for Mirror
17½" x 19"

22¼"

2⅝"   17"   2⅝"

1"/4

18½"

Detail Showing
How Strip Under
Silhouette Is Fas-
tened To Sides of
Frame At A   FIG. 4

FIG. 5

The Proper Way
To Assemble A
Frame. First Drill
Holes So Brads
Will Miss Each Other As
Shown At A & B. Drive
Brad A First To Make
Corners Even

Slotted Holes
For Screwing
Bottom & Top
To Back of
Frame

2"/8

28"

1" Squares

Grain

FIG. 1

15¼"

Screw &
Washer

1"

1½"

31"

⅞"

8¼"

FIG. 2

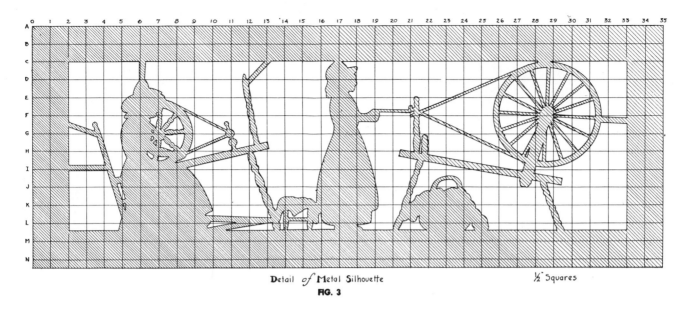

Detail of Metal Silhouette   ½" Squares
FIG. 3

takes place during season changes. If plywood is used for the scroll-sawed pieces (many manufacturers now use plywood), that part of the scroll-sawed pieces against which the frame is placed can be sawed out and the pieces fitted around the frame. However, the attractive volute scrolls shown on this piece cannot be carved on plywood.

The design of the copper silhouette may be drawn at full size on ½-in. graph squares (Fig. 3). Drill holes into every corner of the waste pieces which are to be cut out of the design, and saw them out with a jeweler's saw or a metal-cutting blade and a power jig saw.

Figure 4 shows how the wooden strip below the silhouette is fastened to the frame. Make the rabbeted strip and lay it against the back of the frame in its proper position. Then, with a sharp knife, trace the outline of the tenons on the frame to make the layout for the mortises.

The screws and washers joining the scrolled pieces to the frame should be snug but not too tight or they may interfere with the expansion which must take place.

14.

EARLY GEORGIAN SLANT-TOP DESK

Slant-top desks are much sought after, and a light, nicely proportioned period piece, such as this early Georgian slant-top desk, would be highly prized by anyone who loves fine furniture. This desk has many features to recommend it, such as the gracefully formed and beautifully carved cabriole legs, the richly carved apron, and the interesting cabinet inside the desk with its curved-front and block-front drawers. The carved sunburst adds just the right finishing touch.

The desk is well constructed with deep mortises and long tenons and dovetailing on all drawers and at several other places where important members are joined together. The fine proportions and the harmonious arrangement of the curved members add to the beauty of the desk.

PROCEDURE

The legs should be prepared first from a pattern made from Figure 4, giving the shape of the legs and the carving details. Stock, 3¼ in. square, is used for the main part of the leg. Before sawing the leg proper to shape on a band saw, glue two bracket blocks on two adjacent sides of each leg, 6 in. from the top.

Place the pattern on one of the inner sides of the leg and trace the design. Saw close to these lines on a band saw. Save all waste pieces for they are to be retacked to the leg to form flat surfaces for sawing out the remaining two sides. After tacking on the waste pieces, trace the design on the adjacent inner side of each leg and make the final cuts. This procedure for cutting out a curved leg is illustrated in Figure 7, page 134.

Early Georgian Desk — closed

Early Georgian Desk — open

BILL OF MATERIAL

DESCRIPTION	PIECES	DIMENSIONS
Main Part of Desk		
Honduras or Cuban Mahogany:		
Legs	4	3¼ x 3¼ x 26
Bracket blocks to be glued to upper part of each leg	8	3¼ x 3¼ x 3
Table board	1	⅞ x 16¾ x 35
Carved apron	1	⅞ x 4 x 37
Front rail below upper drawer	1	⅞ x 3 x 35
Front rail above lower drawer	1	⅞ x 3 x 36½
Dovetailed stiles between drawer and slide supports	2	⅞ x 1¼ x 4¼
Slide supports	2	15/16 x 2 15/16 x 17
Top of desk	1	⅞ x 9 x 35½
Upper desk ends	2	⅞ x 17¾ x 19
Lower desk ends, or aprons	2	⅞ x 6 x 17
Desk lid	1	⅞ x 16¼ x 34¾
Cleats at ends of lid	2	⅞ x 2 x 16¼
Drawer front (bottom drawer)	1	⅞ x 3 7/16 x 34 7/16
Drawer front (upper drawer)	1	⅞ x 2 15/16 x 39 11/16
Molding	1	1 x 1¼ x 80 (approx.)
Poplar:		
Long rail at back of frame which supports lower drawer	1	⅞ x 2 x 37
Long rail at front of frame which supports lower drawer	1	⅞ x 2¼ x 37
End rails of frame which support lower drawer	2	⅞ x 2¼ x 14⅝
Long rail at back of frame above lower drawer	1	⅞ x 2 x 37
End rails of frame above lower drawer	2	⅞ x 2¼ x 14⅝
Long rail at back of frame which supports upper drawer	1	⅞ x 2 x 35
End rails of frame which support upper drawer and slide supports	2	⅞ x 3½ x 13¾
Guides for upper drawer and slide supports	2	¾ x 1¼ x 15⅞
Sides for lower drawer	2	½ x 3 7/16 x 17½
Sides for upper drawer	2	½ x 2 15/16 x 16⅝
Back for lower drawer	1	⅜ x 2 11/16 x 33 15/16
Back for upper drawer	1	⅜ x 2 3/16 x 29 3/16
Plywood:		
Bottom for upper drawer	1	⅜ x 16⅜ x 29 3/16
Bottom for lower drawer	1	⅜ x 17¼ x 33 15/16
Mahogany-Veneered Plywood:		
Back of desk	1	½ x 19¾ x 35¼
Cabinet on Inside of Desk		
Mahogany:		
A	2	⅜ x 13¼ x 13⅛
B	2	¼ x 9⅞ x 6 3/16
C	2	¼ x 8¼ x 6 3/16
D	2	¼ x 7⅛ x 6 3/16
E	1	⅜ x 7 x 33⅝
F	2	¼ x 10¼ x 13 11/16
G	1	½ x 13¾ x 33⅝
H	1	½ x 2¾ x 33⅝
I	2	½ x 6¾ x 9
J	2	¼ x 8¼ x 2 11/16
K	2	¼ x 13 x 3¼
L	2	½ x 1½ x 13½
Small door	1	¾ x 6 x 8¾
Outside curved drawer fronts	2	1 x 2 7/16 x 7 1/16
Inside curved drawer fronts	2	1 x 2 7/16 x 7
Outside block drawer fronts (convex)	2	1 x 2 15/16 x 8 15/16
Center block drawer front (concave)	1	1 x 2 15/16 x 14 15/16
Poplar:		
Long sides of outside small curved drawers	2	¼ x 2 7/16 x 10⅛
Short sides of outside small curved drawers	2	¼ x 2 7/16 x 8⅛
Long sides of inside small curved drawers	2	¼ x 2 7/16 x 7⅞
Short sides of inside small curved drawers	2	¼ x 2 7/16 x 6⅜
Backs for small curved drawers	4	¼ x 1 15/16 x 6 5/16
Sides of convex block drawers	4	¼ x 2 15/16 x 12¾
Sides of concave block drawer	2	¼ x 2 15/16 x 12½
Backs for convex block drawers	2	¼ x 2 7/16 x 8 11/16
Back for concave block drawer	1	¼ x 2 7/16 x 14 11/16
Drawer runs for block front drawers: End runs	2	½ x ¾ x 10½
Drawer runs for block front drawers: Middle runs	2	½ x 1½ x 10½
Plywood:		
Bottoms for outside curved drawers	2	¼ x 6 5/16 x 10
Bottoms for inside curved drawers	2	¼ x 6 5/16 x 7½
Bottoms for convex block drawers	2	¼ x 8 11/16 x 12¾
Bottoms for concave block drawers	1	¼ x 14 11/16 x 12¼

Hardware:

Chippendale bail-type drawer pulls, antique finish for large drawers

Chippendale escutcheon plate for lid; same pattern as above handles

Small pulls for drawers and small cabinet door

Desk hinges, special type without round barrel

Small hinges for small door

Desk lid lock

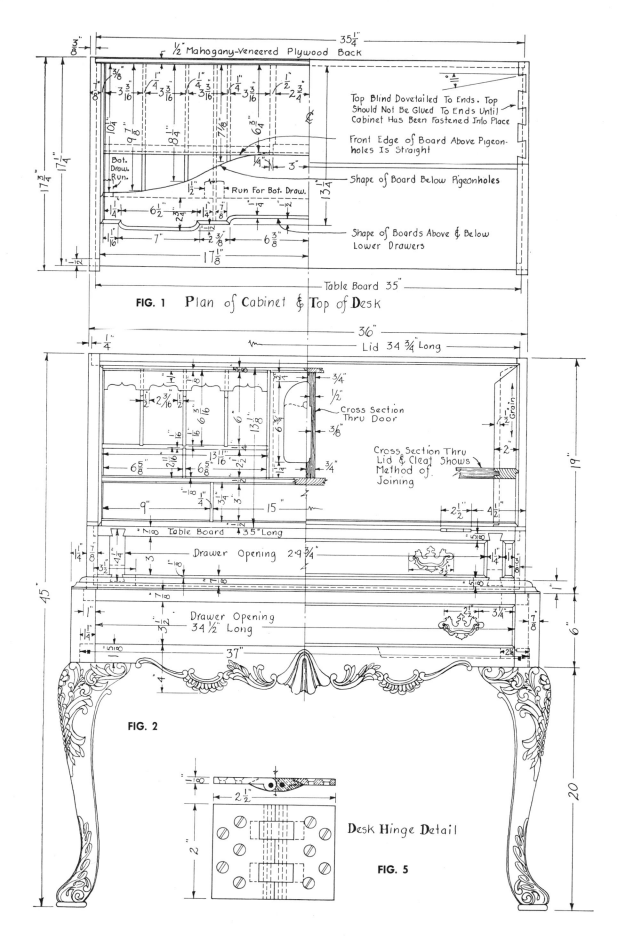

½" Mahogany-Veneered Plywood Back

$35\frac{1}{4}$"

Top Blind Dovetailed To Ends. Top Should Not Be Glued To Ends Until Cabinet Has Been Fastened Into Place

Front Edge of Board Above Pigeon-holes Is Straight

Shape of Board Below Pigeonholes

Shape of Boards Above & Below Lower Drawers

Bot. Draw. Run.

Run For Bot. Draw.

Table Board 35"

FIG. 1   Plan of Cabinet & Top of Desk

36"

Lid $34\frac{3}{4}$" Long

Cross Section Thru Door

Cross Section Thru Lid & Cleat Shows Method of Joining

Grain

Table Board 35" Long

Drawer Opening $29\frac{3}{4}$"

Drawer Opening $34\frac{1}{2}$" Long

37"

FIG. 2

Desk Hinge Detail

FIG. 5

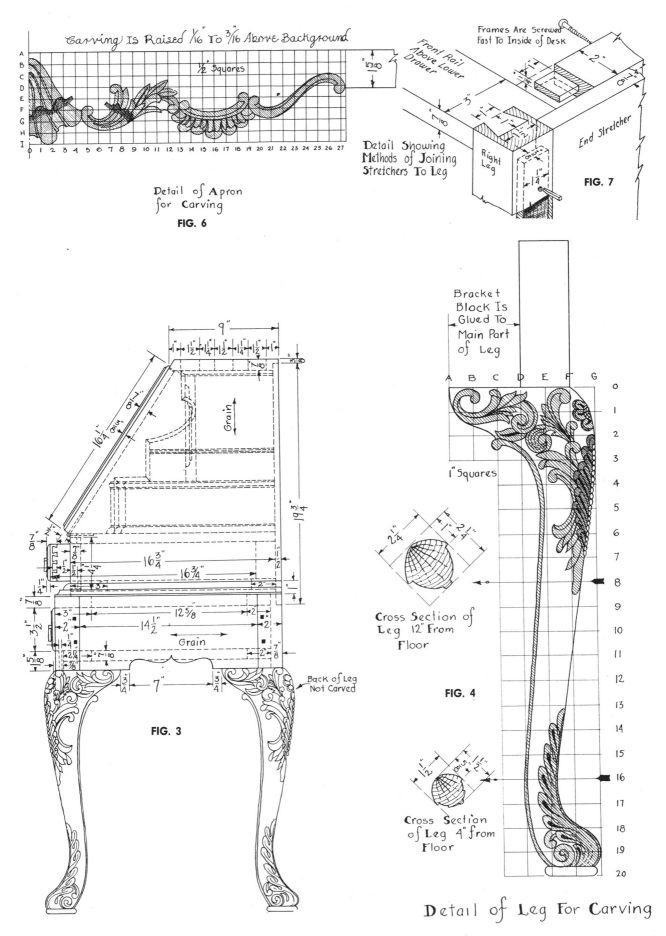

Carving Is Raised ¹⁄₁₆" To ³⁄₁₆" Above Background

½" Squares

Detail of Apron for Carving

FIG. 6

Detail Showing Methods of Joining Stretchers To Leg

Frames Are Screwed Fast To Inside of Desk

Front Rail Above Lower Drawer

Right Leg

End Stretcher

FIG. 7

Bracket Block Is Glued To Main Part of Leg

1" Squares

Cross Section of Leg 12" From Floor

FIG. 4

Cross Section of Leg 4" from Floor

Grain

Back of Leg Not Carved

FIG. 3

Detail of Leg For Carving

Fig. 8. Cut a stencil for carving the legs.

Fig. 9. A close-up of the carved leg.

When sawed out in this manner, the legs are the approximate shape of the finished member, except that they are square in section and need to be shaped as shown in the cross-section views of Figure 4. Shape the pieces with chisels, a spokeshave, scraper blade, or wood file, and sandpaper. Inspect the leg occasionally as the shaping progresses to correct flat or bulging outlines.

Cut a stencil for the carving on the same pattern which was used for cutting the leg to shape. Figure 8 shows how such a stencil should be cut, and Figure 9 gives a good view of how the leg should look after it has been carved. The beauty of the carving will depend largely upon the care with which it is done. Roughing out a carving usually is not difficult, since all you need do is outline the forms with a V tool or a fine veining tool. The beauty of the carving is in the finishing of each individual detail and in the skill with which the craftsman carves these details.

When carving, first remove the background to a depth of from ¼6 in. to ⅜6 in., holding generally to the more shallow depth until most, or all, of the design has been outlined with a V tool or a fine veining tool and the leaves and scrolls have been pretty well shaped. Then cut the background to the greater depths required. Carve the back legs on only one side.

Lay out a pattern for the apron from Figure 6. Transfer the design to the wood and carve it.

Next, plane and sandpaper the back and end

aprons. Lay out and cut the mortises and tenons, and join these members together. Square the frame when gluing these stretchers to the legs. A detail illustrating part of this construction is shown in Figure 7. Holes ¼ in. in diameter are drilled through these joints and square or roughly octagoned straight-grained pins are driven into these holes to help secure the joints. Dip the pins into glue before driving them. Now, cut out the dovetail joints for fastening the upper stretcher to the legs. Fasten together, with mortise and tenon joints, the rails which will be attached to the inside of the assembled lower section to hold the drawer. Screw these rails to the inside of the desk as shown in Figure 7.

Start the work on the upper part of the desk by gluing up the ends and cutting them to shape after planing and sanding the pieces to the proper thickness. Lay out and cut the grooves for the table board and the frame which supports the upper drawer. These ⅜-in. deep grooves are to stop ½ in. from the front edges of the end boards, as shown in Figure 3. In making the frame, fasten the drawer and slide-support guides to the end rails before gluing the frame and table board to the desk ends (Fig. 10).

Rabbet the back edges of the end boards for the back of the desk. Glue the table board and the frame to the desk ends.

Make the dovetailed stiles which separate the upper drawer from the slide supports. With a sharp knife, trace the shape of the dovetails on the front edges of the table board and the frame. Then saw and chisel out the mortise members of the dovetail joints. Glue these joints. Make the slide supports that hold up the open lid. A detail of a slide support is shown in Figure 11.

The next step is to make the board for the top of the desk, and to lay out, cut, and fit the dovetailed joints which fasten the top to the ends of the desk. Do not glue the top in place until the inside cabinet has been assembled and fastened to the desk. Figures 1, 2, and 3 show many important details of the inner part of the desk. The rather detailed and readily understood assembly drawing (Fig. 12), as well as the photograph which shows the lid of the desk open, will help solve most of the difficulties encountered in constructing this part of the desk. Further details are shown in Figures 13 to 18.

To build the cabinet, dress the two lower horizontal boards (Fig. 12, G and H), and, with

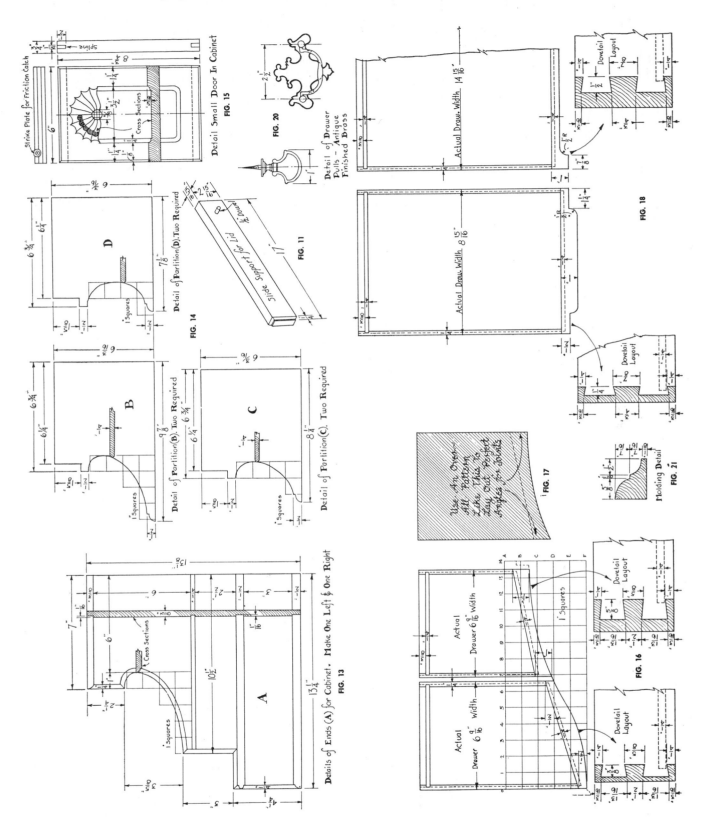

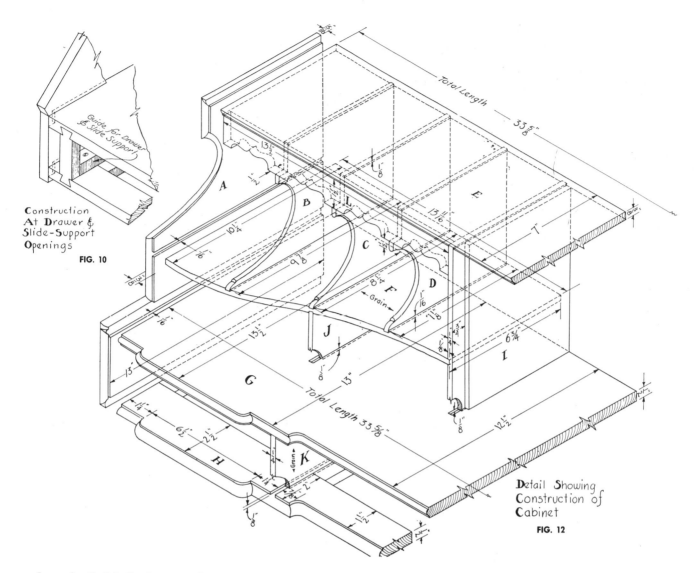

Construction At Drawer & Slide-Support Openings

FIG. 10

Detail Showing Construction of Cabinet

FIG. 12

a sharp knife blade, lay out the grooves into which the vertical partitions are to be fitted. Cut these grooves ⅛ in. deep with a dado saw or a router plane. Fit the partitions. The grain on all vertical partitions should run in a vertical direction.

Lay out the shape of the horizontal boards with a cardboard pattern and cut to shape, using a jig saw or a coping saw. Make the molded front edges with a shaper or wood-carving tools.

Make a pattern for the vertical partitions (Fig. 12, A) at the ends of the cabinet. Cut the partitions, then lay out and cut the grooves into which all horizontal partitions are to be fitted.

Lay out, cut, and fit all the other partitions in the following order (see Fig. 12):

1. The vertical partitions I, on each side of the door, which are ½ in. thick and are rabbeted on the front for the door.

2. The upper horizontal board E.

3. The ¼-in. thick horizontal partition, F, below the pigeonholes; the grooves for vertical partitions B, C, D, and J are to be only 1/16 in. deep.

4. The vertical partitions between the pigeonholes, B, C, and D. Each partition is different and separate patterns have to be made.

5. The vertical partitions between the upper drawers, J.

6. The shaped canopy, L.

In cutting the molding on the end boards (Fig. 12, A), take the following precautions: Do not cut the molding at the joints where the three horizontal boards, E, G, and H, are joined to the front edges of A, until the entire cabinet has been assembled. These points require special shaping (Fig. 12). Carefully square all parts to each other, so that the drawers will slide easily.

When the cabinet has been assembled, fit and fasten it to the desk. A few wood screws, at the

Fig. 19. The shapes of the drawer fronts are the same as the shape of the horizontal partition above each drawer.

back of the desk where they will not show, will hold the cabinet in place. Now glue the top to the ends. Build and fit the large drawers. Dovetail joints fasten the drawer sides to the drawer fronts (Fig. 3). Dovetail joints can be used at the drawer backs also; but, if this is done, the back lengths, as given in the bill of material, will not be quite long enough since these were intended for the dadoed drawer joint.

Build and fit the small drawers. The shapes of the drawer fronts are the same as the shape of the horizontal partitions above them (see Figs. 12, 16, 18, and 19). To make the upper drawers with the curved fronts, cut a template as large as the top of the whole drawer (Fig. 17). This insures correct angles where the sides are joined to the front. These are the most difficult drawers to build. The angles must be absolutely correct or the drawer fronts will not correspond in shape to the partitions above them and the drawer may not fit the opening.

The easiest way to cut the narrow beading around the fronts of the small drawers and the small door is with a wood carver's V tool and a skew chisel. However, the drawers must fit properly and slide easily before cutting the beading.

Lay out and carve the sunburst on the small door. The small door is reinforced with splines at the top and bottom to prevent it from warping (Fig. 15). A friction catch holds the door in place when closed. Prevent the slides, which support the lid, from being pulled out entirely by drilling holes and gluing in dowels near the rear end.

Build the lid. It has two cleats, which are fastened with tongue-and-groove joints to each end for strength and finish. The tongue and groove is also cut on the miter joints at the front of the lid, as shown in Figure 2. Cut the rabbeted edges and the molding after the cleats have been glued to the lid. Fit and fasten the lid.

Cast brass butt hinges can be used to fasten the lid, but a desk hinge in which the surface is perfectly flat when the lid is open is preferable (Fig. 5). The finish for this desk is discussed in the chapter on wood finishing.

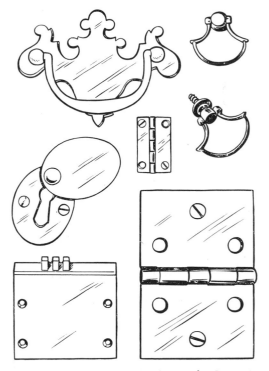

Fig. 22. Hardware for the Early Georgian Slant-Top Desk

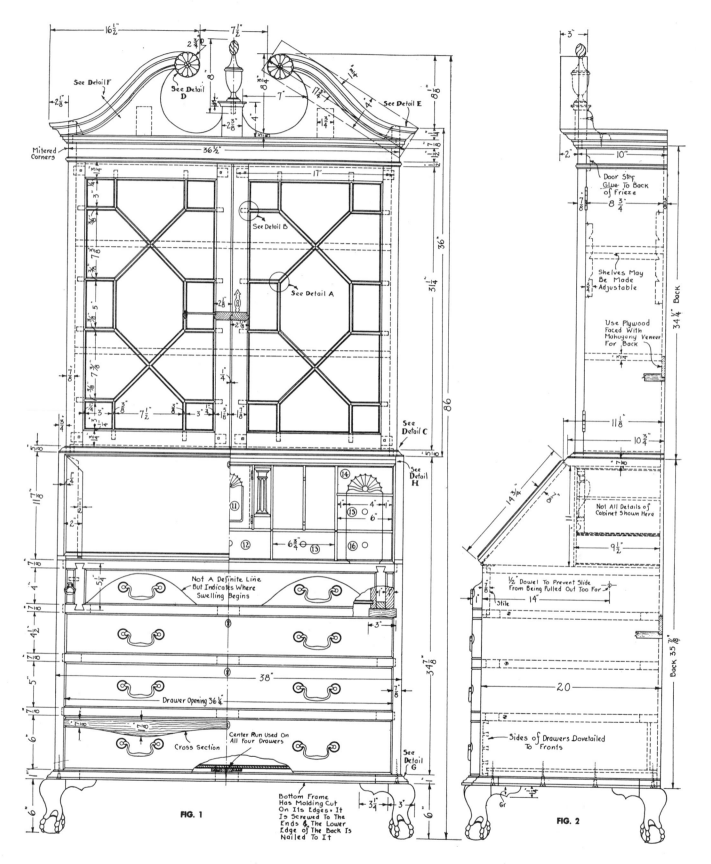

FIG. 1

FIG. 2

15.

GOVERNOR WINTHROP SECRETARY

A Governor Winthrop secretary is a serpentine-fronted piece of furniture of mixed Chippendale and later eighteenth-century motif. It is an American innovation in which two English period styles are rather pleasingly combined.

It is possible that this type of secretary was so named because a similar one was made for, or found in, a home belonging to this famous New England family. The piece is impressive and rich enough to compare favorably with the fine secretaries of the Chippendale, Hepplewhite, Sheraton, and other eighteenth-century styles.

Unlike many of the less expensive Governor Winthrop secretaries now appearing on the market, solid rather than veneered wood is used to make this entire piece of furniture. This includes even the serpentine drawer fronts. These drawer fronts could, however, be veneered over steam-bent core stock. Then the beading around the edges of the drawers (which on solid wood is carved or cut on a shaper) would have to be replaced with cock-beading.

The feet, the shells on the small drawers in the cabinet, the rosettes in the pediment, and the top of the finial should be carved by hand. Doors made according to the directions given here are expensive to build and require considerable care in their construction, but are well worth the effort. On secretaries built to meet price-cutting competition, scroll-sawed veneered stock that stimulates molding is usually placed over a plain piece of glass. This device results in a very inferior product.

Mahogany is the only wood proper for this secretary.

PROCEDURE

To build the lower section or desk part of the secretary, first glue up and dress the two ends.

Governor Winthrop Secretary

BILL OF MATERIAL

DESCRIPTION	PIECES	DIMENSIONS
LOWER SECTION OF SECRETARY		
Ends	2	$7/8$ x $20\frac{1}{2}$ x $34\frac{7}{8}$
Lower drawer front	1	$1\frac{1}{8}$ x $5^{15}/_{16}$ x $36^{3}/_{16}$
Second drawer front	1	$1\frac{1}{8}$ x $4^{15}/_{16}$ x $36^{3}/_{16}$
Third drawer front	1	$1\frac{1}{8}$ x $4^{7}/_{16}$ x $36^{3}/_{16}$
Upper drawer front	1	$1\frac{1}{8}$ x $3^{15}/_{16}$ x $32^{3}/_{16}$
Front rail, lower frame	1	1 x $3\frac{3}{4}$ x $39\frac{1}{2}$
End rails, lower frame	1	1 x $3\frac{1}{2}$ x $18\frac{1}{8}$
Back rail, lower frame	1	1 x $2\frac{3}{8}$ x $39\frac{1}{2}$
Front rails, three frames between drawers	3	$7/8$ x 3 x $36\frac{3}{4}$
End rails, two frames	4	$7/8$ x 2 x $18\frac{1}{8}$
End rails, upper frame	2	$7/8$ x 3 x $18\frac{1}{8}$
Back rails, three upper frames	3	$7/8$ x 2 x $36\frac{3}{4}$
Rail for center run, lower frame	1	1 x $2\frac{1}{2}$ x $18\frac{1}{8}$
Rails for center run, three upper frames	3	$7/8$ x $2\frac{1}{2}$ x $18\frac{1}{8}$
Slides to support lid	2	$^{15}/_{16}$ x $3^{15}/_{16}$ x $19\frac{5}{8}$
Vertical stiles between slides and drawer	2	$7/8$ x 1 x $5\frac{1}{4}$
Top, lower section	1	$7/8$ x $11\frac{1}{8}$ x $37\frac{1}{4}$
Table board	1	$7/8$ x $19\frac{5}{8}$ x $36\frac{3}{4}$
Lid of desk	1	$7/8$ x $14\frac{3}{4}$ x $36\frac{3}{4}$
Molding around top, lower section	1	$5/8$ x $3/4$ x 61
Feet	4	3 x 3 x 6
Feet	6	3 x $3\frac{1}{4}$ x $1\frac{1}{4}$
Feet	4	$5/8$ x $4\frac{3}{8}$ x $7\frac{1}{2}$
Guide strips, center runs	4	$\frac{1}{2}$ x $1\frac{1}{4}$ x $18\frac{3}{4}$
Guide strips, center runs	8	$3/8$ x 1 x $18\frac{3}{4}$
Guide strips between slides and upper drawer	2	$3/4$ x 1 x $18\frac{3}{4}$
Sides, lower drawer	2	$5/8$ x $5^{15}/_{16}$ x $19\frac{3}{8}$
Sides, second drawer	2	$5/8$ x $4^{15}/_{16}$ x $19\frac{3}{8}$
Sides, third drawer	2	$5/8$ x $4^{7}/_{16}$ x $19\frac{3}{8}$
Sides, upper drawer	2	$5/8$ x $3^{15}/_{16}$ x $19\frac{3}{8}$
Plywood:		
Back, lower drawer	1	$3/8$ x $5\frac{1}{16}$ x $35\frac{7}{16}$
Back, second drawer	1	$3/8$ x $4\frac{1}{16}$ x $35\frac{7}{16}$
Back, third drawer	1	$3/8$ x $3\frac{9}{16}$ x $35\frac{7}{16}$
Back, upper drawer	1	$3/8$ x $3\frac{1}{16}$ x $31\frac{7}{16}$
Bottom, three lower drawers	1	$3/8$ x 19 x $35\frac{7}{16}$
Bottom, upper drawer	1	$3/8$ x 19 x $31\frac{7}{16}$
Back, lower section	1	$3/8$ x $35\frac{7}{8}$ x $37\frac{1}{4}$
UPPER SECTION OF SECRETARY		
Ends	2	$7/8$ x 10 x 36
Roof, upper section	1	$7/8$ x $9\frac{1}{2}$ x $35\frac{1}{2}$
Face board, pediment	1	$7/8$ x $12\frac{1}{4}$ x $36\frac{1}{2}$
Floor, upper section	1	$7/8$ x $9\frac{5}{8}$ x $36\frac{1}{2}$
Shelves	2	$3/4$ x $8\frac{3}{4}$ x $34\frac{3}{4}$
Face block, pediment under finial	1	$3/8$ x $2\frac{3}{8}$ x $3\frac{3}{8}$
Cap, pedestal under finial	1	$5/8$ x $1\frac{3}{4}$ x $3\frac{1}{4}$

DESCRIPTION	PIECES	DIMENSIONS
Finial	1	$2\frac{1}{4}$ diam. x 8
Molding above doors	1	$3/8$ x $\frac{1}{2}$ x 58
Curved molding, face of pediment	1	$2\frac{1}{8}$ x 4 x $17\frac{3}{4}$
Molding above frieze	1	$3/4$ x $7/8$ x 60
Door stiles, outside	2	$7/8$ x 2 x $31\frac{1}{4}$
Door stiles, inside	2	$7/8$ x $2\frac{1}{8}$ x $31\frac{1}{4}$
Door rails	4	$7/8$ x 2 x 17
Molding for muntins for doors	1	$3/8$ x $3/4$ x 18 ft.
Back, upper section (plywood, faced with mahogany veneer)	1	$3/8$ x $35\frac{3}{4}$ x $34\frac{1}{4}$

CABINET INSIDE OF DESK (Italicized numbers correspond with circled numbers in Figures 1 and 3.)

	DESCRIPTION	PIECES	DIMENSIONS
1.	Top	1	$3/8$ x $9\frac{1}{2}$ x $35\frac{3}{4}$
2.	Bottom	1	$3/8$ x $9\frac{1}{2}$ x $35\frac{3}{4}$
3.	Ends	2	$3/8$ x $9\frac{1}{2}$ x 11
4.	Horizontal partition	1	$\frac{1}{4}$ x $9\frac{1}{4}$ x $23\frac{1}{8}$
5.	Horizontal partitions	4	$\frac{1}{4}$ x $9\frac{1}{4}$ x $6\frac{3}{16}$
6.	Vertical partitions	2	$\frac{1}{4}$ x $9\frac{1}{4}$ x $10\frac{1}{2}$
7.	Vertical partitions	2	$\frac{1}{4}$ x $9\frac{1}{4}$ x $7\frac{3}{16}$
8.	Vertical partitions	2	$\frac{1}{4}$ x $9\frac{1}{4}$ x $7\frac{3}{16}$
9.	Vertical partitions	2	$\frac{1}{2}$ x $9\frac{1}{4}$ x $7\frac{3}{16}$
10.	Vertical partitions	2	$\frac{1}{4}$ x $9\frac{1}{4}$ x $3\frac{3}{16}$
11.	Door	1	$5/8$ x $4^{15}/_{16}$ x $6^{15}/_{16}$
12.	Drawer front	1	$5/8$ x $2^{15}/_{16}$ x $8^{15}/_{16}$
13.	Drawer fronts	2	$5/8$ x $2^{15}/_{16}$ x $6^{11}/_{16}$
14.	Drawer fronts	2	$5/8$ x $2^{15}/_{16}$ x $5^{15}/_{16}$
15.	Drawer fronts	2	$5/8$ x $3^{11}/_{16}$ x $5^{15}/_{16}$
16.	Drawer fronts	2	$5/8$ x $2^{15}/_{16}$ x $5^{15}/_{16}$
12.	Drawer sides	2	$\frac{1}{4}$ x $2^{15}/_{16}$ x 9
13.	Drawer sides	4	$\frac{1}{4}$ x $2^{15}/_{16}$ x 9
14.	Drawer sides	4	$\frac{1}{4}$ x $2^{15}/_{16}$ x 9
15.	Drawer sides	4	$\frac{1}{4}$ x $3^{11}/_{16}$ x 9
16.	Drawer sides	4	$\frac{1}{4}$ x $2^{15}/_{16}$ x 9
12.	Drawer back	1	$\frac{1}{4}$ x $2\frac{7}{16}$ x $8\frac{11}{16}$
13.	Drawer backs	2	$\frac{1}{4}$ x $2\frac{7}{16}$ x $6\frac{7}{16}$
14.	Drawer backs	2	$\frac{1}{4}$ x $2\frac{7}{16}$ x $5\frac{11}{16}$
15.	Drawer backs	2	$\frac{1}{4}$ x $3\frac{3}{16}$ x $5\frac{11}{16}$
16.	Drawer backs	2	$\frac{1}{4}$ x $2\frac{7}{16}$ x $5\frac{11}{16}$
Plywood:			
12.	Drawer bottom	1	$\frac{1}{4}$ x $8\frac{11}{16}$ x $8\frac{3}{4}$
13.	Drawer bottoms	2	$\frac{1}{4}$ x $6\frac{7}{16}$ x $8\frac{3}{4}$
14.	Drawer bottoms	2	$\frac{1}{4}$ x $5\frac{11}{16}$ x $8\frac{3}{4}$
15.	Drawer bottoms	2	$\frac{1}{4}$ x $5\frac{11}{16}$ x $8\frac{3}{4}$
16.	Drawer bottoms	2	$\frac{1}{4}$ x $5\frac{11}{16}$ x $8\frac{3}{4}$

DRAWERS WHICH HOLD SECRET DRAWERS

DESCRIPTION	PIECES	DIMENSIONS
Half columns[1]	1	$1\frac{3}{4}$ x $1\frac{3}{4}$ x $6^{15}/_{16}$
Drawer fronts	2	$5/8$ x $6^{15}/_{16}$ x $1\frac{11}{16}$
Drawer sides	4	$3/16$ x $6^{15}/_{16}$ x $8\frac{1}{8}$
Spreaders	2	$\frac{1}{4}$ x $\frac{1}{4}$ x $1\frac{11}{16}$

[1] Split single turning in half.

BILL OF MATERIAL

DESCRIPTION	PIECES	DIMENSIONS
Sliding panels	2	³⁄₁₆ x 1⁷⁄₁₆ x 6⁹⁄₁₆ (tongue on three sides)
False bottoms	2	³⁄₁₆ x 1⁷⁄₁₆ x 7³⁄₈
Drawer bottoms	2	³⁄₁₆ x 1⁷⁄₁₆ x 8
SECRET DRAWERS		
Fronts	2	¼ x 1 x 1¼
Sides	4	⅛ x 1 x 6½
Backs	2	⅛ x ¾ x 1⅛
Bottoms	2	⅛ x 1⅛ x 6½

Hardware:

8 pulls for large drawers, No. 1

2 pulls for lid supports, No. 3

5 oval escutcheon plates for drawers and lid, No. 4

12 brass knobs for small drawers in cabinet, ⅝, No. 2

2 brass knobs for secret drawers, ⅜, No. 2

2 escutcheon plates for glass doors, No. 6 (No. 5 could be used on the small door)

1 cabinet door lock for glass doors, No. 7

1 friction catch for small door, ⁵⁄₁₆ (bullet type)

2 small brass butt hinges for small door, 1 in. long (See Early Georgian Slant-Top Desk.)

2 desk lid hinges (See Early Georgian Slant-Top Desk.)

1 desk lid lock (See Early Georgian Slant-Top Desk.)

2 cleats for lid of desk   ⅞ x 2 x 14¾

Single wide boards of mahogany will be the most suitable for obtaining a good grain effect. Cut grooves into these ends for the table board and the frames which are to support the drawers. If the frames and table board are not the *exact* thickness specified, make these pieces first, and then cut the grooves to correspond to the slightest variation in thickness. Any variation in thickness might result in a faulty appearance and poor-fitting drawers which may stick.

The frames are mortised and tenoned together as shown in Figure 6. The end rails on the upper frame must be wider than those on the two frames below it to provide for the slides which they support. The lower frame is thicker, wider, and longer than the other frames because it forms the base upon which the ends and other parts rest (Figs. 1 and 2). This frame is molded around three of its edges. The fronts of the drawers and of all frames are serpentine-shaped. Fasten the center-run guide strips and the guide strips between the slides and the upper drawer. Do this before the frames are fastened to the ends of the desk.

To fasten the back, rabbet the back edges of the ends. Then glue together and assemble the ends, frames, and table board. Do not glue too much of the frame to the ends because some shrinkage or expansion occurs during different seasons. Many desk ends split because the frames were fastened too thoroughly during the building process and no provision had been made for expansion or contraction. The table board can be glued along the entire length of its ends to the grooves in the desk ends because the rate of expansion and contraction for both the table board and the desk ends will be about the same. The ends of the lower section are fastened securely with screws to the lower frame, the top is dovetailed to the ends, and the back is nailed securely to the ends and frames, thus adequately holding all parts together. It will be necessary to glue only the ends of the front rails when fastening the frames to the desk ends. A single wood screw through the end rails into the desk ends will hold the frames in place.

Square the frames and table board to the ends to insure drawers which slide easily. It would be almost impossible to fit the cabinet into the desk if the frame were not properly squared.

Make the feet next. The main part of the foot is a block of wood 3 in. square by 6 in. long. Glue to the rabbeted top of the foot two blocks of wood, 1¼ by 3 by 3¼ (Fig. 9B), with which the legs are fastened to the bottom frame. First, roughly cut the main part of the leg to shape on a band saw and hollow it out for the block which holds the other three parts together. After the ball-and-claw foot has been carved, glue and fasten together with wood screws all four of these pieces. Then complete the shaping at the top of the leg. Make a pattern of the foot from Figure 9A. Fasten the feet securely to the lower frame as shown in Figure 9B.

The board upon which the top of the secretary rests should be dovetailed to the ends of the

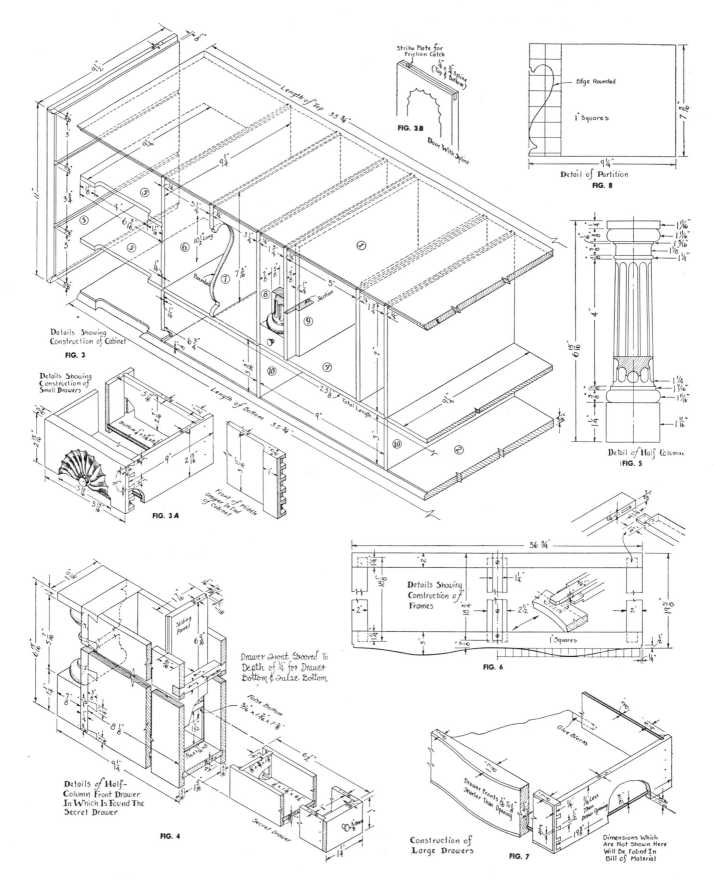

FIG. 3B
Strike Plate for Friction Catch
¼ x ¾ Spline (Top & Bottom)
Door With Spline

Edge Rounded
1" Squares
Detail of Partition
FIG. 8

Detail of Half Column
FIG. 5

Length of Top 35 ¾"

Section
Rounded

Length of Bottom 35 ¾"
Total Length
23⅜"

Details Showing Construction of Cabinet
FIG. 3

Details Showing Construction of Small Drawers

Front of Middle Drawer In End of Cabinet
FIG. 3 A

Details of Half-Column Front Drawer In Which Is Found The Secret Drawer
FIG. 4

Sliding Panel

Drawer Front Grooved To Depth of ¼" for Drawer Bottom & False Bottom

False Bottom

Secret Drawer

Details Showing Construction of Frames
1" Squares
FIG. 6

36 ¾"

Glue Blocks

Drawer Fronts 1" To ⅛" Shorter Than Opening

Construction of Large Drawers
FIG. 7

Dimensions Which Are Not Shown Here Will Be Found In Bill of Material

lower section as shown in Figure 10. Do not fasten it permanently to the ends with glue until the cabinet has been built and fastened to the desk.

Build the large drawers next. The thick planks from which the drawer fronts are made should be of the finest mahogany, with a nicely figured grain, if possible. Lay out the serpentine shape on the edges of the drawers with a cardboard pattern and then saw them to shape on a band saw. Next, dress the drawer fronts with a circular plane on which the bed of the plane can be adjusted for convex or concave surfaces. Go over the surfaces with sharp scraper blades and sand them smooth. Shape the upper drawer in the same manner, but, since the top of this drawer remains straight, form the hood-shaped convex projections with chisels and gouges and finish off with a scraper and sandpaper. The ends of this drawer should be straight and flat so that these surfaces will join nicely with the stiles dovetailed to the table board and the upper frame. As indicated in Figure 1, the swelling on the upper drawer is not bounded by a sharp line, but should curve out gradually, making a smooth curve from the flat plane to the convex. These drawer fronts have no projecting lip; they are beaded around the edges instead.

The drawer sides are dovetailed to the fronts, as shown in Figure 7. No dimensions are given for the dovetailing, except for the size of the pin members, since each drawer will be different because of the varying width. For the nice, neat dovetailing job found on fine, older work, the pins are narrow and the tails wide. This is a mark of superiority which is not duplicated in modern machine-made dovetailing.

When the stiles have been made and fitted with dovetail joints to the desk, make and fit the slides which support the lid. Provide stops at the proper place by gluing short dowels to the slides about 14 in. from the front (Figs. 1 and 2).

Now, make and fit the lid. The ends of the lid are tongued and grooved to the large board, and should be fitted very carefully to make a tight joint. The molded lip of the lid must lie perfectly flat against the slanted edges of the ends and the top. The lid should be fastened and fitted to the desk before the cabinet is put into the desk because making the lid fit may require a slight amount of trimming. Hinges like those shown for the early Georgian desk can be used.

Build and fit the cabinet to the desk next. Dress the boards for the top, ends, and bottom, and mold the front edges with a shaper, or carve the molding by hand. The shape of this molding is clearly illustrated in Figure 3. Note, especially, how it is shaped at the place where the four boards meet. The cabinet ends are rabbeted at the top and bottom for the top and floor of the cabinet. Dress all partitions and then lay out and cut the grooves to fit them together. Lay out the marks for these grooves with a thin-bladed knife whether they are to be cut on the dado head, power router, or by hand with a router plane. Knife lines will set the guide if a dado head is used and prevent splintering at the edges. If a router plane is used, the knife lines are indispensable.

Make a trial assembly of all the parts before gluing and fit this trial assembly to the inside of the lower section to assure a proper fit. See Figure 3A. Since it is difficult to glue all the parts together at once proceed as follows: First, glue together 1, 2, and 3 (four pieces in all). Follow with pieces 6 and 4, in that order. Put in the remaining partitions in any order. All partitions following the first four have to be slid into place, and, to do this, a thin, slow-setting glue must be used. This step will not be difficult if the partitions have been fitted to slide readily into place without sticking. However the joints must not be loose. Such workmanship requires painstaking care.

The construction of the small drawers is shown in Figure 3A. The shape of the carved sunburst is also clearly shown. This same sunburst appears on the small door. Figure 3B shows the method of putting a spline in the top and bottom of the door to strengthen it, and keep it from warping. The door is held closed with a bullet-type friction catch. The front edges of the partitions, against which the door fits, are rabbeted to make a door stop, as shown in Figure 3. A pattern for the shape of partition 7 (Fig. 3) is shown in Figure 8.

The construction of the drawers which hold the secret drawers, as well as of the secret drawers themselves is shown in Figure 4. The column, shown in Figure 5, is turned from a single piece of stock, and then split in half to provide decorative facings for the deep narrow drawers. Glue the half columns to the drawer fronts before assembling the rest of the drawer. Cut grooves for the sliding panel in the back into the sides and bottom

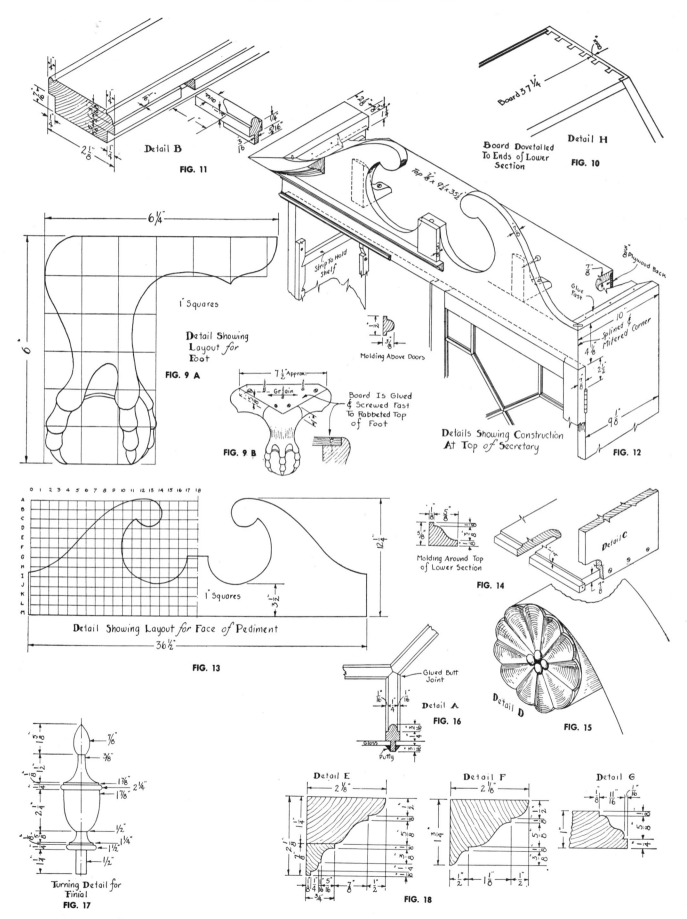

Detail B

FIG. 11

Board Dovetailed
To Ends of Lower
Section

Detail H

FIG. 10

Board 37 1/4"

Top 7/8" x 9 1/2" x 35 1/2"

Strip To Hold
Shelf

1" Squares

Detail Showing
Layout *for*
Foot

FIG. 9 A

7 1/2" Approx.

Grain

Molding Above Doors

Board Is Glued
& Screwed Fast
To Rabbeted Top
of Foot

FIG. 9 B

3/4" Plywood Back

Glue
Fast

10"
Splined &
Mitered Corner

Details Showing Construction
At Top *of* Secretary

9 1/8"

FIG. 12

0 1 2 3 4 5 6 7 8 9 10 11 12 13 14 15 16 17 18

A B C D E F G H I J K L M

1" Squares

3 1/2"

12 1/4"

Detail Showing Layout *for* Face *of* Pediment

36 1/2"

FIG. 13

Molding Around Top
of Lower Section

FIG. 14

Detail C

Glued Butt
Joint

Detail A

FIG. 16

Glass

Putty

Detail D

FIG. 15

7/8"

3/8"

1 7/8"
1 7/8" 2 1/4"

1/2"
1 1/4"

1/2"

Turning Detail for
Finial

FIG. 17

Detail E
2 1/8"

Detail F
2 1/8"

Detail G

FIG. 18

of the deep drawer. The drawers, being narrow, are deep enough so that the presence of a false bottom, with a secret compartment for a drawer underneath, is not easily detected. The drawer must be removed entirely from the cabinet before the panel at the rear can be raised, revealing the tiny secret drawer which is then pulled out from the back. The back of the deep drawer is held together at the top by means of a spreader, dovetailed to the sides.

When the cabinet has been completed, fasten it to the desk with a few small screws or brads. Then glue the top of the lower section to the ends, completing the lower section of the secretary.

To build the upper, or bookcase, part of the secretary, first dress the ends. The ends are 36 in. long and 10 in. wide at the top where a mitered edge joins them to the face board of the pediment. At the top of the doors, the ends are only 9⅛ in. wide; these ends are grooved 1¼ in. down from the top on the inside to a depth of ⅜ in. for the roof board. The back edge of each end board is also rabbeted ⅜ by ½ in. for the plywood back (see Fig. 2). They are rabbeted at the bottom end for the floor board, the rabbet being ⅜ in. deep by ⅞ in. wide.

Prepare the floor board next. Make a door stop at the front edge, with a ¼ by ⅞-in. rabbet, and a tongue at each end to close up the hole at the back of the molding. Detail C, Figure 14, shows this construction.

The face board of the pediment should now be made. Draw a full-size pattern for laying out the pediment (Fig. 13), truing up the curves very carefully so there will be no flat places. These curves, being a principal feature, must be carefully drawn. Cut a ⅜ by ⅞-in. groove into the face board, 2 in. from the inside bottom edge, for joining the roof board to it. The ends of the face board are mitered and grooved for a spline and joined to the ends of the upper section.

When these five pieces have been made, and a trial assembly has shown that they fit together properly, glue them together. Everything must be perfectly square when gluing up these parts, since obtaining a good fit on the doors will depend upon it.

Cut out straight moldings for the secretary on a shaper. Where the proper machinery and the skill required for the job are available, partly carve out the curved molding at the top on a

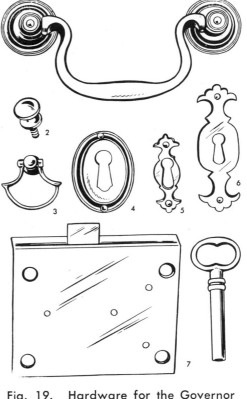

Fig. 19. Hardware for the Governor Winthrop Secretary

machine. The amateur in the average shop will probably hand-carve the molding. If care is taken, there is no reason why it should be inferior to machine work. In any case, the finishing cuts must be done with hand tools. Figures 1 and 12 show most of the construction details for this part of the work. Details for making the molding are given in Figure 18. After the molding has been made, glue it fast with an occasional brad to help hold it in place.

Make and fit the shelves and supporting strips to the inside of the upper section. These shelves are made so they can be adjusted to various heights, and should, therefore, not fit too tight.

Making the doors is, perhaps, the most difficult job in building the secretary. Many cabinetmakers will not attempt it with the limited machinery usually found in the average workshop. However, if the cabinetmaker has the required skill and patience, there is no reason why he should not attempt the job, even with limited equipment.

First, make the wide stiles and rails, and cut the moldings and the rabbets on a shaper or with molding cutters on a variety saw. Make the mortises for the muntins. Detail B, Figure 11, shows how the molding is made and how the muntins are joined. Detail *A*, Figure 16, shows how the muntins are joined together with glued butt joints. These joints are strong enough for all practical purposes once the glass is in place. Carefully cut the angles for the miter joints to make a good fit. It is advisable to make full-size layouts of these joints on a large flat surface, such as Upson board or plywood, and then cut and trim the ends to make a perfect joint.

To assemble the doors, first glue all of the short vertical and horizontal muntins (Fig. 1) to the stiles and rails; then glue the rails and stiles together. Next, fit and glue the short pieces in the middle in place. Do this while the door is lying on a perfectly flat surface.

Put a lock on the right-hand door only. The escutcheon on the left-hand door balances the design. Fasten the doors to the ends with hinges and put a good elbow catch at the bottom of the left-hand door. Sometimes, sliding bolt catches are used to hold the left-hand door on fine pieces of furniture. These catches are superior to the more easily applied elbow-catches.

Details still to be attended to include making and putting on the face block and cap block under the finial, turning and carving the finial, attaching the brace blocks and corner strips in back of the pediment board, and putting glass in the doors. Fit and place drawer pulls but remove them when finishing the secretary. The plywood back should also be put on if this has not already been done.

16.

DUNCAN PHYFE ROLL-TOP DESK

Duncan Phyfe furniture has become very popular, both commercially and with amateur cabinetmakers. While Phyfe built furniture to meet practically every household need, the greater part of his output seems to have been tables, chairs, and sofas. The Duncan Phyfe style, particularly that part which was inspired by his English contemporaries, Sheraton and Hepplewhite, has numerous merits. It is simple, but does not lack elegance; the lines are clean, the proportions excellent, the scale refined. The carving and reeding, the typical ornamentation found on this type of desk, is dignified and restrained. Duncan Phyfe furniture, if properly designed and carefully constructed, has the qualities of the great period styles.

The desk shown here is exceptionally beautiful and distinctive. In this particular instance, the roll top is a unique feature, appropriate to the spirit of the Duncan Phyfe style. Not many years ago, the roll-top desk was standard office equipment. Although it has been replaced by the flat-topped desk in modern offices, the roll-top idea has advantages for a desk in the home. No matter how littered with papers the desk may be, it can instantly be made presentable by pulling the top shut.

PROCEDURE

To build this desk, first turn the columns and stretchers (Figs. 3 and 4). The columns require four pieces of stock, 2 in. square and at least 17 in. long. Turn the stretchers from stock 1¾ by 1¾ by 36 in. Carve these members while they are in the lathe, since the position can be adjusted easily while transferring and carving the design.

To lay out the reeds, cut strips of paper to fit exactly once around the circumference of the column at the upper and lower ends of the reeded part (see the left-hand column, Fig. 1).

Duncan Phyfe Roll-Top Desk — closed

Duncan Phyfe Roll-Top Desk — open

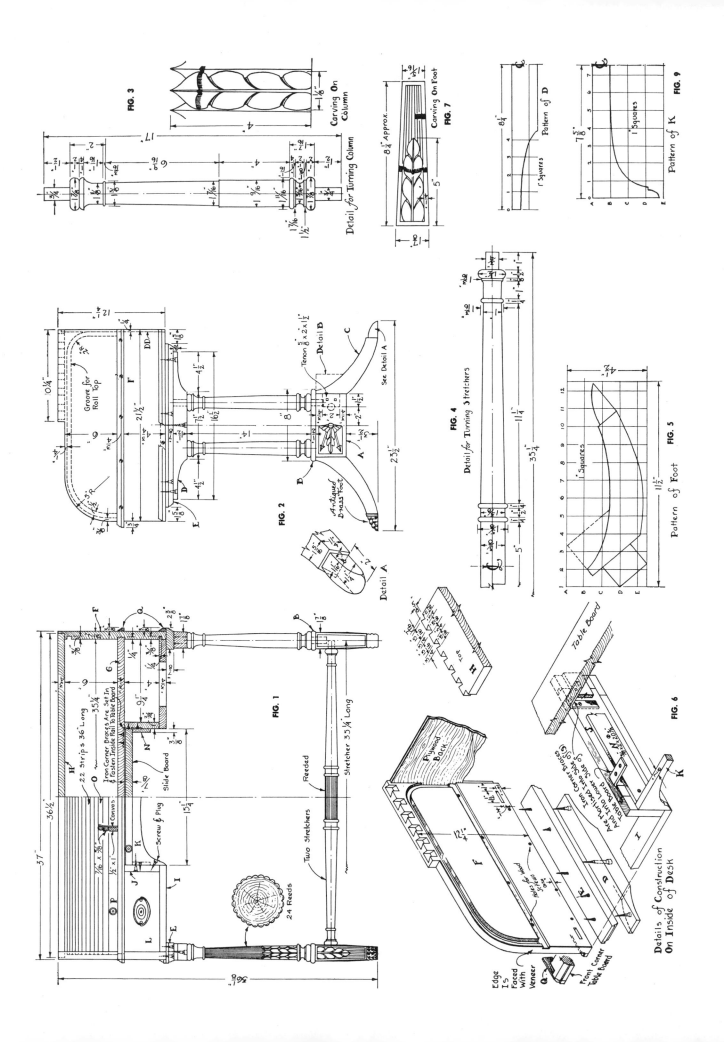

FIG. 3

Carving On Column

1 1/2"

4"

Detail for Turning Column

17"

2"

2 1/2"

1 1/2"

1 1/16"

6 9/16"

4"

3/4"

1 1/2"

1 7/16"

9 1/16"

9/16"

9/16"

Carving On Foot

FIG. 7

8 1/4" Approx.

5"

1 5/8"

1 7/8"

Pattern of D

FIG. 9

Pattern of K

7 5/8"

1" Squares

8 1/4"

1" Squares

FIG. 2

12 1/4"

10 1/4"

Groove for Roll Top

21 1/2"

6"

4 1/2"

4 1/2"

14"

8"

23 1/2"

DD

F

E

D

A

B

C

Tenon 5/8" x 2 x 1 1/2"

Detail B

See Detail A

Antiqued Brass Foot

Detail A

FIG. 4

Detail for Turning Stretchers

35 1/4"

11 1/4"

5"

FIG. 5

Pattern of Foot

4 1/2"

11 1/2"

1" Squares

FIG. 1

37"

36 1/2"

36 1/8"

35 1/4"

22 Strips 36" Long

Iron Corner Braces Are Set In & Fasten Inside Inside Rail To Table Board

Slide Board

Reeded

Stretcher 35 1/4" Long

Two Stretchers

24 Reeds

Canvas

Screw & Plug

9"

9 1/4"

15 1/4"

3/8"

H

O

N

P

J

I

K

L

E

A

B

G

7/16 x 7/8"

1/2 x 1

FIG. 6

Details of Construction On Inside of Desk

Table Board

Plywood Back

Iron Corner Braces Are Mortised Into Lower Table Board And Into Side Of Slide Board

Front Corner Table Board

Edge Is Faced With Veneer

Holes for Wood Screw

12 1/4"

F

K

I

H

N

Q

Remove the paper strips from the column and divide each strip into 24 equal parts with a pencil. The diameter at the top of the reeding is less than at the bottom, therefore the strip and the divisions for the upper part will be smaller than the strip and divisions for the lower end. Again wrap the strips around the column and mark the divisions on the wood. Then connect the points with straight lines, drawing the first line exactly vertical, so that the reeds will not lean to one side or the other. Carve the reeds by hand. First, use a V tool to cut a sharp groove between each reed. With the heel of a wood carver's skew chisel, round out the reeds between these lines to the shape shown in the cross section, Figure 1.

Wrap another piece of paper around the column where the leaves are to be carved. Remove the paper after its ends have been made to meet exactly, and on this paper draw at full size the leaf pattern shown in Figure 3. Transfer this design to the column by cutting out parts of the leaf veins and outlines to form a stencil, or by using carbon paper under the pattern.

Next, make the feet, composed of pieces A and C (Fig. 2). Fasten the pieces together with mortise-and-tenon joints. Draw a pattern for the feet from Figure 5. To clamp the curved feet to the section between them, allow a squared

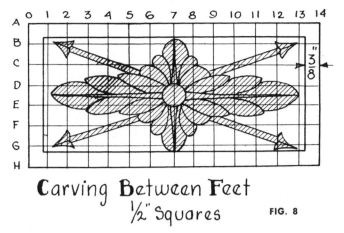

Carving Between Feet
½" Squares   FIG. 8

waste section near the top (Fig. 2, B) to provide a place to fasten the clamps. This waste piece is a part of the foot pattern (Fig. 5). Figure 10 shows the clamps in place.

After the pieces have been glued together, saw off the waste and carve the feet. The design for carving the feet is shown in Figure 7. Also make the pattern shown in Figure 8, transfer it to the outside surface of pieces A (Fig. 2) and carve these members. Detail A, Figure 2, shows how to form the bottom of the foot so that it will exactly fit the claw-foot socket. Purchase these sockets from firms that stock period-furniture hardware.

When the feet have been glued together,

BILL OF MATERIAL

DESCRIPTION		PIECES	DIMENSIONS
Mahogany:			
Fig. 2	A.	2	1⅞ x 3½ x 7
	B.	2	½ x 2¼ x 8
	C.	4	1⅞ x 4½ x 11½
	D.	2	1½ x 1⅞ x 16½
	E.	2	⅞ x 2⅜ x 18¼
	F.	2	⅞ x 12¼ x 21½
Fig. 1	G.	1	¾ x 22 x 37
Fig. 6	H.	1	¾ x 10¼ x 36½
Fig. 12	I.	4	¾ x 2½ x 10⅜
Fig. 13	J.	4	¾ x 1¾ x 4
Fig. 1	K.	1	⅞ x 3¾ x 15¼
	L.	2	¾ x 3¹⁵⁄₁₆ x 9⁹⁄₁₆
Fig. 14	M.	1	¾ x 15³⁄₁₆ x 19¼
Fig. 6	N.	2	⅜ x 2 x 20⅜
Fig. 1	O.	22	⁷⁄₁₆ x ⅝ x 36
	P.	1	½ x 1 x 36
	Q.		⅜ x ¾[1]
Fig. 14	R.	2	¾ x 2½ x 15³⁄₁₆
Fig. 13	S.	2	¾ x 4 x 18½
Fig. 12	T.	4	¾ x 2½ x 18¾

DESCRIPTION		PIECES	DIMENSIONS
Fig. 18	U.	2	¼ x 8 x 35
	V.	2	¼ x 8 x 5⅛
	W.	6	¼ x 8 x 4⅞
	X.	2	¼ x 8 x 6¼
	Y.	1	¼ x 8 x 7¼
Mahogany-Veneered Plywood:			
Fig. 18	Z.	1	¼ x 5⅛ x 35¼
Fig. 17	B-B.	2	¼ x 8¹¹⁄₁₆ x 20¾
Fig. 2	D-D.	1	¼ x 12 x 36¼
Poplar:			
Fig. 17	A-A.	4	½ x 3¹⁵⁄₁₆ x 21
	C-C.	2	½ x 3³⁄₁₆ x 9⁹⁄₁₆
Columns		4	1⅞ diam. x 17
Stretchers		2	1⅜ diam. x 35¼

Hardware:

2 oval drawer pulls, antique finish No. 3

4 pulls for roll-top and slide board No. 2

4 iron corner braces   3 x 3

4 brass feet, open type, No. 1

---

[1] Length as needed.

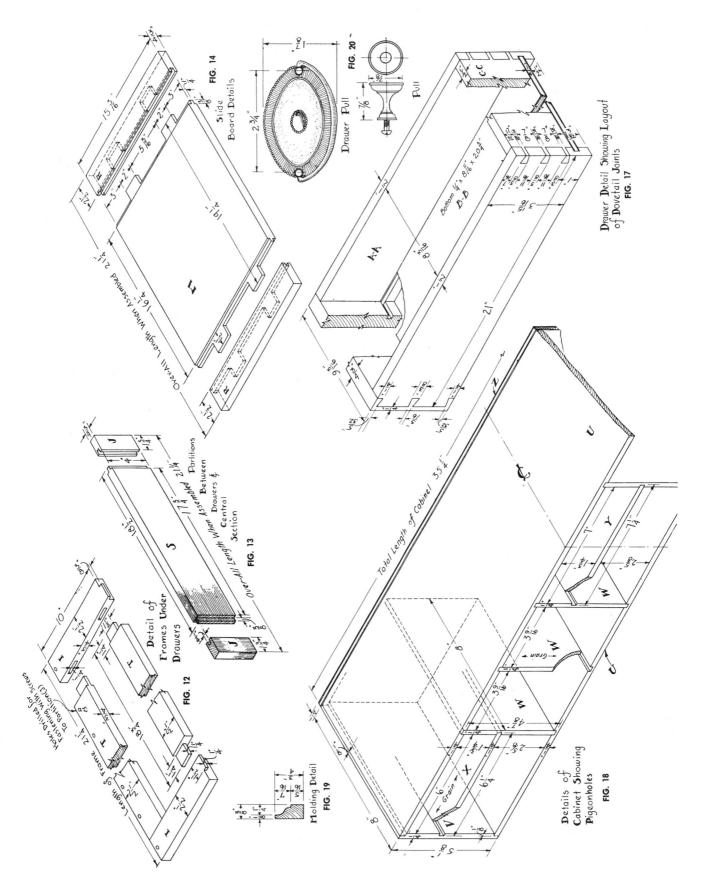

FIG. 14

Slide Board Details

Drawer Pull
FIG. 20

Pull

Drawer Detail Showing Layout of Dovetail Joints
FIG. 17

Overall Length When Assembled 16¼"

Detail of Frames Under Drawers
FIG. 12

Over-All Length When Assembled 21¼" Between Partitions
Central Section
FIG. 13

Molding Detail
FIG. 19

Details of Cabinet Showing Pigeonholes
FIG. 18

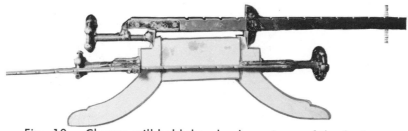

Fig. 10. Clamps will hold the glued-up pieces of the foot
assembly firmly in place until dry.

carved, and fitted with the sockets, bore the holes for the stretchers and columns. Make pieces *D*, Figures 2 and 9. The pattern for shape *D* is found in Figure 9. Next, make the plain pieces, *B*, between the foot and the columns.

When all these pieces have been made, glue up the lower framework (Fig. 11, *A*).

Now, make *F*, the ends of the desk (Fig. 6). Most of the dimensions for *F* are found in Figures 1 and 2. Cut the grooves for the table board and for the roll top with a power router, or score the outlines with knife cuts and cut the grooves with a router plane. Cut the mortises. Dovetail the top first, then place the top on the ends and trace an outline with the sharp point of a knife. Since the dovetailing in pieces *F*

is cut into an edge of the boards instead of an end, careful trimming and fitting will be necessary to keep from splitting the dovetails off. Once glued up, this joint will have adequate strength. Sandpaper the groove for the roll top. In finishing the desk, do not varnish this groove, but apply several thin coats of shellac, rub down with steel wool, and wax. Veneer the curved, front edges of *F* for added strength and appearance before gluing the table board to the ends. Rabbet the other end of *F* for the plywood back.

Glue up the table board, extending the molded front ¾ in. (Figs. 2 and 6). Now glue and assemble the top, ends, and table board (Fig. 11, *B*).

Make the drawer frames (Fig. 12) and the partitions (Fig. 13). Glue and screw the frames to the partitions, and fasten the partitions to the table board with iron corner braces, sunk flush into the table board and the partitions. File all screw heads smooth so they will not protrude and scratch the slide board. Fasten the pieces *N* in place to support the slide board and the arched stretcher *K* (Fig. 1).

To make the roll top, rip and dress 22 strips,

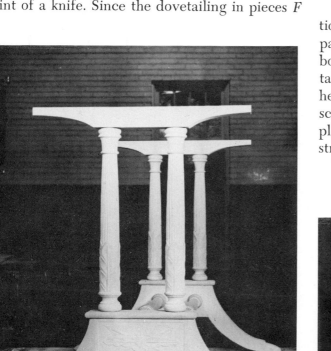

Fig. 11. Assembly details. A, left, shows the lower framework glued up. B, right, shows the
assembly of the desk top, ends, and table board.

Fig. 15. To make the roll top, glue the strips to medium-weight canvas, employing a jig to hold the strips firmly against the canvas.

Fig. 16. The strips are exposed for a distance of 1 in. at each end of the roll top.

squaring the bottom sides and rounding the top sides. Glue these 22 strips and the 1-in. bottom strip to medium-weight canvas (Fig. 15). To simplify this work, set up a jig as shown in Figure 15. A jig consists of two boards, B, nailed to a wide, fairly heavy board, A, to line up the ends of the strips. Two wide boards, C, are screwed or clamped to the jig to hold the strips firmly against the canvas and to keep the strips from buckling when they are glued to the canvas. Two strips, D, are planed to the same thickness as the strips of the roll top. Place a piece of heavy wrapping paper, E, under the canvas to prevent the canvas from being glued to the jig.

A cold casein or resin glue is preferable to hot glue, since it allows more time before setting. Spread the glue on the canvas, not on the strips, to avoid getting glue on the strip edges. Nail or

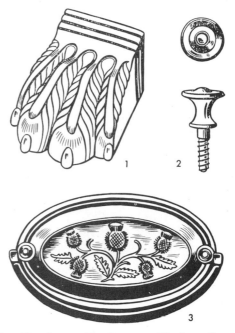

Fig. 20. Hardware for Duncan Phyfe roll-top desk.

screw strip D (Fig. 15) to A. Arrange the strips as shown, clamp boards C over the strips, and pull the strips tightly together with the bar clamps. The canvas, being only 34 in. wide, leaves the strips exposed for a distance of 1 in. at each end of the roll top (Fig. 16). When the glue has dried, remove the top from the jig and be certain that it slides freely in the grooves. Place the roll top into the desk from the back.

Next make the drawers (Fig. 17). The drawers are blind-dovetailed at the front and through-dovetailed at the back. Yellow poplar is good for the drawer sides and backs. If finished without stain, it contrasts in a pleasing manner with the mahogany drawer fronts.

Make the slide board shown in Figure 14. Fasten two short dowels at the back, letting them protrude about ½ in. underneath the slide board to keep it from being pulled out completely after it has been fitted to the desk.

Now complete the inside cabinet containing pigeonholes and compartments (Fig. 18). Fasten the cabinet into the desk so that the roll top will not slide around the sharply curved corner at the back.

Cover the screws in the desk ends with moldings, Q (Figs. 1 and 2). A detail of this molding is shown in Figure 19. Fasten the plywood back to the desk and attach the antique-finished brass hardware shown in Figure 20. The proper finish for this desk is discussed in Chapter 27.

17.

SPINET DESK

Spinet desks originated during the past two decades when it was the vogue to reclaim and rejuvenate furniture of outmoded design and put them to new, and sometimes entirely different, uses. While this hobby resulted in many poorly designed pieces, there were also a few happy innovations. Among the latter are desks made from spinets, the musical instruments which were the forerunners of our modern piano. The spinet called for a much smaller and lighter case than the piano. Once the instrument has been removed from the case, the case is converted readily into a writing desk.

Soon after the remodeling idea caught on, furniture manufacturers responded to popular demand by introducing their own designs. Unfortunately, many of these designs were poorly conceived although the original idea was not altogether lacking in merit.

Thomas Sheraton is famous for his ingenuity and inventiveness in making furniture serve more than one function. Duncan Phyfe lived during the Sheraton era, but was not as ingenious as Sheraton in this respect. Phyfe did, however, develop a fine spinet desk and it is his design which is imitated here. This design and the Duncan Phyfe roll-top desk design were developed by students in furniture design taught by the author.

The spinet desk should be built of mahogany or walnut. Use appropriate hardware of the types shown, dulled to an antique brass finish. The feet are fitted like a sheath over the ends of the curved feet. The hinges are of the invisible type shown in the drawings. Featured on this desk are beautifully colored inlays and marquetry.

PROCEDURE

First turn the columns and carve them (see Figure 3, Roll-Top Desk). The reeding on the columns, on the stretchers (Fig. 1), and on the feet (Fig. 7, Roll-Top Desk), is done with a V tool and a skew chisel. The columns and stretchers are carved most easily if left on the lathe, since the work can be turned from one position to another. To make a full-sized pattern for the carved leaves on the columns, find the distance around the circumference with a piece of string. Cut a piece of drawing paper 4 in. high, and as wide as the string showed the circumference to be. Divide this into four equal parts for the leaves, and lay out a full-size stencil pattern to transfer the design to the column.

Next, prepare the feet. The proper procedure for making and assembling feet like these is

Spinet Desk — closed

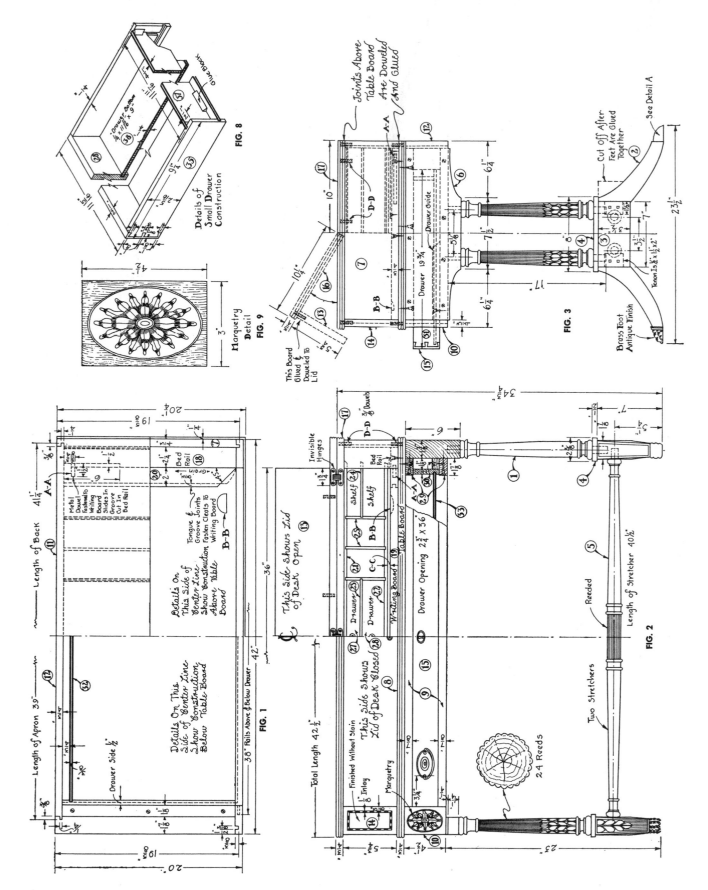

described in the chapter on the Duncan Phyfe roll-top desk.

Now, cut and shape the ends below the table board. A tongue is cut on the front end, which fits into a groove in the block which is faced with marquetry (Figs. 1, 6, and 9). A groove is cut also into the side of this member at the rear of the desk, as shown on the left side of Figure 1; while the rear apron has a tongue cut on its end which fits into this groove.

If the inlay and marquetry are glued in place before assembling the desk, carefully protect these surfaces with smooth blocks of wood when applying the clamps. Glue the rails above and below the large drawer to the end blocks before gluing the end blocks to the ends of the desk.

Fit the drawer runs and the drawer guides. Then build the large drawer, details of which are shown in Figure 7. Glue up the table board,

Spinet Desk — open

BILL OF MATERIAL

(The italicized numbers correspond with the encircled numbers in Figures 1, 2, 3, 5, 6, 7, and 8.)

DESCRIPTION	PIECES	DIMENSIONS
Mahogany:		
1. Columns	4	1⅞ diam. x 17¹
2. Curved feet	4	1⅞ x 4½ x 11½
3. Blocks between feet	2	1⅞ x 3½ x 7
4. Caps above feet	2	½ x 2⅜ x 8
5. Stretchers	2	1⅝ diam. x 40½
6. Ends below table board	2	1⅞ x 6 x 19⅝
7. Ends above table board	2	¾ x 5¾ x 19⅝
8. Table board	1	¾ x 20¼ x 42½
9. Rails below table board	2	¾ x ⅞ x 38
10. Blocks faced with marquetry	2	¾ x 3 x 4½
11. Back above table board	1	¾ x 5¾ x 41¼
12. Back below table board	1	¾ x 4½ x 39
13. Front of lid	1	¾ x 5¾ x 36
14. Inlaid face blocks	2	¾ x 3 x 5¾
15. Front, large drawer	1	¾ x 2¹¹⁄₁₆ x 35¹⁵⁄₁₆
16. Lid	1	¾ x 10¼ x 42½
17. Top	1	¾ x 10 x 42½
18. Bedrails	2	¾ x 2¼ x 18½
19. Writing board	1	¾ x 18½ x 36
20. Cleats, writing board	2	¾ x 2 x 18½
21. Upper board, cabinet	1	¼ x 9¼ x 40¼
22. Lower board, cabinet	1	⅜ x 9¼ x 40¼
23. Shelf between drawers, cabinet	1	¼ x 9¼ x 12¼
24. Shelves, cabinet	2	¼ x 9¼ x 7½

DESCRIPTION	PIECES	DIMENSIONS
25. Partitions of pigeonholes	6	¼ x 9¼ x 4⅜
26. Ends, cabinet	2	¼ x 9¼ x 5
27. Small drawer front	1	½ x 1⁷⁄₁₆ x 11¹⁵⁄₁₆
28. Small drawer front	1	½ x 2⁵⁄₁₆ x 11¹⁵⁄₁₆
Poplar:		
29. Runs above and below large drawer	4	⅞ x 1⅞ x 18½
30. Drawer guides	2	¾ x 1⅛ x 18½
31. Sides, large drawer	2	½ x 2¹¹⁄₁₆ x 19½
32. Sides, small drawer	2	¼ x 2⁵⁄₁₆ x 9⅛
33. Sides, small drawer	2	¼ x 1⁷⁄₁₆ x 9⅛
Plywood:		
34. Back, large drawer	1	⅜ x 1¹³⁄₁₆ x 35⁷⁄₁₆
35. Bottom, large drawer	1	⅜ x 19¼ x 35⁷⁄₁₆
36. Back, small drawer	1	¼ x ¹⁵⁄₁₆ x 11¹¹⁄₁₆
37. Back, small drawer	1	¼ x 1¹³⁄₁₆ x 11¹¹⁄₁₆
38. Bottoms small drawers	2	¼ x 11¹¹⁄₁₆ x 9

Hardware:

2 oval drawer pulls (See Fig. 20, Roll-Top Desk.)
1 drawer lock
1 desk lid lock
2 pulls for small drawers. (See Fig. 20, Roll-Top Desk.)
2 pieces marquetry (See Fig. 9.)
⅛ in. inlay banding, about 30 in.
3 Soss invisible hinges, 1¾ in.
4 brass claw sheath feet

¹ Turn from stock 2 in. square.

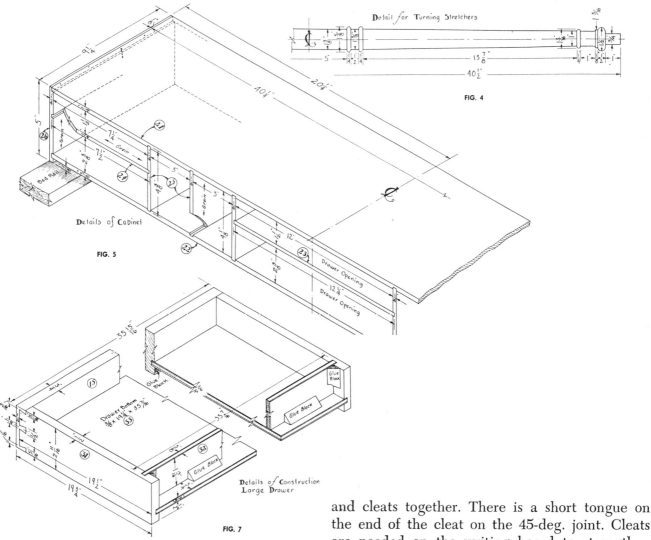

Detail for Turning Stretchers

FIG. 4

Details of Cabinet

FIG. 5

Details of Construction
Large Drawer

FIG. 7

molding its edges either with wood-carving tools or with the proper cutter on a power shaper. Wood screws through the upper drawer runs, through the rail above the drawer, and through a strip fastened to the upper edge on the inside of the back rail (not shown in the drawing), will secure the table board firmly to the frame.

Begin the upper part of the desk by cutting the tongues-and-grooves on the end boards, the inlaid face blocks, and the back. Glue these together, carefully squaring the corners; then fasten this assembled unit to the table board with dowels and glue as shown at *D-D*, Figures 2 and 3.

Next, make the writing board. The construction is shown in Figures 1 and 6. The board will slide back and forth more easily if the cleats are slightly thicker on the bottom than the board itself. Tongue-and-groove joints hold the board

and cleats together. There is a short tongue on the end of the cleat on the 45-deg. joint. Cleats are needed on the writing board to strengthen it and to keep it from warping. Cut two depressions or fingerholds (Fig. 2, *B-B*) on the writing board. It is important that the wood used for this board and for the bedrails is well seasoned and that the board slides easily, or these pieces may swell during damp weather. Use metal dowels as shown at *A-A*, Figure 2.

Cut and fit the bedrails. These rails have grooves cut near the rear of the inside edges for the sliding dowels which are fastened to the writing board. These grooves are reinforced with band iron screwed to the bedrails (Fig. 6). Fasten the bedrails to the table board with wood screws. The holes for these screws are counterbored to sink the screwhead below the surface. When the writing board is in place, the holes are closed with wooden plugs (Fig. 6). Do not insert the plugs until the bedrails can be fastened permanently. These rails cannot be tightened

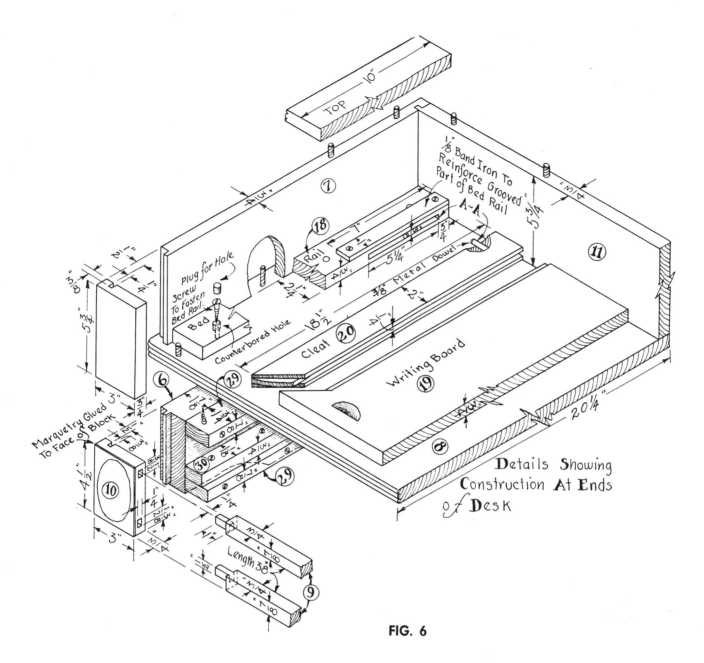

FIG. 6

until the writing board has been fitted properly to insure easy sliding and the writing board and the surface of the table board beneath it have had the finish applied.

Build the cabinet for the inside of the desk next. The construction is shown in Figure 5. The ¼-in. space (Fig. 2, *C-C*) is necessary to give clearance to the writing board and provides a place for a large blotter-paper writing pad. The

ends of the cabinet rest directly on the bedrails.

After fitting the cabinet to the desk, fasten the top as indicated at *D-D*, Figure 2. Fasten the lid to the top with invisible hinges. Attach the face board to the lid with dowels and glue.

Now, construct the small drawers (Fig. 8), and complete the desk. Apply the finish which has not already been applied. Attach the hardware after the finishing has been done.

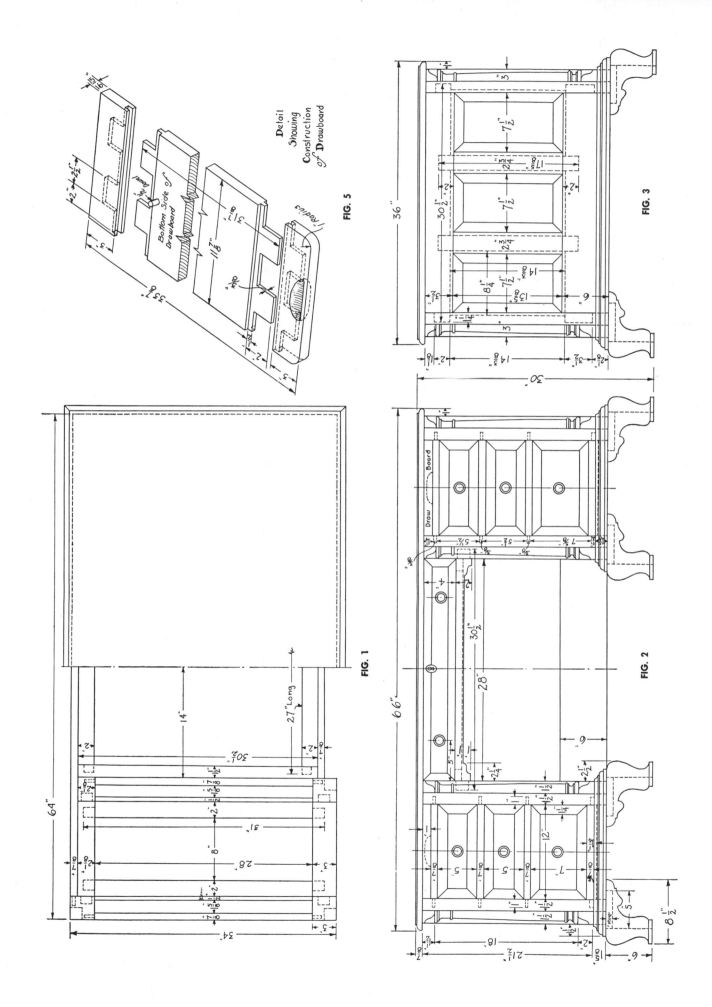

Detail Showing Construction of Drawboard

FIG. 5

FIG. 3

FIG. 1

FIG. 2

18.

EARLY AMERICAN FLAT-TOP OFFICE DESK

"Impressive" is the word to describe this handsome flat-top desk. The beauty of the paneled sides and drawer fronts and the generous proportions make it a truly remarkable piece of furniture. The desk will serve equally well in a business office or in the study of a private residence.

The maple desk shown here was built for the library of the Science Building at Martha Berry College. Either oak or walnut could be substituted for maple.

PROCEDURE

First make the corner posts, consisting of pieces X and Y (Fig. 6). Glue X and Y together; then cut the mortises for the rails, and the grooves for the panels. Layouts for the mortises and grooves are given in Figures 1, 2, 3, and 4.

Construct the frames which hold the paneling next. The rails and stiles are mortised, tenoned, grooved, and then glued together after the panels have been made and put into place. To raise panels such as these, see the method of performing the operation, Figure 8, page 144. The panels are never glued, but are left free in the grooves of the frames. Plane about $\frac{1}{16}$ in. off each edge of the panel, after it has been fitted to the frame, to permit expansion in damp weather.

Glue the paneled frames which form the desk ends and insides to the corner posts and to the two posts on the inside back. Peg these mortise-and-tenon joints with $\frac{1}{4}$ in. roughly octagoned, hardwood pegs to further strengthen them. Drill the holes for these pegs about $\frac{1}{32}$ in. smaller than the peg's rough diameter so that the peg will fit very tightly when it is driven through the joint. On antique pieces of this type, the joints were drawbored[1] to pull them tightly together when the pegs were driven in, but with

---

[1] Drawboring consisted of drilling the hole for the peg closer to the shoulder on the tenon member of a mortise-and-tenon joint than it was bored on the mortise member. Thus, when the peg was driven home, it pulled both members of the joint tightly together.

Early American Desk — front view

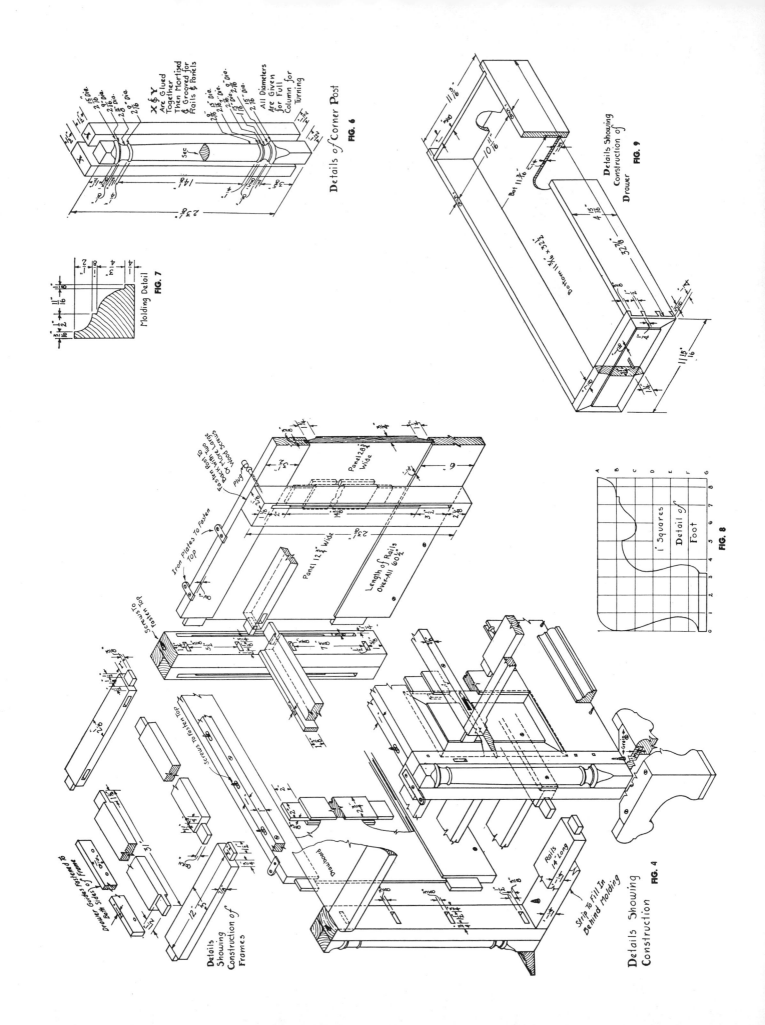

Details of Corner Post FIG. 6

Molding Detail FIG. 7

Details Showing Construction of Drawer FIG. 9

Detail of Foot FIG. 8

Details Showing Construction of Frames

Details Showing Construction FIG. 4

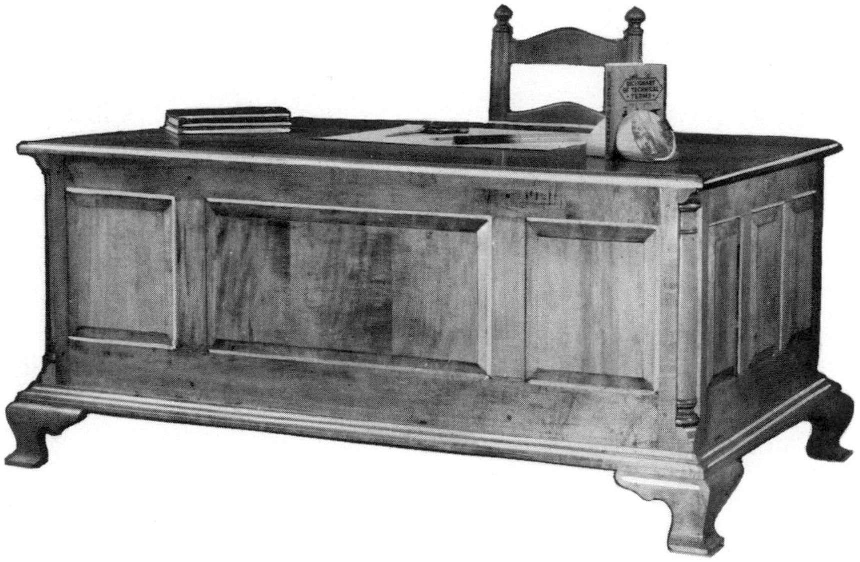

Early American Desk — rear view

BILL OF MATERIAL

DESCRIPTION	PIECES	DIMENSIONS
Corner posts	6	1½ x 3 x 23⅛
	6	1½ x 1½ x 23⅛
Posts at rear of desk	2	2⅛ x 3 x 23⅛
Quarter columns	6	3 x 3 x 23⅛[1]
Rails for the back	1	⅞ x 3½ x 60½
	1	⅞ x 6 x 60½
Rails for ends and for inside	4	⅞ x 3½ x 30½
paneling	4	⅞ x 6 x 30½
Stiles for ends and for inside paneling	8	⅞ x 2¾ x 17⅝
Stiles for back	2	⅞ x 3 x 17⅝
Rail below wide drawer	1	⅞ x 2 x 30½
Frames to Hold Drawers		
Long rails for six frames	12	⅞ x 2 x 31
Front rails	6	⅞ x 3 x 14
Back rails	6	⅞ x 2⅛ x 14
Drawer guides	12	½ x 1⅜ x 28
Frames Under Lower Drawers		
Long rails for two frames	4	1¼ x 2 x 31
Front rails	2	1¼ x 3 x 14
Back rails	2	1¼ x 2⅛ x 14
Drawer guides	4	½ x 1¾ x 28
Frame Under Wide Drawer		
Rails	2	⅞ x 1½ x 30½
Rails	2	⅞ x 2 x 27
Strips[2]	2	1¼ x 3 x 12
12 feet[3]	1	1⅞ x 6 x 102

[1] Made from two turned columns.
[2] To fill in behind molding under lower frames.
[3] From one piece molded on its face to the shape of the outside foot.

DESCRIPTION	PIECES	DIMENSIONS
Corner blocks for tops of feet	6	¾ x 4⅞ x 8½
Drawboards	2	15/16 x 11⅞ x 31⅞
	4	15/16 x 3 x 11⅞
Panels for sides	12	¾ x 8¼ x 14⅜
Panels for back	2	¾ x 12¾ x 14⅜
Panel for back	1	¾ x 28¾ x 14⅜
Top of desk	1	⅞ x 36 x 66
Strips to hold top to rails	4	1 x 1 x 28
Drawers		
Fronts	4	1¼ x 4 15/16 x 11 15/16
Fronts	2	1¼ x 6 15/16 x 11 15/16
Front	1	1¼ x 3 15/16 x 27 15/16
Sides	8	⅝ x 4 15/16 x 32⅞
Sides	4	⅝ x 6 15/16 x 32⅞
Sides, wide drawer	2	⅝ x 3 15/16 x 31⅛
Bottoms	6	¼ x 11 3/16 x 32½
Bottom	1	¼ x 27 3/16 x 30¾
Backs	4	⅜ x 4 3/16 x 11 3/16
Backs	2	⅜ x 6 3/16 x 11 3/16
Back, wide drawer	1	⅜ x 3 3/16 x 27 3/16
Molding		1½ x 1⅝ x 183 (plus allowance for waste in cutting)

Hardware:

8 No. 1 brass drawer pulls, antique brass finish, No. 3
1 No. 2 or 3 brass escutcheon, No. 1
1 drawer lock, No. 2

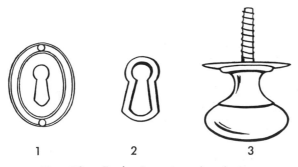

Fig. 10. Early American hardware

modern, efficient clamping devices the drilling and pegging can be done before the clamps are removed.

Make the frames which support the drawers and drawboards next. The frames are mortised and tenoned together, and, in addition, the frames themselves are fastened to the posts with mortise-and-tenon joints. The lower frames are thicker than the others, as are the joints with which they are fastened together and to the posts. Fasten the guide strips which keep the drawers in line to the sides of the frames with screws before gluing the frames to the posts.

When all the joints on the frames have been sanded smooth to permit free sliding of the drawers and drawboards, glue the drawer frames to the previously assembled panel frames and posts. It would be wise — and simpler — to fasten the strips to which the desk top is later fastened before gluing the frames to the ends of the desk.

Assemble the paneled back. Make the bracketed rail which goes in the middle of the desk. Also make and assemble the frame which supports the drawer.

Using long bar clamps, glue up the desk which consists of the two end compartments, the bracketed stretcher, and the paneling for the back. Fasten the frame which supports the middle drawer to the inside with wood screws (Fig. 4). Use several large, No. 14 wood screws to fasten the inside rear posts to the upper and lower rail of the paneled frame. Counterbore the holes on the outside of the rails and plug the holes (Fig. 4).

Make and fit the drawers and drawboards to the desk at this point. Fit the drawers before fastening the top in place. Figure 9 shows the drawer construction. In the desk shown here,

only the wide drawer was fitted with a lock. A mechanism for locking all drawers by locking the center drawer could be installed in this desk. However, to do this, a number of changes would have to be made on the inside, such as shortening the drawers and frames at the back to provide room for the locking device.

The construction of the drawboards is shown in Figure 5, where the bottom side is shown to better illustrate how the handhold cavity is chiseled into the front cleat. Notice the dowel which keeps the board from being drawn entirely out of the desk.

After the drawers and drawboards have been fitted to the desk, make and attach the top. Do this before the quarter columns are fastened in place, since it is desirable to drive wood screws on an angle through the tops of the corner posts (Fig. 4) to keep the edges of the top from curling up or warping, and to hold the top more securely in place. Use an extension with a screw-driver bit in a brace to drive the screws through the strips into the top. Lay the top face down on a clean floor and place the assembled desk in its proper position on top of it. The extension must be long enough to reach from the bottom frame to the top of the desk. For assembling this particular desk, a special screw driver with a blade of the required length was made in the blacksmith's shop.

Turn and then split the columns in the manner described for the construction of the Jacobean chest of drawers (Fig. 12, page 142). Glue the columns into their respective niches. Then fasten the molding to the bottom of the desk with wood screws at the sides and back, finish with nails, and glue the front.

Make and attach the feet next. By making a long piece of Ogee molding of the required thickness, width, and length, all of the parts of the feet can be sawed to length, mitered for the corner joints, and then sawed to the bracket shape on a band saw. The joint is glued and further strengthened by driving corrugated fasteners into the top and bottom of the foot. Mortise the foot at the top for the corner block with which it is fastened to the desk before the corrugated fastener is hammered in.

Put on the drawer pulls and lock and finish the desk.

19.

CHIPPENDALE WING CHAIR

A wing chair is as comfortable and cozy a chair as anyone could wish to have. The price of a good one comes high. The design of this chair, inspired by the finest Chippendale types, has vigorous, free-flowing curves on the wings, arms, and cabriole legs; beautifully carved feet and knees; and a generously proportioned seat and back.

The front leg is carved from heavy, solid mahogany, 3 in. square, with extra blocks glued to the top on two sides to extend the width of the beautifully carved knee. The back legs are from a single piece of mahogany from bottom to top, and not joined to a less expensive wood under the upholstery as is sometimes the case with manufactured furniture. Mortise-and-tenon joints unite the various members, and adequate braces of iron and wood strengthen the frame. For the covered frame use birch, gum, soft maple, or other wood, not too soft or too hard, that will hold tacks well without splitting. The material used on this chair is cotton and rayon damask.

PROCEDURE

First, make and carve the front legs from pieces of solid mahogany, 3 in. square and 14½ in. long. Glue two blocks of mahogany, 2¾ by 3 by 3¼ in., to each leg, 2½ in. from the top, after the upper 2½ in. of the leg has been cut down to 1⅞ in. square (Fig. 4). After cutting the mortises and gluing on the blocks, mark one inside surface of each leg for sawing, using a pattern made from the outline of Figure 5. Band-saw two sides of the leg to shape. Mark the adjacent inside surface for the next sawing. The leg has now been shaped, but is still square in section. Round the leg with a spokeshave, chisels, file, scraper blades, and sandpaper. In carving the foot, block out the toes and complete them after the ball has been formed. When carving the toes, keep the knuckles lined up horizontally. The carving on the knee requires time and care, but is not as difficult to carve as the foot. Outline each leaf with a V tool, then cut away the background, and finally model the leaves (Fig. 6).

There should be no great difficulty in making the rest of the frame. The back legs come next. Lay out a full-sized pattern for the side of the leg from Figure 7. Cut two legs from a plank of the size specified in the bill of material, if the legs are marked off side by side. After the legs have been sawed and dressed to the proper shape, lay out and cut all mortises. Make all stretchers for the back, cut the tenons, and glue up the back. Assemble the vertical strips and the rails to which they are fastened in the back. Glue the rails to the back legs. Make the front seat rail and glue it to the front legs. Then make the side rails and glue to the front and back of the chair.

Chippendale Wing Chair

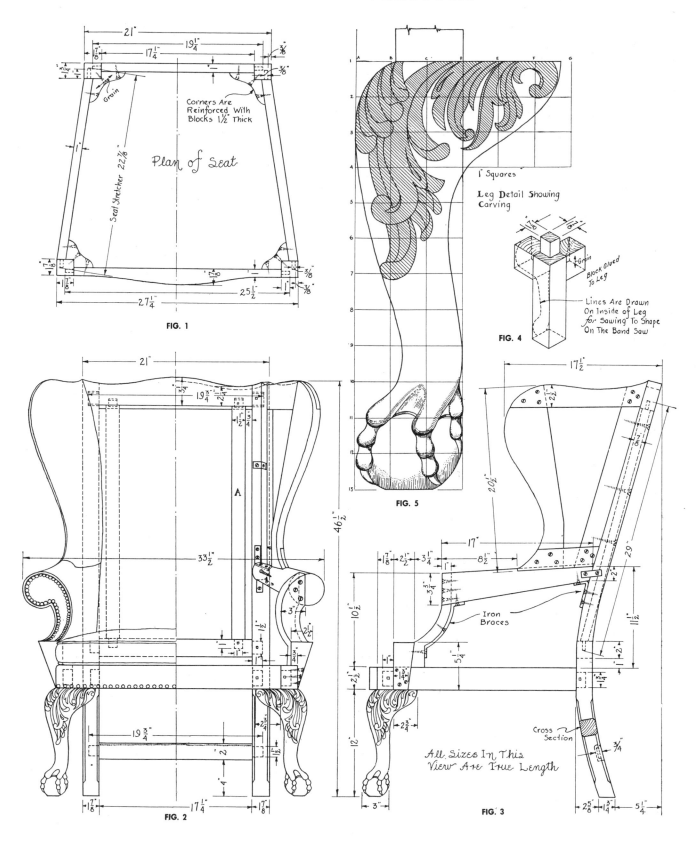

Plan of Seat

Corners Are Reinforced With Blocks 1½" Thick

Grain

Seat Stretcher 22⅞"

FIG. 1

Leg Detail Showing Carving

1" Squares

Block Glued To Leg

Grain

Lines Are Drawn On Inside of Leg for Sawing To Shape On The Band Saw

FIG. 4

FIG. 5

Iron Braces

Cross Section

All Sizes In This View Are True Length

FIG. 2

FIG. 3

Turn the arms and the vertically placed, cone-shaped cylinders near the front of the seat. Saw the arm support first to the shape shown in Figure 3, then to the shape shown in Figure 2. Save the waste from the first sawing and tack it back on, and the second sawing will be easy to do. Assemble, fit, and fasten the three-piece arms to the chair.

Make and assemble the wings. Lay out full-sized patterns for the various parts from Figure 8. The construction of the entire frame should be easily understood after studying Figure 9.

Apply all finishing materials to the lower parts of the chair before starting the upholstering. Furniture finishing is discussed in Chapter 27.

To upholster the chair, proceed as follows: Tack good webbing to the bottom of the seat frame, stretching it tight with a webbing stretcher (Fig. 10). Also tack webbing to the inside of the back (Fig. 13), to the inside of the arms (Fig. 12), and the inside of the wings. The webbing must be interwoven, stretched, and tacked as shown in the drawings. When starting, double the ends of the webbing and tack through the double thickness. Tack only one piece of webbing to the inside of the arm. Draw a piece of burlap over the arm, and a piece of webbing

Fig. 6. Detail of the beautifully carved cabriole legs.

over the burlap. When all of the upholstering material has been placed over the inside of the arm, pull the material down over the outside of the seat stretcher and tack it (Fig. 12).

By fastening the upholstering material, muslin, and webbing to the outside of the seat stretcher, the tops of the seat stretchers are left free to tack the burlap and other covering material over the springs of the seat.

BILL OF MATERIAL

DESCRIPTION	PIECES	DIMENSIONS
Mahogany:		
Front legs	2	3 x 3 x 14½
Blocks on front legs	4	2¾ x 3 x 3¼
Back legs	2	1⅞ x 9 x 48[1]
Rear stretcher near floor	1	¾ x 2 x 19¾
Birch, Gum, or Soft Maple:		
Front seat stretcher	1	1⅞ x 2½ x 25½
Side seat stretchers	2	1 x 2½ x 22⅞
Back seat stretcher	1	1 x 2½ x 19¼
Bottom rail, back (above seat rail)	1	1¾ x 2 x 19¼
Upper rail, back	1	1¾ x 3¼ x 19¼
Vertical strips, back	2	⅞ x 1½ x 29
Arms	2	3¾ diam. x 17
Arm fronts	2	3 x 4¾ x 10½
Turned vertical cylinders, lower arms	2	2½ diam. x 5¼
Wing fronts	2	⅞ x 5¼ x 20½
Wing backs	2	⅞ x 2 x 22½
Wing tops	2	⅞ x 2¾ x 15

[1] Both legs are cut from this plank.

DESCRIPTION	PIECES	DIMENSIONS
Blocks for bracing seat	2	1½ x 2 x 5½
	2	1½ x 2 x 4½
Upholstering Materials:		
3½-in. webbing, best quality jute fiber		
12 No. 2 broad-block springs for seat		
9 4-in. cushion springs for back		
10-oz. burlap, approx. 3 yd.		
Upholstering tacks 16 oz., 12 oz., 10 oz., 6 oz., 3 oz.		
Muslin		
Moss filling		
Cotton felt (no seeds)		
Spring twine and sewing twine		
Sponge rubber for cushion		
6 yd. upholstering material 54-in. wide, and matching, heavy-duty mercerized thread		
⅛-in. band iron for bracing		
Wood screws		

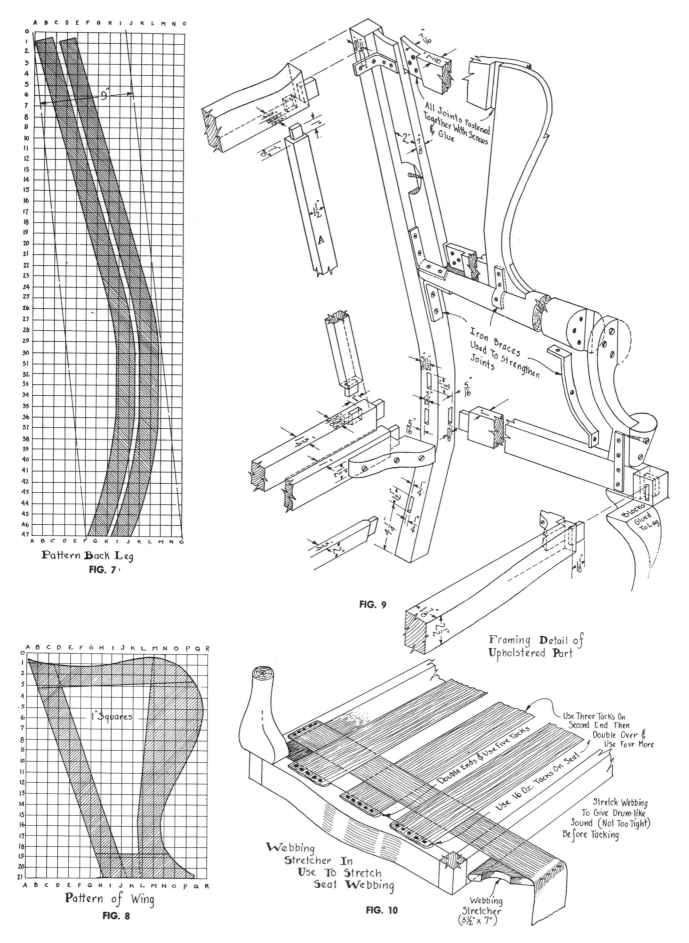

Pattern Back Leg
FIG. 7

Pattern of Wing
FIG. 8

All Joints Fastened
Together With Screws
& Glue

Iron Braces
Used To Strengthen
Joints

Blocks
Glued
To Leg

FIG. 9

Framing Detail of
Upholstered Part

Double Ends & Use Five Tacks

Use Three Tacks On
Second End Then
Double Over &
Use Four More

Use 16 Oz. Tacks On Seat

Stretch Webbing
To Give Drum-like
Sound (Not Too Tight)
Before Tacking.

Webbing
Stretcher In
Use To Stretch
Seat Webbing

Webbing
Stretcher
(3½" x 7")

FIG. 10

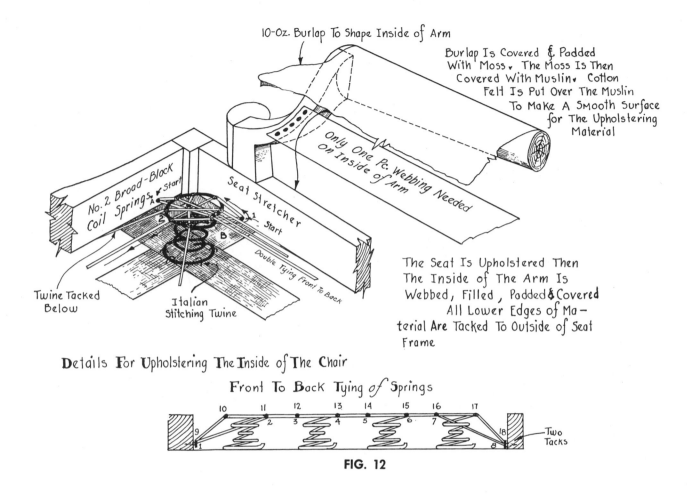

10-Oz. Burlap To Shape Inside of Arm

Burlap Is Covered & Padded
With Moss. The Moss Is Then
Covered With Muslin. Cotton
Felt Is Put Over The Muslin
To Make A Smooth Surface
for The Upholstering
Material

No. 2 Broad-Block Coil Springs

Seat Stretcher

Only One Pc. Webbing Needed On Inside of Arm

Start

Double Tying Front To Back

Twine Tacked Below

Italian Stitching Twine

The Seat Is Upholstered Then
The Inside of The Arm Is
Webbed, Filled, Padded & Covered
All Lower Edges of Ma-
terial Are Tacked To Outside of Seat
Frame

Details For Upholstering The Inside of The Chair

Front To Back Tying of Springs

Two Tacks

FIG. 12

For the back of the chair, sew nine 4-in. pillow springs with twine to the webbing where the strips intersect. Sew twelve No. 2 broad-block coil springs to the seat webbing. Tie all seat springs eight times, as shown in Figure 12, with weaver's knots. Stretch and tie the twine in such a way that the springs can be compressed without tearing or loosening the twine where it is tacked.

Tack the twine where it says "start" in Figure 12, leaving the short end to tie to the front of the spring later. Proceed from the tack through the spring to the top of the far side, and from there to the second spring where it is knotted to both sides. Proceed in this manner to the spring on the opposite side of the chair, tie a knot to the inside wire, and then go through the spring to the bottom edge of the seat stretcher and tack it fast. From there go to the top of the spring, tying the twine to the part of the coil closest to the last tacking. Then tie the short end, left at "start," to the top of the spring on the opposite side from the first tie. Use this method to tie all the seat springs, pulling them down about level with the tops of the seat stretchers.

The short pieces of twine on the corner springs, which are tacked to the bottoms of the seat stretchers, are put on after the long pieces are in place. Tie them to both sides of the coils on top of the springs.

The springs in the chair back are tied only two ways, to keep them from being too stiff (Fig. 13).

Cover the tied springs with about 3 yds. of heavy burlap. Pull the burlap through the opening between the back legs and the vertical strips, Figure 2, A, and tack it with 6-oz. tacks to the backs of the strips. Lay the filling material on the back, cover it with muslin and the remaining upholstering material and draw these materials through this opening and tack in a similar manner. At the bottom of the back, draw the materials through the opening between the seat rail and the stretcher, and tack to the latter. Draw the upholstery materials tight at the top and tack them to the back. Cover the webbing on the arms and wings with burlap, and sew the filling to it.

After the burlap has been tacked in place, lay the chair on its back and evenly distribute a

5- or 6-in. thick layer of moss over it. This thickness will be reduced considerably once the muslin has been stretched over the filling material. Sew long loops of twine all over the burlap. Work some of the moss into these loops to prevent it from sliding out of place. The moss is first picked (pulled apart) to form a springy mass. Do not pull all of the moss through the loops, only enough to hold the rest of the moss in place.

Pad the insides of the wings and arms in the same manner, varying the thickness of the filling from about 1 in., or a little more, around the tops of the arms, to greater thicknesses where needed. Take great care to keep the filling springy and uniform. Stretch the muslin over the filling, one surface at a time. Now stuff the seat. A stuffing regulator can be used to shift the moss after the muslin has been stretched, if this is necessary to get a smooth surface. All surfaces will be improved considerably by placing a layer of 10- or 12-oz. cotton felt over the muslin. The cotton felt helps keep dust, which may form on the inside of the chair, from coming through the cloth.

The seat, at the front, has a built-up roll edge, consisting of a roll of moss encased in burlap and tacked to the top of the seat stretchers (Fig.

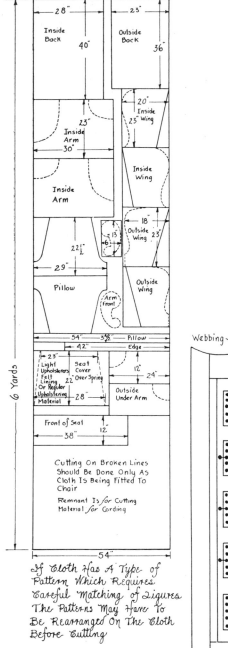

Plan for Cutting Upholstering Material

FIG. 11

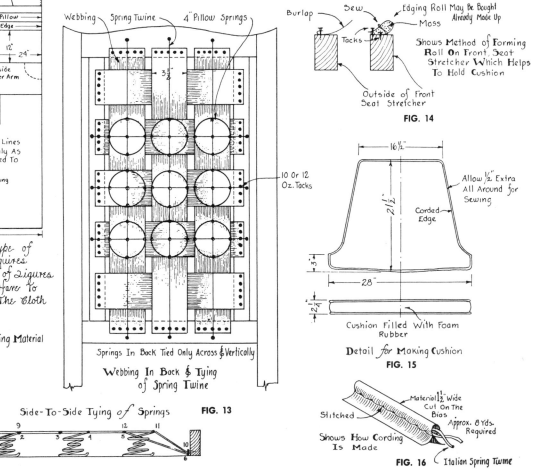

Shows Method of Forming Roll On Front Seat Stretcher Which Helps To Hold Cushion

FIG. 14

Cushion Filled With Foam Rubber

Detail for Making Cushion

FIG. 15

Springs In Back Tied Only Across & Vertically

Webbing In Back & Tying of Spring Twine

FIG. 13

Shows How Cording Is Made

FIG. 16 Italian Spring Twine

Side-To-Side Tying of Springs

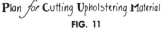

14). Make this roll fairly hard by sewing a running stitch along its entire length after it has been tacked in place. Since these rolls can be bought already made up at a low cost, it is hardly worth the trouble of making one.

The outside of the frame, the back of the chair, the outsides of the wing frames, and the places below the arms are filled and then covered with muslin. Cotton felt goes over the muslin. Now, the chair is ready for the upholstering material.

As shown in the diagram, Figure 11, about 6 yds. of 54-in. material are needed. All patterns in Figure 11 are large enough to provide for seams and for turning under at the edges. It will be simpler to cut all edges straight at first, leaving each piece sufficiently large to put it in its place on the chair and then mark it for cutting. With the machine, sew the inside wing piece to the piece on the inside of the arm before tacking it to the chair. Slip-tack the material to the chair; that is, do not completely drive in the tacks at first. Allow for their removal, and the restretching of the cloth as the fitting progresses. Use 3-oz. tacks, and always tack from the center of the cloth toward the ends. Draw inside wing cloth around and tack it to the outside of the wings.

Draw down and tack the material covering the inside arms to the outside of the seat stretcher. Do the same to the webbing and other covering material. Tack the material under the arms on the outside, below the arm roll, then sew it to the material above it with a curved needle using the blind stitch. Fasten the cloth for the inside back to the rear of the vertical strips, A.

The cording, or piping is made by covering Italian spring twine with upholstering material (Fig. 16). The cording starts under the arm, goes around the front outside edge of the wing, around the upper edge of the top rail at the back of the chair, down the edge of the other wing, and then on below the arm. To this cording is sewn the outside wing covering, and the top edge of the material used for the outside back of the chair. Sew the blind stitch with a small curved needle. Sew the vertical edges of the cloth on the back of the chair to the outside wing material and to the other material which was drawn around from the side. Sew these seams, which are also blind-stitched, as close to the edges as possible. Cord the top and bottom edges of the seat cushion (Fig. 16). Fill the seat cushion with one or two layers of foam rubber, cut to the proper shape and size.

Next cut and then sew the material to the fronts of the arms. This material is folded under around its edges and blind-stitched to the other material. Finish the chair with large-headed brass upholstery nails. A row of nails around the bottom of the upholstered part puts a nice finishing touch to this part of the chair.

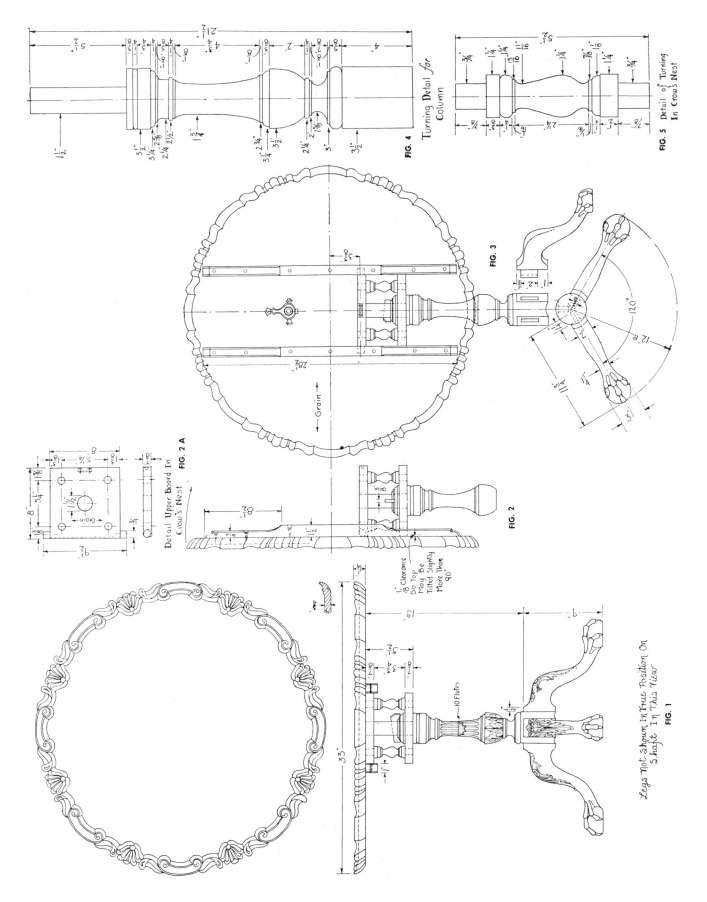

FIG. 4   Turning Detail for Column

FIG. 5   Detail of Turning In Crow's Nest

FIG. 3

FIG. 2 A   Detail Upper Board In Crow's Nest

FIG. 2

FIG. 1   Legs Not Shown In True Position On Shaft In This View

20.

PIECRUST TABLE

Tilt-top piecrust tables are among the most exquisite of all furniture pieces. They are as decorative as they are useful. Placed next to a deep, comfortable easy chair, such a table serves as a side table for a reading lamp, books, or decorative pieces. Placed in the corner of a room or alongside a fireplace, with the top tilted vertically, it becomes a purely decorative accessory. Either way, it will add a very distinctive note to a room.

The top of a good piecrust table should be made, if possible, of a single, wide, well-seasoned board. The carving around the edge should not be glued on, but carved from the solid board. Therefore, stock 1¼ in. thick will be required, and the middle portion must be lowered in the carving process. The center can be hollowed on a large lathe, if the lathe is equipped with a large faceplate fastened to the outside of the headstock. Otherwise, it will have to be carved out with gouges and then scraped flat and smooth.

Unlike most antique piecrust tables the legs of this one have been designed by the author to be fastened to the base of the shaft with mortise-and-tenon joints. A running dovetail joint is usually used because it can be fitted to the shaft without using clamps. The joints, however, are not always sufficiently strong to bear the loads re-

quired, and many an otherwise worthy design has been damaged by a split shaft. Mortise-and-tenon joints are much stronger, but must be clamped while the glue hardens. This is possible if the legs are sawed first to the shape shown in Figure 10, then glued to the shaft, and the waste sawed or chiseled off.

Use top-grade Honduras or Cuban mahogany. Black walnut or hard maple are second-choice woods.

PROCEDURE

First, turn the shaft, using solid stock, if possible. On the base of the shaft, lay out the three places where the legs are to be joined to

Piecrust Table

BILL OF MATERIAL

DESCRIPTION	PIECES	DIMENSIONS
Feet	3	3 x 6 x 15
Shaft	1	3½ diam. x 21½
Top	1	1¼ x 33 diam.
Upper board, crow's nest	1	⅞ x 8 x 9½
Lower board, crow's nest	1	⅞ x 8 x 8
Wooden washer	1	⅞ x 3½ diam.
Key	1	⅜ x 1 x 3¼
Spindles, crow's nest	4	1¼ diam. x 5½
Cleats to fasten top to crow's nest	2	1 x 1½ x 28½
1 piecrust-table latch (brass)		

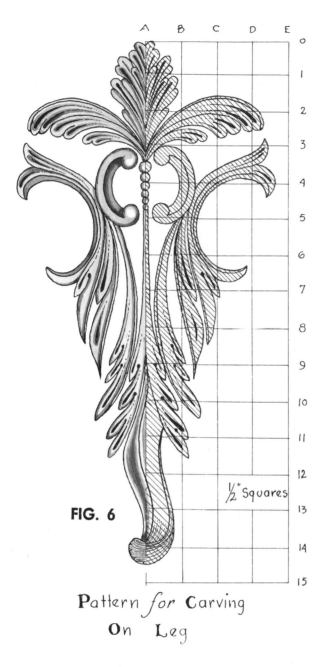

FIG. 6

½" Squares

Pattern *for* Carving
On Leg

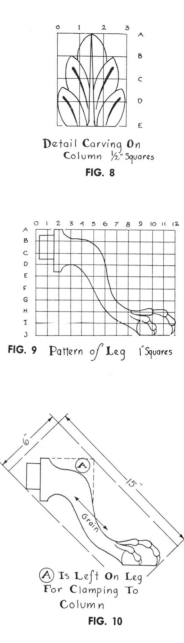

Detail Carving On
Column ½" Squares
FIG. 8

FIG. 9 Pattern *of* Leg 1" Squares

Ⓐ Is Left On Leg
For Clamping To
Column
FIG. 10

the shaft, flatten them, and cut the mortises (Fig. 3).

Make a pattern for the legs (Figs. 9 and 10). Shape the legs on a band saw, as shown in Figure 10, then trim off ½ in. on both sides above the foot, leaving a thickness of only 2 in. on all of the leg except the foot. Cut the tenon on each leg and fit the legs to their respective mortises. Finish shaping the legs with the exception of the knees where pieces A are to be kept until the legs have been glued to the shaft. Carve the shaft and then glue the legs to it. Cut off waste pieces A, and carve the legs and feet. Patterns

for all carvings on the legs and shaft are given in Figures 6, 8, and 9.

Make the board for the crow's nest. Allow ¾-in. dowels to protrude on both ends of the upper board to form the fulcrum of the hinge for swinging the top. Slant the back edge of the top board to allow the top to be raised slightly more than 90 deg. Trim off ⅛ in. of the edge of the board below it for the same reason (Fig. 2).

Turn the spindles shown in Figure 5, and assemble the crow's nest. Turn the wooden washer and cut the slot in it for the key. Place the crow's nest and washer on the shaft and see that they turn freely on the shaft. Make the hole for the

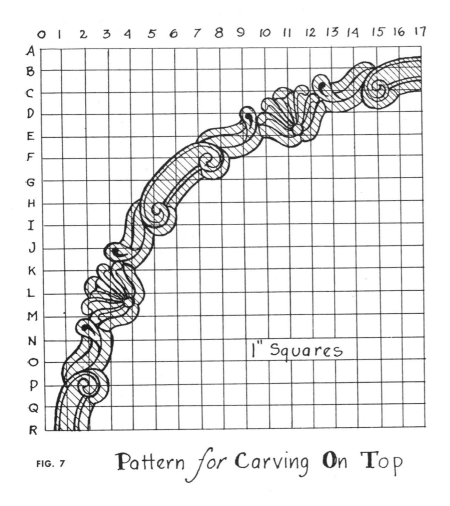

FIG. 7 Pattern for Carving On Top

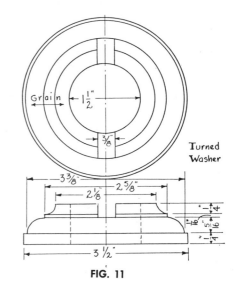

Turned Washer

FIG. 11

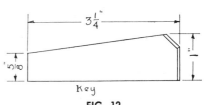

Key

FIG. 12

key on the shaft, and mortise the hole through the shaft (Figs. 2 and 3).

Band-saw the top to a diameter of 33 in. Using a full-sized pattern made from Figure 7, lay out the carving around the rim of the top. Mount the top on a large faceplate, which has been fastened to the outside of a heavy lathe. If this machine is not available, gouge out the waste, leaving the central portion of the top ¾ in. thick. Scrape smooth and level, and then carve the piecrust rim. Also shape this rim carefully on the back, as shown in Figure 3, since this should show the same fine workmanship as the carved upper side.

When the top has been carved, make the two cleats and fasten them across the grain under the top (Fig. 3). Fasten the cleats with wood screws into counterbored holes and plug with wooden plugs. Be sure the top swings freely on the dowels of the upper board in the crow's nest. Fasten the latch, and the table is ready to stain.

Fig. 13. Hardware for Piecrust Table

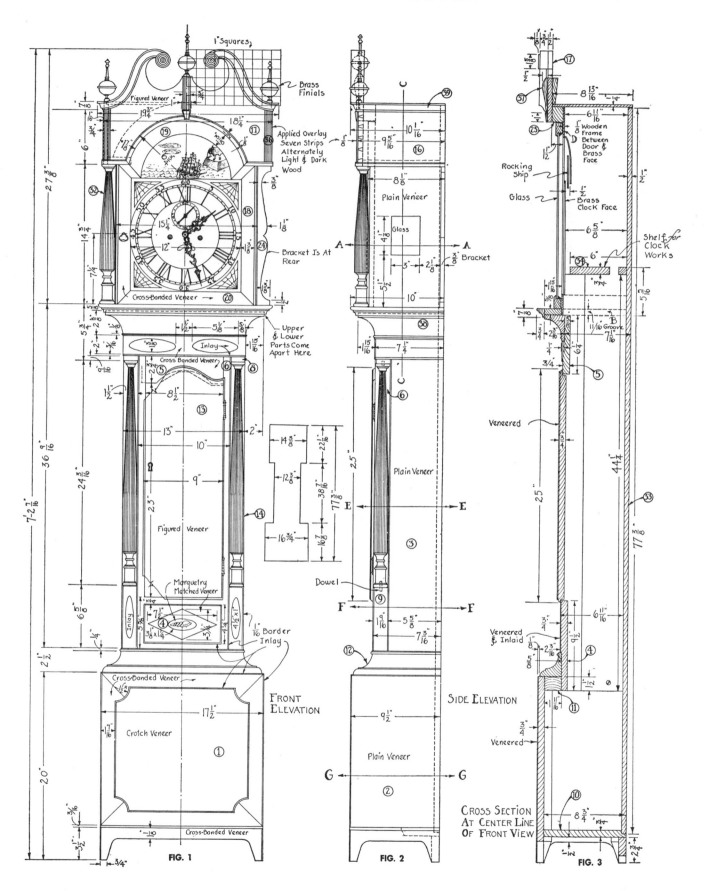

FRONT ELEVATION

FIG. 1

SIDE ELEVATION

FIG. 2

CROSS SECTION AT CENTER LINE OF FRONT VIEW

FIG. 3

21.

SHERATON-TYPE GRANDFATHER'S CLOCK

This beautifully veneered and inlaid masterpiece among clocks is designed in the Sheraton style, but is of American workmanship. This particular example is built of mahogany, veneered with both plain and figured veneers, and embellished with marquetry and inlays.

This clock could very well be built of solid mahogany, cherry, or even walnut, without veneering any part of the case. Even the narrow line inlays could be dispensed with. By making the case of solid stock instead of veneer, the job will be simplified considerably since veneering and inlaying entails a great deal of additional work.

Purchase the works for the clock before building the clock cabinet, so as to make sure the works will fit the case.

Veneering and inlaying are almost a trade in themselves and our "Procedure" properly starts with directions on this phase of the work.

Veneers and marquetry can be purchased in made-to-order patterns, or from stock patterns, similar to the desired design. For anyone unfamiliar with the processes of matching and making up veneers to a pattern, this course is recommended.

PROCEDURE

Veneering usually comes in sheets which are ⅟₂₈ in. thick. For panels like the one on the bottom of the clock case, select the veneer, cut it to shape, and join the individual pieces together with veneer tape. Cut a thin veneer with a very sharp, thin-bladed knife, firmly holding the straightedge over the veneer. Saw a thicker veneer with a fine-toothed saw such as a dovetail saw. Include the inlay strips found between the border and the central portion of the panel at the time the veneering is made up for laying. To do this matching and joining, lay the veneer (central part first) on a large flat board and drive a few veneer

pins through the edges to hold it down. Veneer pins are very thin steel pins without heads. Do

Sheraton-Type
Grandfather's Clock

111

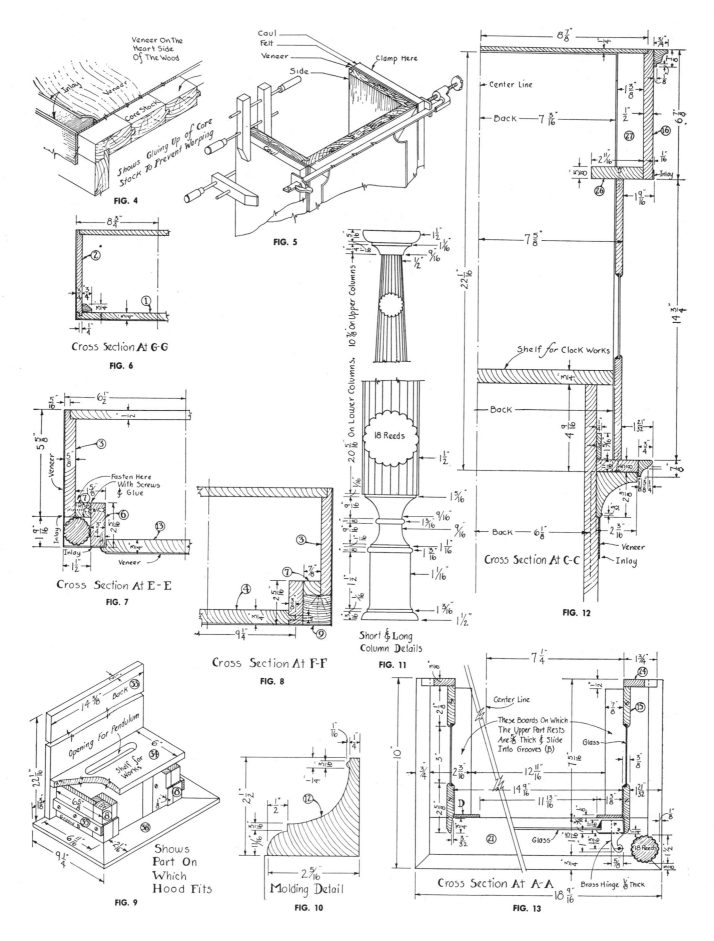

FIG. 4

FIG. 5

Cross Section At G-G
FIG. 6

Cross Section At E-E
FIG. 7

Cross Section At F-F
FIG. 8

Short & Long
Column Details
FIG. 11

Cross Section At C-C
FIG. 12

Shows
Part On
Which
Hood Fits
FIG. 9

Molding Detail
FIG. 10

Cross Section At A-A
FIG. 13

not drive the veneer pins in completely since they will be removed when the panel is finished.

Next, fit the inlay strip around the central portion. To do this, lightly glue the inlay tight against the center part, curving and fitting it carefully around the corners, and drive veneer pins at intervals along the outside edge, holding it in place until the glue has dried. Then remove the pins and lay the cross-banded veneer for the border, fitting it carefully around the inlay strips and tacking it down with veneer pins. When this has been done, tape all joints with veneer tape, or glue paper strips over each joint, and remove all veneer pins. The veneer is now ready for gluing to the core stock.

The best wood to use for core stock in this instance is Honduras mahogany. It warps and shrinks less than most woods, and does not absorb glue too fast. American yellow pine is a good second choice for the same reasons. Whichever wood is used, it should be clean and dry. Veneer the heart side of the wood since veneering exerts a slight pull on the surface, tending to warp the wood. The natural pull of the core stock away from the heart side will counteract this pull of the veneer. Other ways of reducing this pull are to glue up the core stock in fairly narrow strips (Fig. 4) or to veneer the core stock on the back, as well as the face side, but with a cheaper veneer.

Some veneers, especially the highly figured varieties, are likely to buckle before they are used. If this happens, straighten the veneer before using it by dampening the wood slightly and pressing out the "bumps" between two hot cauls on a veneer press or with clamps. The cauls for the veneering on this clock should be flat, smooth boards at least 1 in. thick. Heat the cauls over a

BILL OF MATERIAL

(The italicized numbers correspond with the circled numbers in the drawings.)

DESCRIPTION		PIECES	DIMENSIONS
1.	Front, lower section	1	¾ x 17½ x 20
2.	Ends, lower section	2	¾ x 9 x 20
3.	Ends, middle section	2	⅝ x 5⅝ x 44¼
4.	Rail below door	1	¾ x 9½ x 9¼
5.	Rail above door	1	¾ x 6¼ x 9¼
6.	Stiles on both sides of door	2	¾ x 2 5/16 x 44¼
7.	Fill-in strips back of columns	2	¾ x ⅞ x 44¼
8.	Blocks above columns	2	1½ x 1 9/16 x 10⅝
9.	Blocks below columns	2	1½ x 1 9/16 x 10⅝
10.	Floor	1	¾ x 8¾ x 16
11.	Battens	1	1½ x 1 11/16 x 16
		2	1½ x 1 11/16 x 6 9/16
12.	Molding between lower and middle section	1	2 5/16 x 2½ x 37 (approx. length)
13.	Door, middle section	1	¾ x 9 x 25
14.	Columns, middle section	2	1½ diam. x 24 3/16
15.	Sides, hood	2	⅜ x 7¾ x 14¾
16.	Sides, crown of hood	2	½ x 6⅞ x 9 5/16
17.	Front of pediment	1	½ x 12⅝ x 18¼
18.	Door stiles	2	11/16 x 1⅜ x 14¾
19.	Arched rail, door	1	11/16 x 6¼ x 14¾
20.	Lower rail, door	1	11/16 x 1⅜ x 14¾
21.	Front, hood base	1	⅝ x 1 15/16 x 17 1/16
22.	Sides, hood base	2	⅝ x 2 3/16 x 7 5/16
23.	Molding around hood base	1	¾ x ⅞ x 39 (approx. length)
24.	Brackets, back of hood	2	⅜ x 1¾ x 14¾
25.	Arch inside hood	1	1½ x 5⅞ x 16
26.	Strips inside crown of hood	2	⅝ x 2 11/16 x 8 13/16
27.	Fill-in blocks, back of hood	2	½ x 1⅜ x 5⅞
28.	Side frame around clock dial	2	⅛ x 1 13/32 x 12
29.	Bottom frame around clock dial	1	⅛ x 2 1/16 x 14 9/16
30.	Top frame around clock dial	1	⅛ x 7⅞ x 14 9/16
31.	Top of hood (plywood)	1	¼ x 8 13/16 x 17¾
32.	Columns on hood	2	1½ diam. x 14¾
33.	Back of clock	1	½ x 16¾ x 77⅜
34.	Shelf for works	1	¾ x 6 x 14⅜
35.	Strips to hold hood	2	¼ x 1 5/16 x 6 11/16
36.	Overlay strips (glued-up stock)	2	⅛ x ¾ x 5⅞
37.	Curved decorative strip under finial at center of pediment	1	½ x ¾ x 3⅝ (approx. length)
38.	Large molding under hood	1	2 3/16 x 2⅜ x 36½
39.	Molding, top of hood at sides	2	¾ x ⅞ x 10 1/16
40.	Curved Ogee molding on pediment	1	¾ x 3¼ x 9¾

Hardware:

3 No. 1 brass finials

1 No. 3 brass pull for upper door

1 No. 2 escutcheon for lower door

1 lock for lower door

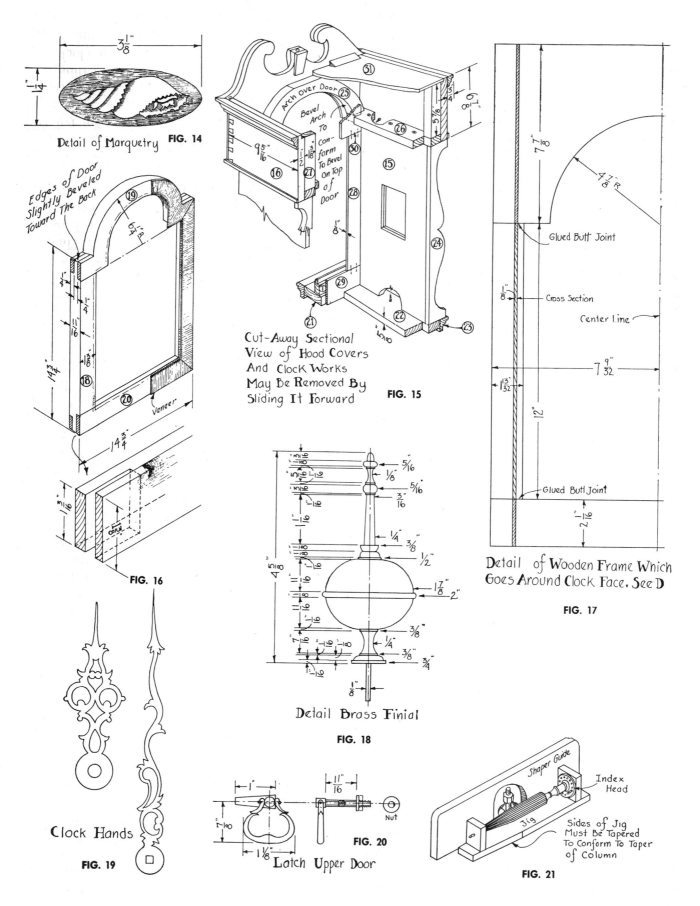

3 1/8"

1 1/4"

Detail of Marquetry   **FIG. 14**

Edges of Door Slightly Beveled Toward The Back

6 1/4" R.

14 3/4"

14 3/4"

Veneer

FIG. 16

Arch over Door

Bevel Arch To conform To Bevel On Top of Door

9 5/16"

Cut-Away Sectional View of Hood Covers And Clock Works May Be Removed By Sliding It Forward   **FIG. 15**

Detail Brass Finial

4 5/8"

5/16"
1/8"
5/16"
3/16"
1/4"   3/8"
1/2"
1 7/8"
2"
3/8"
1/4"
3/8"
3/4"
1/8"

FIG. 18

Clock Hands

FIG. 19

1"
11/16"
Nut
7/8"
1 1/8"
Latch Upper Door

FIG. 20

Glued Butt Joint

7 7/8"

4 7/8" R

1/8"

Cross Section

Center Line

7 9/32"

1 13/32"

12"

Glued Butt Joint

2 1/16"

Detail of Wooden Frame Which Goes Around Clock Face. See D

FIG. 17

Shaper Guide

Index Head

Jig

Sides of Jig Must Be Tapered To Conform To Taper of Column

FIG. 21

stove or steam pipes, or by any other convenient method.

Prepare the core stock by planing it perfectly flat. Level, or fill all holes, and then go over the entire surface with a toothing plane. The cutting edge of a toothing plane is milled or grooved so that it has saw-like teeth. Hold the blade upright in the plane to properly "tooth" or roughen the surface to hold the glue better. This "toothing" should be done in several directions. Size the surface with very thin glue, and, after the glue has dried, lightly tooth it again. Also size the reverse side of the core stock to help prevent warping.

A veneer press is invaluable in veneering work since pressure can be applied more quickly and distributed more evenly over the entire surface than by merely using clamps. However, whether a veneer press or clamps are used have everything ready for quickly applying pressure to the work after it has been glued. Too long an interval between the application of glue and clamping will result in failure. The cauls should be hot and ready at hand; the room temperature should be quite warm, about 80 deg.; and the glue should be clean and fairly thin. Have sheets of clean newspaper and felt ready to use. Veneer pins should also be handy.

When everything is ready, spread the glue quickly and evenly over the entire surface of the core stock with a wide brush. Let the glue set just a little. This prevents sliding and too much swelling of the veneer. Then carefully lay the veneer, face down, on the glue. Smooth the surface quickly and thoroughly with the hand, then fasten the edges with several veneer pins to prevent slipping when the clamps are applied. Cover the veneer on the taped side with newspapers, and the papers with a layer of felt. This will press the veneer more firmly to the core stock than the hard surface of the caul alone could do. Lay the hot caul over the felt. Lose no time in applying the pressure of the veneer press or clamps, first near the center of the panel and then toward the ends.

The marquetry below the door should be bought already made up. The individual craftsman can make it up himself, if he so desires, but the process requires so much skill, that in view of the relatively low cost at which beautiful marquetry can be bought it hardly seems worth the effort.

Veneering the sides of the lower part presents something of a problem, since the whole end cannot be veneered until the front has been joined to it (Fig. 4). A method for veneering the sides is shown in Figure 5; use enough clamps to insure a good job. Veneer the ends of the middle section and the hood before these are assembled. It is permissible to veneer the front of the clock case only and not the ends without materially detracting from its beauty.

To construct the clock case, proceed with the lower part first. The methods for joining the parts together are shown in the cross-section views, Figures 3 and 6. Make a ¼-in. rabbet-and-groove joint to unite the front with the ends, then cut a rabbet on the back edge of each end to join it to the back.

Do not place the back on the clock until the middle section has been made and joined to the lower section. Otherwise it will be difficult to fasten the two sections together. Glue thick battens, *11*, around the upper edges on the inside of this lower part, then fasten the front rail, *4*, of the middle section and the bottoms of the ends, *3*, to these battens with glue and wood screws (Figs. 2 and 3).

To make the middle section, cut the ends, *3*, and rabbet them on the back. Then glue the fill-in strips, *7*, to the ends, fastening them further with a few wood screws (Figs. 7 and 8). Make the door frame next, of two stiles, *6* (Fig. 2), and rails, *4* and *5* (Fig. 3). These rails have a tenon ⅜ in. long on both ends and are joined to mortises of ⅜-in. depth in the stiles. Glue up the frame, glue on the marquetry and veneer, and fasten it with glue and wood screws to the fill-in strips shown in Figures 7 and 8. The cross-banded veneer with the oval inlays above the door can consist of either two layers of veneer, one over the other, or a thicker piece of veneer. There is a slight offset here, as shown in Figures 1 and 2; to use a single piece of thicker veneer is the better practice. This veneering cannot be done until after block 8 has been glued in place. Now veneer the blocks below and above the columns and glue the lower ones, 9, into place.

The proper procedure in placing the column into this niche is, first, to provide a dowel joint (Fig. 2) for holding the column in place. If the column is fastened to the clock at this time, the finishing operations on this part of the clock will be difficult. On old clocks, these columns often were fitted and installed after all parts had been finished, but it is for that reason that many columns came loose and were damaged or lost. Glue, alone, will not hold since it does not adhere well to a finished surface. So, it is suggested that the columns and the niche behind the columns be finished entirely before they and the upper blocks, 8, are fastened to the middle section. In this way, the columns can be held in place with dowels as well as glue.

Once the columns, 14, and blocks, 8 and 9, have been fastened to the case, glue on the veneer with the oval inlays and the molding, 38. The parts against which the upper molding, 38, and the lower molding, 12, are fitted are to be rabbeted to a depth of ⅛ in. for these moldings. This is necessary to keep the parts of the molding with the astragal from being too thin.

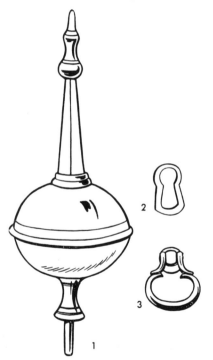

Fig. 22.   Correct hardware for the Sheraton-Type Grandfather's Clock.

Assemble the middle section and fasten it to the lower section, then attach the back to the clock. Put on the shelf for the clock works, 34, and the strips to hold the hood, 35 (Fig. 9).

Make the hood next. Details for this are shown in Figures 12, 13, and 15, as well as in Figures 1, 2, and 3. Start with the sides, 15. Notice that the rabbeting on the front edges of these sides is slanted and the rabbet has a very shallow offset which is cut along its inside edge to hold the thin wooden clock-face frame, 18. This rabbet

and offset are shown in Figure 13. This ³⁄₃₂-in. slant or bevel is cut also on the underside of the arch, 25, and will be found on two sides and the top of the door, permitting the door to be closed tightly without binding. The fronts of pieces 26 are slanted and curved to complete the bottom of the arch (Fig. 15).

The wooden frame, Figure 17, which is placed in front of the dial, is only ⅛ in. thick. Therefore, nothing but simple glued butt joints are practical to join parts 28, 29, and 30 together. Drill thin holes for veneer pins and use them as metal dowels to strengthen the joints. To glue these joints so they will stay together, apply glue to the joint, glue paper to each side of the joint until the glue has hardened, and then sandpaper off the paper. It is practical now to substitute a single piece of veneered plywood for a frame such as this. Veneered plywood was not available when this clock was made. Piece 29 is gained into the hood base, 22, at the front and into pieces 26 at the top.

To show the dovetailed joint by which the front of the pediment 17 is joined to the sides 16, the joint has not been covered by the zebra-striped overlay, 36, on the front of the clock. It is important that this joint be shown.

The Ogee moldings, faced with turned rosettes at the top, can be partly formed on the shaper if proper cutters are available. However, carve the moldings with carving chisels rather than go to the trouble and expense of making new knives.

Join the pieces of the door together with bridle joints (Fig. 16). Veneer the door face after the pieces have been joined together.

Cut the reeding of the columns with a jig having an index head on the shaper (Fig. 21). Carve these reeds by hand or use a shaper.

The finials on the clock are spun and turned brass. The stem is solid brass, the ball, spun. Finials such as this may be purchased.

Obtain a rich, mahogany color for this clock by brushing on a coat of whitewash or quick-lime. Then wash off this coat with boiled linseed oil that has been thinned with turpentine. The color produced is strikingly rich. The advantage of this coloring method is that, while the lime and mahogany react chemically, coloring the mahogany a rich red, there is no change in the color of the other woods found in the inlays. Remove every trace of the lime. Apply the succeeding finishing coats of shellac or varnish.

22.

WILLIAM AND MARY DRESSING TABLE, MIRROR, AND STOOL

During the eighteenth century, the golden age of furniture, a lady's dressing table was an important article. The earliest furniture deserving the name "dressing table" are the handsome lowboys of the William and Mary period. In fact, the William and Mary style may be called the first humanized style of period furniture.

The William and Mary lowboy lends itself particularly well to the design of a dressing table. The shaped apron with its handsome cyma curves and high arch in the center is found on all of the best examples. The distinctive and handsome crossed stretcher, with its interesting finial at the intersection, adds character and gives the needed rigidity and bracing without interfering with intended service. The clean-cut lines, the interesting curved elements, the effective relation of major and minor masses, and the carefully planned proportions combine into a table which any craftsman should be proud to build and own.

Walnut is the proper wood to use in building this dressing table.

This handsome hand-carved mirror frame and the upholstered stool, together with the William and Mary dressing table, constitute a very interesting ensemble for a bedroom. In designing the three pieces, special attention has been paid to the development of details and proportions, so that there will be perfect harmony when the pieces are grouped together.

The bench, or stool, strongly resembles the table because of the striking likeness of the X stretcher, and the turnings on the two pieces. The arch at the middle of the table apron is repeated at the top of the mirror frame.

The mirror can be used separately in a hallway or some other room. The hand-carved molding and shell, and the unique shape of the frame, make this an unusually nice mirror.

PROCEDURE

Start constructing the dressing table by sawing out the legs. Saw 3-in. square of walnut stock to 2-in. square at one end, for a length of 9 in. (Fig. 2). This 2-in. section remains square while the balance of the leg is turned to the dimensions given. The author turned the legs and feet from single pieces of stock, and

William and Mary Dressing Table and Mirror

117

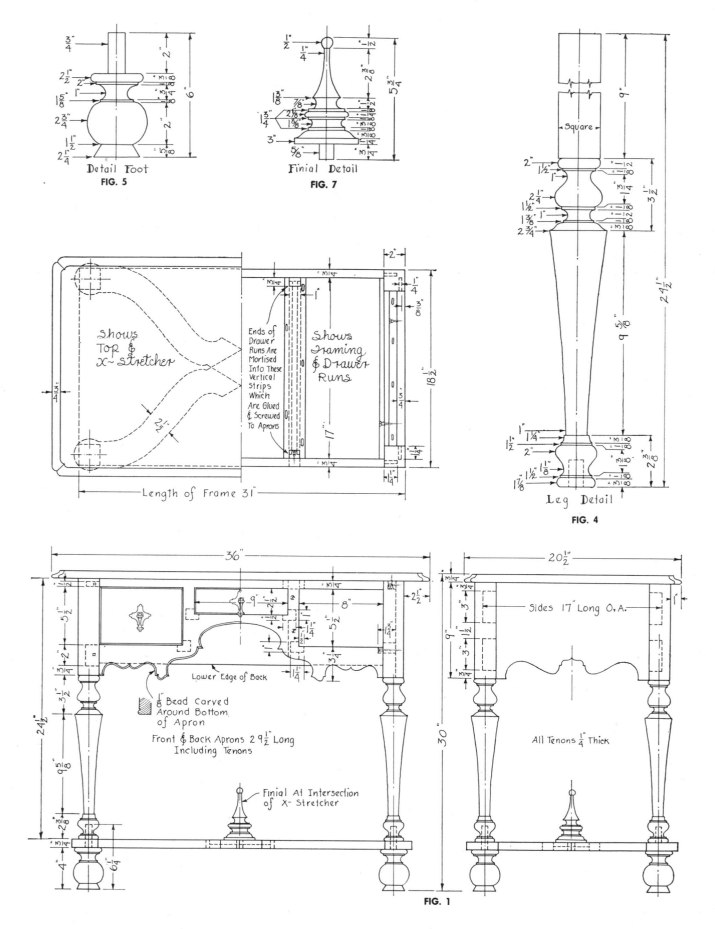

Detail Foot
FIG. 5

Finial Detail
FIG. 7

Leg Detail
FIG. 4

shows
TOP &
X-stretcher

Ends of
Drawer
Runs Are
Mortised
Into These
Vertical
Strips
Which
Are Glued
& Screwed
To Aprons

Shows
Framing
& Drawer
Runs

Length of Frame 31"

Square

Lower Edge of Back

⅛" Bead Carved
Around Bottom
of Apron

Front & Back Aprons 29½" Long
Including Tenons

Finial At Intersection
of X-Stretcher

Sides 17" Long O.A.

All Tenons ¼" Thick

FIG. 1

turned dowels between these two parts. This method is quicker than turning the feet separately, but greater care is required because the added length increases the vibration when the thin sections are being turned. Therefore, it is wise to turn the thinnest sections last. After a trial assembly of the frame (or even before this), saw the foot from the other part of the leg and bore a ¾-in hole into the bottom of the leg for the dowel. Pass the dowel through the stretcher and into the leg. When turning the legs, take proper care to turn the dowels exactly ¾ in. in diameter so that they will fit snugly into bored holes of that size.

When the legs have been turned, lay out and cut the mortises. The places for the mortises are indicated on the drawings in Figures 1 and 6. Then plane and square the aprons to size, fit the tenons to their respective mortises, and cut the lower edges of the front and end aprons to shape on a band saw. Draw patterns for the aprons and the X stretcher by laying them out on a large sheet of graph paper with 1-in. squares.

The strips for fastening the drawer runs to the front and back apron should be glued and screwed fast to the inside of each apron (Fig. 6) after cutting the mortises which hold the drawer runs.

BILL OF MATERIAL

DESCRIPTION	PIECES	DIMENSIONS
DRESSING TABLE		
Walnut:		
Legs and feet	4	3 x 3 x 30½ (or longer)[1]
Top	1	¾ x 20½ x 36
Front apron	1	¾ x 9½ x 29½
Back apron	1	¾ x 8 x 29½
End aprons	2	¾ x 9 x 17
Stretchers	2	¾ x 4½ x 36¼
Finial	1	3 diam. x 6
Middle drawer front	1	¾ x 2⁷⁄₁₆ x 8¹⁵⁄₁₆
End drawer fronts	2	¾ x 5⁷⁄₁₆ x 7¹⁵⁄₁₆
Pegs for joints	16	³⁄₁₆ x ³⁄₁₆ x 1
Yellow Poplar:		
Middle drawer sides	2	½ x 2⁷⁄₁₆ x 17½
End drawer sides	4	½ x 5⁷⁄₁₆ x 17½
Drawer runs	4	1 x 1¼ x 17
Drawer runs	2	1 x 1¾ x 17
Strips above drawers	2	¾ x 2 x 17
Strips inside ends to hold top	2	¾ x ¾ x 14½
Vertical strips inside front apron to hold drawer runs	2	¾ x 1 x 7½
Vertical strips inside back apron to hold drawer runs	2	¾ x 1 x 8
Three-Ply Veneered Plywood:		
Middle drawer bottom	1	¼ x 8⁷⁄₁₆ x 17¼
End drawer bottoms	2	¼ x 7⁷⁄₁₆ x 17¼
Middle drawer back	1	⅜ x 1¹³⁄₁₆ x 8⁷⁄₁₆
End drawer backs	2	⅜ x 4¹³⁄₁₆ x 7⁷⁄₁₆
18 glue blocks to reinforce drawers (see Fig. 11)		
Hardware:		
1, 1¼, 2¼ No. 8 f.h. bright, wood screws to fasten drawer runs and top		

DESCRIPTION	PIECES	DIMENSIONS
Three trumpet-shaped pendant-type antique brass drawer pulls (Fig. 19)		
STOOL		
Walnut:		
Legs and feet	4	2½ x 2½ x 19⅜[2]
X stretcher	2	⅝ x 3¼ x 27¼
Finial	1	2 x 2 x 4
Poplar:		
Side rails	2	⅞ x 3 x 22½
End rails	2	⅞ x 3 x 11½
Upholstering Materials:		
Tapestry, damask, or brocade cover, ⅔ yd. of 36-in. material		
Six 6-in. seat springs		
Webbing, approximately 10 ft.		
Spring twine		
4-oz. and 12-oz. tacks		
Upholsterer's burlap		
Cotton felt		
Heavy muslin		
Curled hair or moss filling		
Stitching twine		
MIRROR		
Walnut:		
Top	1	1 x 8½ x 16
Sides	2	1 x 1½ x 20⅛
Bottom	1	1 x 1½ x 16
Three ³⁄₁₆-in. splines for joints		
Plywood:		
Plywood back	1	¼ x 13¾ x 24½[3]
Plate-glass mirror	1	13¾ x 24½[3]

[1] Turn the legs and feet from one stick, as shown in Figures 2 and 3. After turning, saw the feet off from the leg, and bore a ¾-in. hole into the bottom of the leg (Fig. 4).

[2] Add a few extra inches to the length for turning.

[3] Cut to shape shown by dotted lines in Figure 20.

Fig. 2. Top: To shape legs, first saw a 3-in. square of stock to 2-in. square for a length of 9 in. Bottom: Turn the balance of the leg to the dimensions given.

Indicate the layout for the drawer openings on the inside of the front apron so the face of this piece can rest flat on the band-saw and jig-saw tables during the sawing process. Bore or drill holes at each corner of these openings to permit the easy turning of corners while sawing. The openings at each end can be done quickly on a band saw, but the opening for the middle drawer must be done on a jig saw.

When the drawer openings have been sawed out, filed, and sanded smooth, glue the frame together (Fig. 3). When assembling the frame, adjust the clamps in such a way that the frame will be square, otherwise there will be trouble in fitting the drawers and making them slide easily. Glue

Fig. 3. Glue the frame together before constructing the X stretcher.

the front and back legs to their respective end aprons and drill ³⁄₁₆-in. holes through the joints to a depth of about 1 in. With a knife, trim square ends on walnut pegs, dip the pegs in glue, and drive them into these holes. All joints of legs and aprons should be flush on the outside as were the fine, early pieces of furniture. Such joints permit longer mortises and tenons and are easily dressed and cleaned after gluing.

Next, make the X stretcher. Lay out a full-sized pattern from the pattern in Figure 9, trace it on a planed and squared board, 4½ in. wide (Fig. 8), and saw it to shape on the band saw. File and sandpaper the edges very carefully, and, only after this has been done, make the layout for the half-lap joint (Fig. 8). Clamp the stretcher pieces together so that they cross properly, and mark the edges of the joint on both pieces with a sharp knife. Remove the clamp and mark the depth of the cut on each stretcher. Make saw cuts on the waste side of the knife lines to this depth and chisel out the waste. Glue and assemble the stretcher, and join it to the frame.

Now, make and fit the drawer runs. Rabbet these runs with a dado head on a variety saw. Glue the runs and screw fast to the inside of the frame (Fig. 6). The 2-in. strips above the middle drawer prevent the tilting of the drawers when they are being drawn out, and help hold the top. Slots, instead of round holes, are drilled into these upper strips to allow for expansion and contraction of the top during change of seasons.

When the drawer runs are all in place, prepare

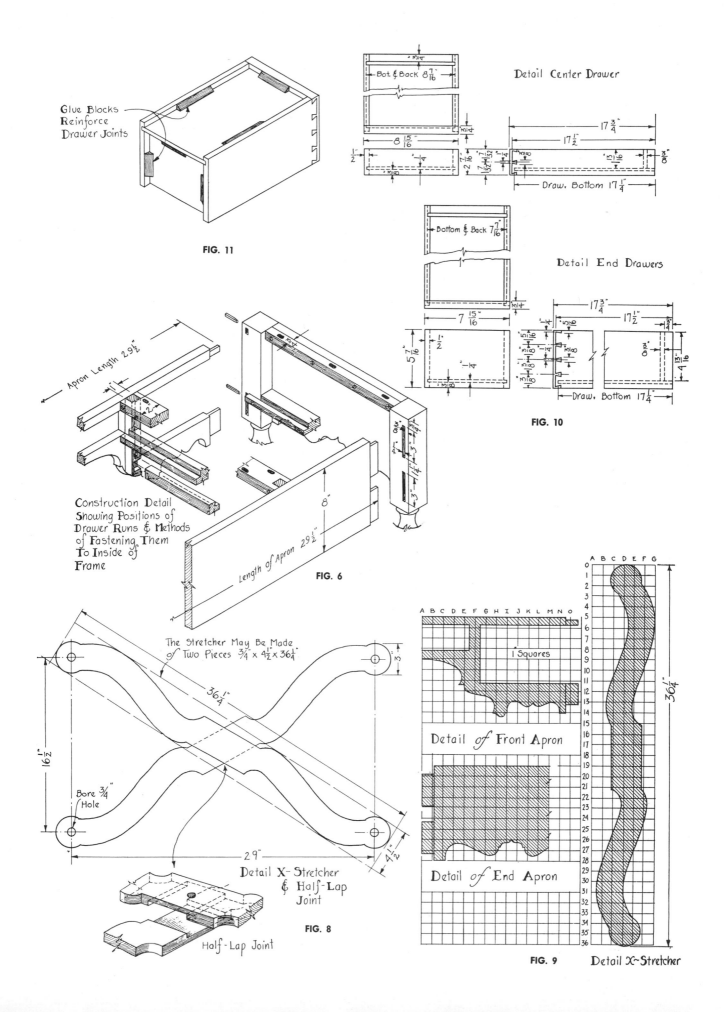

Glue Blocks
Reinforce
Drawer Joints

FIG. 11

Detail Center Drawer

Bot. & Back $8\frac{7}{16}$"

$8\frac{15}{16}$"

$17\frac{3}{4}$"

$17\frac{1}{2}$"

Draw. Bottom $17\frac{1}{4}$"

Bottom & Back $7\frac{7}{16}$"

Detail End Drawers

$7\frac{15}{16}$"

$17\frac{3}{4}$"

$17\frac{1}{2}$"

$5\frac{7}{16}$"

$4\frac{13}{16}$"

Draw. Bottom $17\frac{1}{4}$"

FIG. 10

Apron Length $29\frac{1}{2}$"

Construction Detail
Showing Positions of
Drawer Runs & Methods
of Fastening Them
To Inside of
Frame

Length of Apron $29\frac{1}{2}$"

8"

FIG. 6

The Stretcher May Be Made
of Two Pieces $\frac{3}{4}$" x $4\frac{1}{2}$" x $36\frac{1}{4}$"

$36\frac{1}{4}$"

$16\frac{1}{2}$"

Bore $\frac{3}{4}$"
Hole

3"

$4\frac{1}{2}$"

29"

Detail X-Stretcher
& Half-Lap
Joint

FIG. 8

Half-Lap Joint

A B C D E F G

1 Squares

Detail of Front Apron

Detail of End Apron

$36\frac{1}{4}$"

FIG. 9   Detail X-Stretcher

Fig. 19. William and Mary Dressing Table pull.

the drawers. Dovetail the drawer sides and fronts together (Fig. 10). Wide dovetails fitted to narrow pins present the best looking job, as on all old work. Such construction is not possible, however, if made on a dovetailing machine.

After fitting the drawers, dress the top and mold the edges. The author cut the molding on the edges of this top with wood-carving chisels, though it can be done more quickly on a shaper with the proper cutters. The corners, however, must be carved by hand. Fasten the top and the finial at the intersection of the stretchers. Carve the narrow beading around the drawer fronts and on the lower edge of the front apron for a satisfactory finishing touch, and to soften sharp corners. A wood carver's V tool and skew chisel are needed to perform this operation. Finish the dressing table.

To Make the Stool

Start the dressing table stool by turning the legs. Turn the foot and leg in one piece, as was done on the table. Fasten and glue the rails and legs together with mortise-and-tenon-joints. The construction of the X stretcher is also the same as for the table. Bore holes in the ends of the X stretcher. Cut the feet off the legs and bore holes in the bottoms of the legs. Assemble all parts and complete the frame by applying the finish before upholstering.

To upholster the seat, tack a good grade of webbing to the underside of the rails, two strips

William and Mary Dressing Table Stool

lengthwise and three crosswise, and stretch it tight with a webbing stretcher (Figs. 12 and 13). Sew seat springs to the intersections of the strips with stitching twine. With twine, tie down the springs from the original 6-in. height to 1 or 1½ in. above the seat frame. Run twine from the tack to the top of the spring on the far side, as from 1 to 2, in Figure 13. When reaching the spring at the far side of the seat, tie the twine to the nearest side of the spring, go from there to the rail and tack, pulling the spring down as this is done. Double back from the seat stretcher to the far side of the same spring, tying and leveling it at the same time; then double back and tie to the first side of this same spring. Repeat these steps with the loose end left at the start. Each spring should be tied eight times as shown in Figure 13. Tack burlap over the springs after they have been tied, and follow this with a thick layer of curled hair or moss. Hold the moss or hair in place by tucking some of it into large loops of twine that have been sewed all over the burlap. "Pick" the moss and distribute it evenly over the entire surface. Cover the moss with muslin, drawing the muslin tight and smooth before tacking it. Start tacking the muslin at the center of each rail and tack to the corners. Then fold the corners under and tuck them in, sewing the ends together. Tack the ends fast and cover the muslin with a layer of cotton felt (Fig. 13).

Figure 18 shows the best way of fitting and sewing the cover. Place the cover on the stool with the inside turned out. Then fold the corners as at A, B, and C. Bring A and C together and sew them on a machine. When the cover is turned right side out, it should fit the top of the stool perfectly. Fasten the cover to the stool with large-headed antiqued brass upholsterer's nails (Fig. 13).

To Make the Mirror

Construction of the mirror frame requires careful and accurate workmanship. Saw the top on a band saw from a piece of walnut, 1 by 8½ by 16 in. Saw only the inside of the top before gluing the frame together. This allows the use of clamps to pull the joints tight when gluing. Do not cut the corners on the bottom of the frame either, until after gluing the joints (Fig. 21).

Molding cutters can be made to do the straight members of the frame on a shaper, or the shaping of the molding can be done almost as quickly by

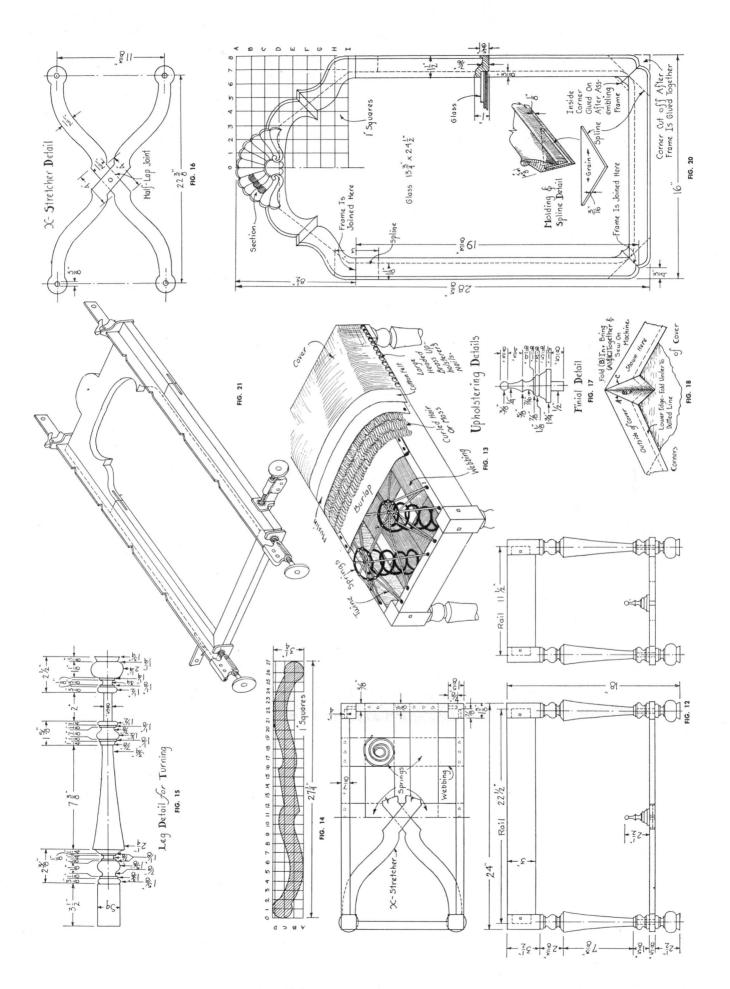

X-Stretcher Detail

11"

22 3/8"

Half-Lap Joint

5/8"

FIG. 16

Section

1" Squares

Frame Is Joined Here

Spline

19 3/8"

1 1/8"

3/4"

28 3/8"

3/8"

Glass 13 3/4" x 24 1/2"

Glass

1 1/2"

3/4"

1/8"

16"

Inside Corner Glued On After Assembling Frame

Grain

Spline

3/16"

Molding & Spline Detail

Frame Is Joined Here

Corner Cut off After Frame Is Glued Together

FIG. 20

FIG. 21

Cover

Lodge Headed Up Brass Covered 3/8 Nails

Cotton Felt

Curled Hair Or Moss

Webbing

Burlap

Twine Springs

Muslin

Upholstering Details

FIG. 13

Finial Detail

FIG. 17

Fold (B)In, Bring (A)&(C)Together & Sew On Machine.

Shown Here

Outside of Cover

Lower Edge Fold Under to Dotted Line

Cover

Corners

FIG. 18

Rail 11 1/2"

2 1/2"

2 1/4"

1 5/8"

2"

7 3/8"

2 3/8"

Leg Detail for Turning

FIG. 15

3 1/2"

5/8"

3 1/4"

1 Squares

2 1/4"

FIG. 14

3/8"

X-Stretcher

Springs

webbing

24"

Rail 22 1/2"

3"

19"

2 1/2"

3 1/2"

2 7/8"

7 3/8"

FIG. 12

Fig. 22. Shaping the molding by hand with carving tools.

William and Mary Dressing
Table Mirror

hand with carving tools. Since the top and the corners at the bottom of the frame must be carved entirely with hand tools, the remainder of the work may be done just as easily. Therefore, first cut the inside of the top to shape on a band saw, then make the joints and glue the frame together before shaping or carving the face of the frame.

Cut the recesses for the splines which join the top to the sides on the circular saw. These recesses, or mortises, open at each side and are $\frac{3}{16}$ in. thick, but are sawed only $\frac{1}{8}$ in. from the rear side of the frame. Cut the recesses and fit the splines before gluing the frame together. The recesses for the splines at the bottom are cut more easily after the joints have been glued together and the corners have been sawed off flat at a 45-deg. angle. Let all the splines protrude when gluing, then trim even with sides.

Perfectly fit all joints, then glue and clamp them. Figure 21 shows how to arrange the clamps.

When the glue has hardened, remove the clamps carefully, saw the cuts for the splines at the bottom, and glue these in place to strengthen the joints. Next, glue small corner blocks to the inside corners at the bottom of the frame. The grain of these blocks should run at a 45-deg. angle to that of the frame.

After the frame has been glued up and the splines are in place, lay out the rabbet for the glass and the plywood backing. The straight sides can be done with a dado head but the top should be done with a hand router or on a mortising machine. Now the top can be sawed to shape and carved.

Preparatory to carving, gauge the thickness at the outside of the frame. Plane a bevel on the face of the frame from the high part of the molding to this line. Then, after gauging the width of the bead cut a deep V groove with a wood carver's V tool inside this gauge line. Hollow out the concave portion of the molding with gouges and trim the convex portion to shape with a skew chisel. Carve the ornament at the top of the frame in the same manner.

Finish the frame. Buy a plate-glass mirror and have it cut to the shape shown by the dotted lines in Figure 20. Also cut $\frac{1}{4}$-in. plywood to the same shape to place in back of the mirror. Lay the frame on its face, place the glass and plywood in it, and drive brads into the sides of the rabbeted edge with a heavy chisel, holding them in the frame.

23.

FOUR-POSTER BEDS

Few pieces of furniture are more impressive than a fine, four-poster bed. The designs of the two beds presented here were inspired by the two great eighteenth-century designers, George Hepplewhite and Thomas Sheraton. The four-poster double bed was built by the author for his own use, while the Sheraton four-poster bed (three-quarter size) was built under the author's direction by students of the Berry Schools. Both are attractively hand-carved.

The greatest difficulty encountered when making poster beds is finding a lathe bed long enough to turn the high posts. To turn the post in one piece is best, but an 8-ft. lathe bed is needed. The next best thing is to turn the post in two or more sections, as shown in Figures 4 and 16. If the holes for the dowels, which join the two parts together, are bored straight and true, and if the joining and gluing of the two sections is done properly, the post will be as strong, as a one-piece post.

PROCEDURE

Decide whether the post can be turned in one piece or if it must be done in sections. Then cut the pieces for the posts and place them in the lathe for turning. If the lathe being used is equipped with an index head, it will be fairly easy to lay out the fluting or reeding on the posts

Hepplewhite Four-Poster Double Bed

125

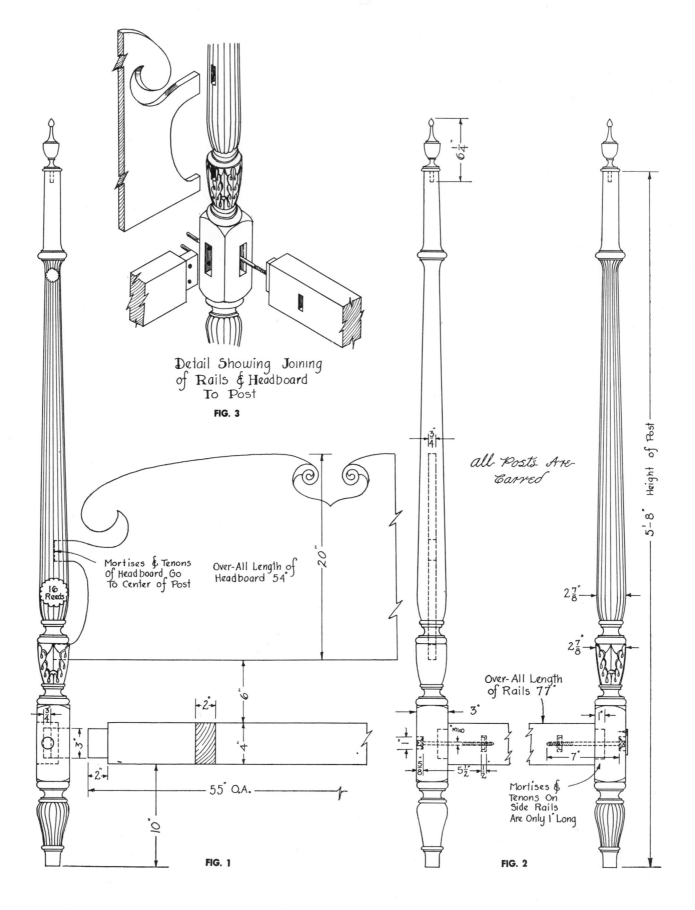

Detail Showing Joining
of Rails & Headboard
To Post

FIG. 3

all Posts Are
Carved

Mortises & Tenons
Of Headboard Go
To Center of Post

Over-All Length of
Headboard 54"

20"

16
Reeds

6"

3"

2"

4"

2"

55" O.A.

10"

FIG. 1

3"
4

5' - 8" Height of Post

2 7/8"

2 7/8"

Over-All Length
of Rails 77"

3"

5 1/2"

Mortises &
Tenons On
Side Rails
Are Only 1" Long

1"

7"

FIG. 2

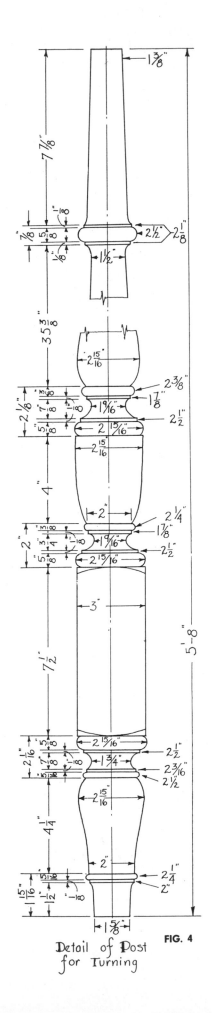

1 3/8"

7 7/8"

1/8"
7/8" 5/8"
1/8"
2 1/2" 2 1/8"
1 1/2"

35 3/8"

2 15/16"

2 3/8"
1 7/8"
2 1/8" 3/100
7/8
1/8 1 9/16"
5/8 2 1/2"
2 15/16"
2 15/16"

4"

2" 2 1/4"
1 7/8"
2" 3/100
3/4 1 9/16" 2 1/2"
5/8
2 15/16"

3"

7 1/2"

5'-8"

2 15/16" 2 1/2"
2 1/16" 5/8
7/8 1 3/4" 2 3/16"
1/8 2 1/2"
5/8

4 1/4"

2 15/16"

2" 2 1/4"
2"
15/16" 5/8
1/2 1/8

1 5/8"

FIG. 4

Detail of Post
for Turning

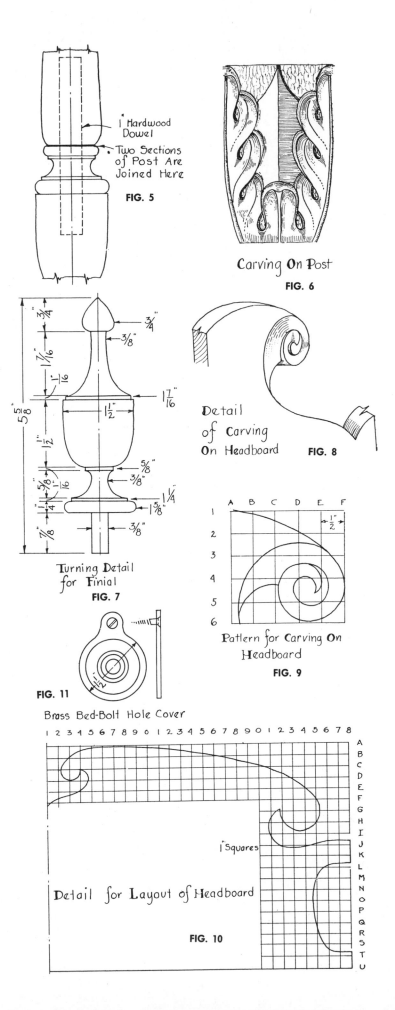

1" Hardwood
Dowel

Two Sections
of Post Are
Joined Here

FIG. 5

Carving On Post

FIG. 6

Detail
of Carving
On Headboard

FIG. 8

3/4"
3/4"
3/8"
1 7/16"
1 1/16"
1"
1/16
1 1/2"
5 5/8"
1 1/2"
5/8"
5/8" 3/8"
1/16
1 1/4"
1/4
1 5/8"
7/8" 3/8"

Turning Detail
for Finial

FIG. 7

A B C D E F
1
2
3
4
5
6
1/2"

Pattern for Carving On
Headboard

FIG. 9

1/2"

FIG. 11

Brass Bed-Bolt Hole Cover

1 2 3 4 5 6 7 8 9 0 1 2 3 4 5 6 7 8 9 0 1 2 3 4 5 6 7 8

A B C D E F G H I J K L M N O P Q R S T U

1" Squares

Detail for Layout of Headboard

FIG. 10

BILL OF MATERIAL

DESCRIPTION	PIECES	DIMENSIONS
HEPPLEWHITE FOUR-POSTER DOUBLE BED		
Honduras or Cuban Mahogany:		
Posts	4	3 x 3 x 68
		or
	4	3 x 3 x 23⅞
		and
	4	3 x 3 x 44⅛
Footrail	1	2 x 4 x 55
Headboard	1	¾ x 20 x 54
Finials	4	1¾ x 1¾ x 6
Birch or Maple:		
Side rails	2	2 x 4 x 77[1]
Headrail	1	2 x 4 x 55

[1] The size of box springs and mattresses has been standardized only quite recently. For double beds, the size is approximately 54 by 74 in. They are designed for the more modern-type beds with thin side rails. For these two beds, special box springs should be made with 2-in. rabbets at both edges on the lower side (Fig. 12) to fit over the wide rails and come flush with the outside of the rails. For the double bed, the box spring and mattress should be 56 by 76 in.; for the three-quarter bed, 45 by 75 in. Box springs and mattresses with recessed corners at the foot which fit around the posts would make it possible for the springs and mattress to come flush with the outside of the rail at the foot of the bed.

DESCRIPTION	PIECES	DIMENSIONS
Hardware:		
4 bed bolts		⅜ x 7
4 antiqued brass bed-bolt hole covers		
SHERATON FOUR-POSTER THREE-QUARTER BED		
Honduras or Cuban Mahogany:		
Posts	4	3½ x 3½ x 77¾
		or
	4	3½ x 3½ x 42⅛
		and
	4	3½ x 3½ x 39⅝
Finials	4	2 x 2 x 6½
Footrail	1	2 x 4 x 42½
Headboard	1	¾ x 23 x 42
Birch or Maple:		
Side rails	2	2 x 4 x 76
Headrail	1	2 x 4 x 42½
Hardware:		
4 bed bolts		⅜ x 7
4 antique brass bed-bolt hole covers		

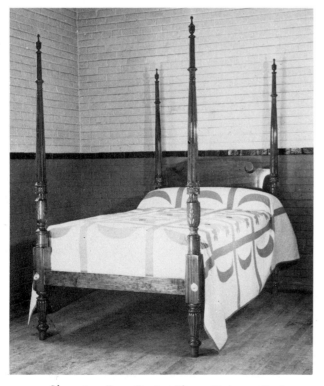

Sheraton Four-Poster Three-Quarter Bed

simply by counting off a certain number of holes on the index head and drawing the lines with a straightedge fastened to the lathe near the post. Since most index heads have 48 holes, it will be easy to determine how many holes apart to make each flute or reed.

After the flutes, reeds, acanthus leaves, and other decorations have been laid out on the post, carve these designs with the post fastened in the lathe, since it will be possible to hold the post in any convenient position with the index head.

The reeding, fluting, and all other decorations on the two original beds were carved by hand with wood-carving chisels. Another way of cutting the flutes and reeds is to make a jig with an index head, such as the one shown in Figure 21, page 114, and then, with the proper cutters, cut them on a shaper. Expert workmanship will be required in this operation, both to properly mount the stock in the jig and to do the actual shaping, since both the fluting and the reeding are tapered. Finish the cutting at the ends by hand.

When the carving on the posts has been done, mortise for the rails and the headboard. Note that, while the mortises for the rail under the headboard and for the rail at the foot of the bed are

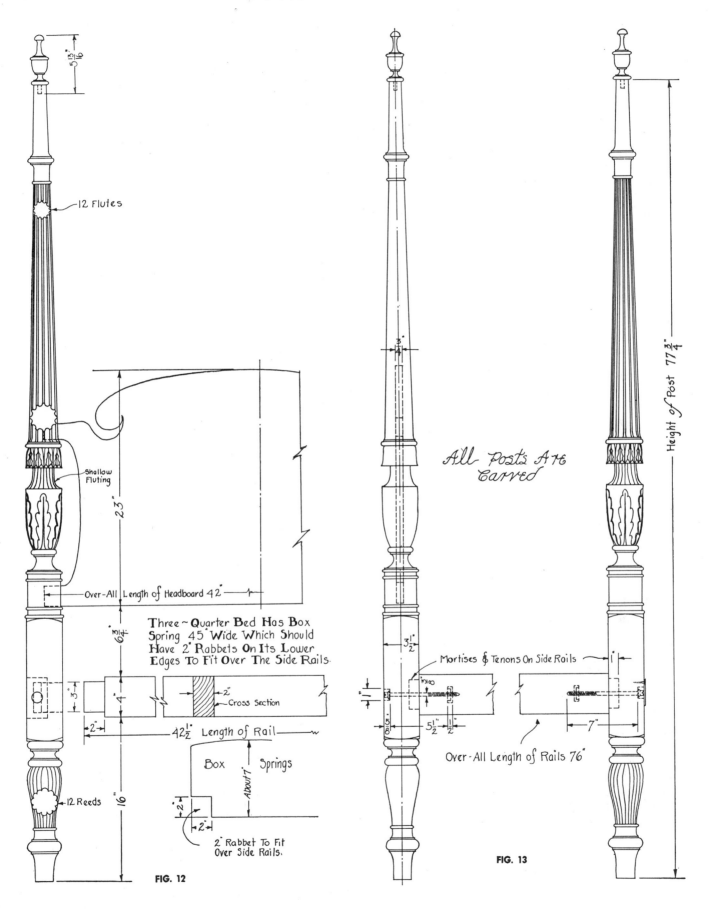

$5\frac{13}{16}$

12 Flutes

Shallow Fluting

23"

Over-All Length of Headboard 42"

Three ~ Quarter Bed Has Box
Spring 45" Wide Which Should
Have 2" Rabbets On Its Lower
Edges To Fit Over The Side Rails.

$6\frac{3}{4}$"

3"

4"

2"

Cross Section

$42\frac{1}{2}$" Length of Rail

Box   Springs

About 7"

2"

2"

2" Rabbet To Fit
Over Side Rails.

16"

12 Reeds

FIG. 12

All Posts Are Carved

3"

$3\frac{1}{2}$"

Mortises & Tenons On Side Rails

1"

$5\frac{5}{8}$"

$5\frac{1}{2}$"

$1\frac{1}{2}$"

Over-All Length of Rails 76"

1"

7"

FIG. 13

Height of Post $77\frac{3}{4}$"

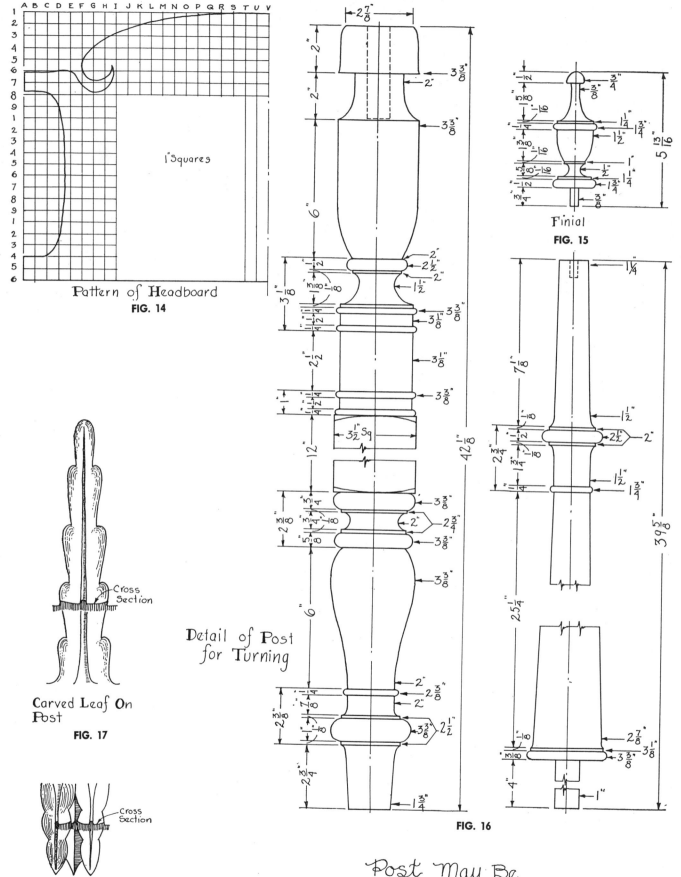

Pattern of Headboard
FIG. 14

Finial
FIG. 15

Carved Leaf On
Post

FIG. 17

Detail Carving On
Post

FIG. 18

Detail of Post
for Turning

FIG. 16

Post May Be
Turned In Two
Parts As Shown

2 in. deep, the mortises for the side rails are only 1 in. deep on both beds. The reason for this is that the wall of wood between the mortise and the head of the bolt will then be strong enough so that the bolt can be tightened sufficiently without danger of breaking or weakening the joint (Figs. 2 and 13).

After the rail under the headboard and the rail at the foot of the bed have been tenoned and glued into the post, peg the joint (Fig. 5).

When the rails have been made and fitted to the mortises, cut out the headboards. Prepare the patterns from Figures 10 and 14. The headboard on the double bed has carved scrolls at the top (Figs. 8 and 9).

After the headboard has been made and the ends fitted into their respective mortises, glue up two ends of the bed.

Fit the long rails to the posts so that they can be removed whenever the bed needs to be dismantled. Special bed bolts are used for this purpose. Mortise the holes for the nuts into the inside face of the rail at each end (Figs. 2, 3, and 13). The heads of the bolt are slotted so they can be tightened with a large screw driver, or, better

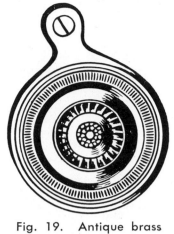

Fig. 19.   Antique brass bed-bolt hole cover

still, with a socket wrench. Cover the holes made for these bolts with brass covers (Fig. 11).

Turn the finials. The finial is always made separately, even though the balance of the post is of one piece. It is too delicately proportioned to be turned as a part of the post. Do not glue the finials to the posts, but insert them by the dowel on their lower end into the small holes bored into the tops of the posts.

Finish the bed.

24.

QUEEN ANNE HIGHBOY

A highboy is a fine and imposing piece of furniture if it has good proportions and its other components are combined properly. Considerable thought and work will go into a highboy as fine as this one, but, once built, it will become a cherished family heirloom. Great cabinetmakers of the past rated tall pieces of furniture such as this among their finest creations. The highboys of Chippendale, John Goddard, and John Townsend of Newport, and of others in Philadelphia and Baltimore are famous. They are featured possessions of our finest museums.

The design of this highboy, though rich, is still conservatively plain when compared with some of the very richly ornamented and superbly executed pieces built by the above cabinetmakers.

The proper wood for a Queen Anne highboy is walnut, though many fine highboys designed in this style have been built of mahogany, curly maple, and cherry. Curly maple and cherry are especially prized for these pieces in America.

The sunburst carvings on the drawers, the carved rosettes on the pediment, and the flame-like carving on the finials are distinguishing characteristics. Cyma-curved moldings, such as those on the pediment, are partly, and often wholly, carved by hand.

Although the lower section of a highboy resembles a lowboy, both in construction and appearance, it is always higher. The height of lowboys seldom exceeds 30 in. There have been instances in which remodeled highboy bases have been sold as lowboys to unsuspecting novice antique collectors. Needless to say, a genuine lowboy of similar design is considerably more valuable than a base from which the upper part has been lost or removed. It would be far better to restore the missing part of such a highboy.

PROCEDURE

Begin with the lower section by first making the legs. The use of solid stock is preferred (Fig. 7), although it is possible to glue pieces for the knee and foot projections to stock of a smaller size before sawing the legs to shape. However,

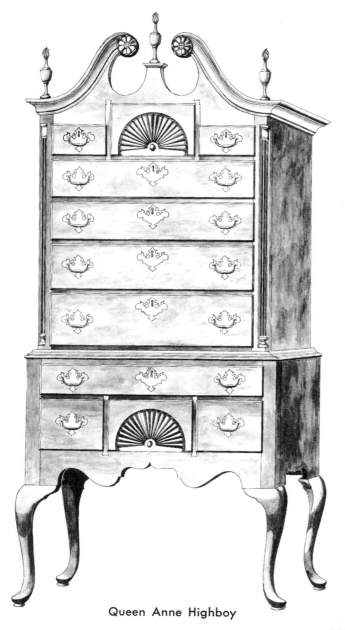

Queen Anne Highboy

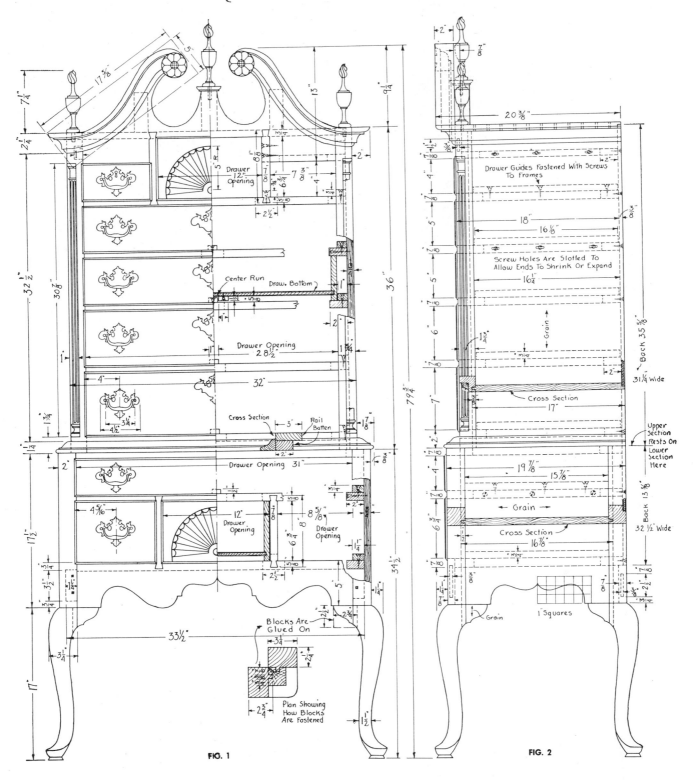

FIG. 1

FIG. 2

a piece of furniture as fine as this deserves the best material, and so solid stock is suggested for the legs.

Lay out and cut all mortises on these legs before sawing them to shape with the exception of the dovetail mortises at the tops of the legs. Cut the dovetail mortises after the rest of the

frame has been assembled. Determine the positions of the mortises on the legs by referring to Figures 1, 2, and 3. Remember to pair the legs, right and left, both front and back.

Make a cardboard pattern for sawing the leg from the graph in Figure 6. Trace the pattern on one side of the stock (Fig. 7, A). Saw the leg

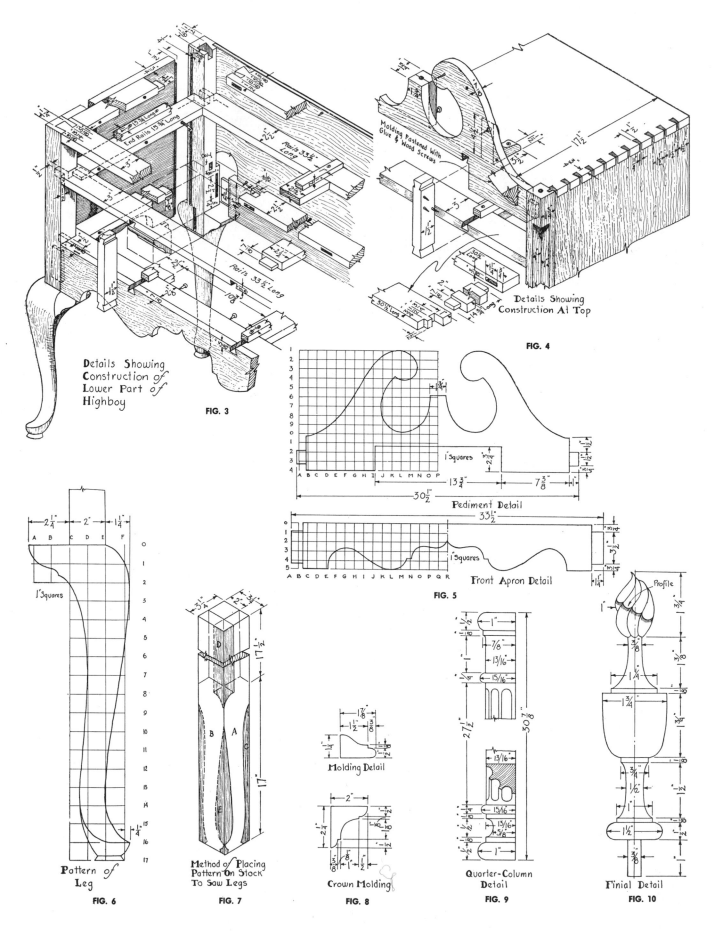

Details Showing
Construction of
Lower Part of
Highboy

FIG. 3

Details Showing
Construction At Top

FIG. 4

Pediment Detail

Front Apron Detail

FIG. 5

Pattern of
Leg

FIG. 6

Method of Placing
Pattern On Stock
To Saw Legs

FIG. 7

Molding Detail

Crown Molding

FIG. 8

Quarter-Column
Detail

FIG. 9

Profile

Finial Detail

FIG. 10

BILL OF MATERIAL

DESCRIPTION	PIECES	DIMENSIONS
LOWER SECTION		
Walnut:		
Legs	4	3¼ x 3¼ x 34½[1]
Blocks for brackets to be glued to legs	8	2¾ x 3¼ x 2½
Ends	2	¾ x 17½ x 16⅞
Front apron	1	⅞ x 5 x 33½
Lower rail, back	1	⅞ x 4⅛ x 33½
Front rails, upper two frames	2	⅞ x 3 x 33½
Front rail, lower frame	1	⅞ x 2⅛ x 33½
Back rails	3	⅞ x 2½ x 33½
End rails	6	⅞ x 2 x 15¾
Rails above and below small drawer[2]	5	⅞ x 2½ x 15¾
Drawer guides, ends of frames	4	¾ x 1¼ x 15¾
Drawer guides between small drawers	2	¾ x ⅞ x 18
Center-run drawer guides	3	½ x 1 x 18 15/16
Upper drawer front	1	⅞ x 4 7/16 x 31⅜
Carved drawer front	1	⅞ x 7 3/16 x 12⅜
Small drawer fronts	2	⅞ x 7 3/16 x 9
Upper drawer sides	2	⅝ x 3 15/16 x 19¼
Small drawer sides	6	⅝ x 6 11/16 x 19¼
Upper drawer bottom (plywood)	1	⅜ x 18 11/16 x 30¼
Carved drawer bottom (plywood)	1	⅜ x 11¼ x 18 11/16
Small drawer bottoms (plywood)	2	⅜ x 7⅞ x 18 11/16
Molding on top of lower section	1	1¼ x 1⅞ x 78
Stiles between drawers	2	⅞ x 1½ x 8
Back (plywood)	1	⅜ x 13⅜ x 32½
UPPER SECTION		
Walnut:		
Ends of cabinet	2	¾ x 17 x 36
Corner posts	2	1¾ x 1¾ x 36
Finials	3	2 x 2 x 9
Quarter columns	1	2 diam. x 30⅞[3]
Stiles between small drawers	2	⅞ x 1½ x 8⅛
Pediment	1	⅞ x 13 x 30½
Top, upper section	1	¾ x 17½ x 32
Front rails, five large frames	5	⅞ x 3 x 30½
Back rails, five large frames	5	⅞ x 2 x 30½
End rails, large frames	10	⅞ x 2 x 14¾

[1] Preferably solid stock, but may be glued up.
[2] Including center-run rail.
[3] Glue up column for turning and subsequent splitting into four sections as shown in Figure 12, page 142.

DESCRIPTION	PIECES	DIMENSIONS
Batten under lower front rail	1	1⅛ x 2 x 28½
Middle rails, large frames	6	⅞ x 2½ x 14¾
Center runs	12	½ x 1 x 17 7/16
Drawer guides, ends of frames	10	¾ x 1 x 16⅛
Front and back rails, small frames above small drawers	4	⅞ x 2 x 7
Side rails, small frames	4	⅞ x 2 x 17⅛
Block under center finial	1	⅞ x 1¾ x 4½
Braces back of pediment	2	1½ x 3½ x 4½[4]
Cyma-curved crown molding on face of pediment[5]	2	2 x 5 x 17⅝
Crown molding on ends	2	2 x 2¼ x 20⅜
Lower drawer front	1	⅞ x 7 7/16 x 28⅞
Second drawer front	1	⅞ x 6 7/16 x 28⅞
Third and fourth drawer fronts	2	⅞ x 5 7/16 x 28⅞
Small drawer fronts	2	⅞ x 4 7/16 x 7¾
Carved drawer front	1	⅞ x 7 3/16 x 12⅜
Lower drawer sides	2	⅝ x 6 15/16 x 17¾
Second drawer sides	2	⅝ x 5 15/16 x 17¾
Third and fourth drawer sides	4	⅝ x 4 15/16 x 17¾
Small drawer sides	4	⅝ x 3 15/16 x 17¾
Carved drawer sides	2	⅝ x 6 11/16 x 17¾
Lower drawer back	1	½ x 6 15/16 x 28⅜
Second drawer back	1	½ x 5 15/16 x 28⅜
Third and fourth drawer backs	2	½ x 4 15/16 x 28⅜
Small drawer backs	2	½ x 3 15/16 x 7¼
Carved drawer back	1	½ x 6 11/16 x 11⅞
Plywood:		
Large drawer bottoms	4	⅜ x 17 3/16 x 27¾
Small drawer bottoms	2	⅜ x 6⅝ x 17 3/16
Carved drawer bottom	1	⅜ x 11¼ x 17 3/16
Back of cabinet	1	⅜ x 31¼ x 35⅝

Hardware:

Two escutcheon plates with handles, antique colored brass, No. 1[6]
5 escutcheon plates[6]
12 bail plates, No. 1 or 3[6]
2 brass knobs, No. 2
7 drawer locks

[4] Grain direction as shown in Figure 4.
[5] See Figures 1 and 8.
[6] Whichever pattern is chosen, all plates should be of the same design. Numbers 1 and 3 are different designs, though they belong to the same general type commonly found on highboys of this period.

to shape on a band saw. Make a second layout (Fig. 7, B). Before sawing this second side, tack waste piece C back on the stock, driving the nails where they will not interfere with the cutting and where the nail holes will not appear in the leg after it has been cut out. Save waste stock D at the top of the leg, tack it back into place when gluing on the bracket blocks (Fig. 1). This makes it easier to apply the clamps when

gluing the blocks to the leg. Tack waste block E to the leg to properly lay out the leg shape at B and to eliminate the necessity for drawing a new elongated pattern for the second cut.

Finish shaping the leg from this point on by first cutting it to an octagon shape and then rounding it with a spokeshave, chisels, scraper, and file, to the shape shown in Figures 1 and 2.

The ends should now be glued up, sawed, and planed to size. Cut and fit the tenons on the ends to the mortises in the legs, then glue these members together.

Next, make the frames which will support the drawers. Their 7/8-in. thickness will bear the weight of the wide drawers, and the tenons cut

Queen Anne Highboy
Drawer Construction

FIG. 11

Detail Small Frames
FIG. 12

on the ends of the frames will hold the lower section of the highboy securely together. Make the front and back bottom stretchers and the stiles with the dovetails at each end. Cut the dovetails on the stiles, then trace their outline on the rails into which the mortise members will be cut. Saw and chisel out the mortise members on the shaped apron. However, on the front rails of the frames, the mortise members can be only partly sawed or cut on a mortising machine. Chop out the remainder of the waste with chisels.

As soon as these dovetails have been properly fitted, the lower part of the highboy, consisting of the assembled ends, two lower frames, front and rear stretchers, and dovetailed stiles, can be assembled. Fasten all drawer runs to the frames before this assembling takes place. Join the upper frame to the assembled members last, so that the tenon members can be traced on the tops of the legs and the mortises accurately cut. When the mortises have been sawed and chiseled out, glue the frame to the legs. Fasten the plywood back; drive in all the wood screws; and begin the upper section.

The molding which holds the upper section in place on the lower section should not be fastened to the lower section until the upper section has been made. (Do not fasten this molding to the upper section of the highboy!)

In making the upper section, start with the corner posts. Lay out and cut the mortises and grooves for joining the frames and ends after the posts have been squared, and before the corners, into which the quarter columns are later fastened, are cut out. Consult Figures 2 and 4 for laying out these grooves and mortises. Cut out of each post the section 1 in. square by 30⅞ in. long for the quarter columns. Most of the corner can be sawed out on a circular saw. Square the upper and lower end on a mortising machine, or chisel by hand.

Make the end boards and the top for the upper section. Lay out, cut, and fit together the dovetail joints for joining these parts together. Rabbet out the back edges of the ends for the plywood back of the cabinet which will be attached later. Do not glue on the top until the frames and the pediment have been joined to the ends and corner posts. When the dovetailed joints have been fitted, glue the end boards to the corner posts.

Now, make all frames for the upper section. Connect them with mortise-and-tenon joints; a

detail of the frame is shown in Figure 4. The over-all width and length of the large frames is 18 by 30½ in. Figure 12 is a detailed drawing of the small frames. Fasten all drawer runs to these frames before assembling the chest. Make the stiles. Cut the dovetail mortises and fit with the stiles before assembling the chest. Lay out the dovetail mortises from the tenons cut on the ends of the stiles.

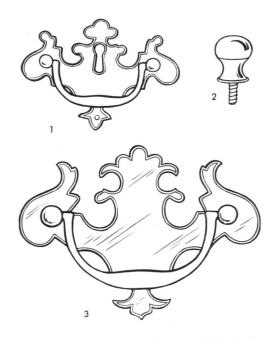

Fig. 13.   Escutcheon plates and knob for Queen Anne Highboy.

Make a full-sized pattern of the pediment from the drawing, Figure 5. Cut the tenons at both ends then saw to shape on the band saw.

To assemble the upper section, fasten the large frames and the pediment to the assembled ends and corner posts. Glue the mortise-and-tenon joints and screw the remaining joints. The holes for these screws are slotted, providing for expansion and shrinkage of the ends during the various seasons and preventing splitting or warping of these wide boards (Fig. 2). Next, fasten the small frames with wood screws. Hold the front of the small frame in place with two screws through the front rail into the pediment, and with another screw through the dovetailed stile which separates the small drawers.

When the frames, ends, and pediment have been assembled, fasten the top to the ends by gluing the dovetail joints. Fasten a batten, 1⅛ in. thick, with wood screws to the bottom of the lower rail to fill in behind the molding which divides the upper and lower section. Now fasten the back with wood screws.

Turn the column from which the quarter columns are to be made. The column is first glued up as shown in Figure 12, page 142, with wrapping paper glued between four 1-in. strips. Then turn and flute as shown in Figure 9. The four sections are separated easily after the column has been turned; two are fastened with glue and wood screws to the niches in the corner posts.

The cyma-curved molding for the top of the pediment is sawed to shape on a band saw and carved. Carve each molding from a plank 2 in. thick, 5 in. wide, and 17⅝ in. long (Fig. 1). The rosettes, at the tops of these moldings can be carved on a thin piece of stock and glued on, although the author prefers to carve the rosettes and the molding from the same stock. Cut the return molding on the ends on a shaper or carve by hand.

Fasten the braces and block to the back of the pediment, turn and carve the finials, and the upper section is finished except for the drawers.

First, cut the molding for the drawer fronts on a shaper. The rabbeted edges can be cut on a shaper or with a dado head on a variety saw. Poplar is accepted generally as a good wood for drawer sides, though some cabinetmakers prefer a harder wood such as oak. The construction of a drawer is shown in Figure 11. The upper and lower dovetail pins are somewhat wider than the remaining ones. Make all upper and lower pins this wide, and divide the remaining distance into the required number of equal parts with center lines to indicate where the remaining pins go. The dovetailing then is laid out easily. The remaining distance will not be divided into 1¼-in. spaces on all drawers, but the distances can be determined by dividing the remaining distance by the number of pins to be cut.

On drawers which have been designed properly the grooves holding the drawer bottoms always will be cut through a tail rather than a pin member of a dovetail joint (Fig. 11). The amount of clearance given to drawers varies somewhat according to the kind of wood used. Hardwoods, such as walnut, maple, and especially mahogany, shrink and expand very little if properly seasoned before being used. Poplar needs more clearance than oak, though the clearances indicated for this highboy will prove quite satisfactory. Center runs, while not absolutely necessary, insure easy sliding for heavily loaded drawers and are advised for a piece with drawers as wide as these.

25.

JACOBEAN CHEST OF DRAWERS

Before there were chests of drawers, blankets, clothing, and other household gear were stored in chests. Chests were found even in the simplest cottages, while the wealthier manor houses had them in abundance. We venture the guess that chests of drawers came into existence in the following manner:

The chest, a wooden box with a lid, for the storage of various household goods, must have been quite annoying at times to the homemaker who constantly had to remove a large part of the contents to find some desired article. Thus, it probably occurred to her that the task could be accomplished with less effort if trays were made that could be removed and replaced easily. Since this still necessitated the removal of all or most of the contents to find an article stored at or near the bottom, the next logical step was to make trays that could be drawn out without disturbing

the others. And so the chest of drawers came to be. This seems the more logical if we consider the fact that many old chests had one or more drawers at the bottom of the box.

The Jacobean chest shown here is a chest-on-chest; so called because the narrower upper section appears to have been placed upon the lower section and to be removable. Indeed, some early chest-on-chests were provided with substantial iron bails, fastened to both ends of the upper section to facilitate its removal, and were held in place by nothing more than the molding on top of the lower section.

The author designed and built this Jacobean chest. The admiration which it evokes in visitors has increased his pride of ownership.

The French-type bracket feet are a digression from the usual ball, bun, or ordinary bracket feet usually found on chests of drawers of so early a

Jacobean Chest of Drawers

139

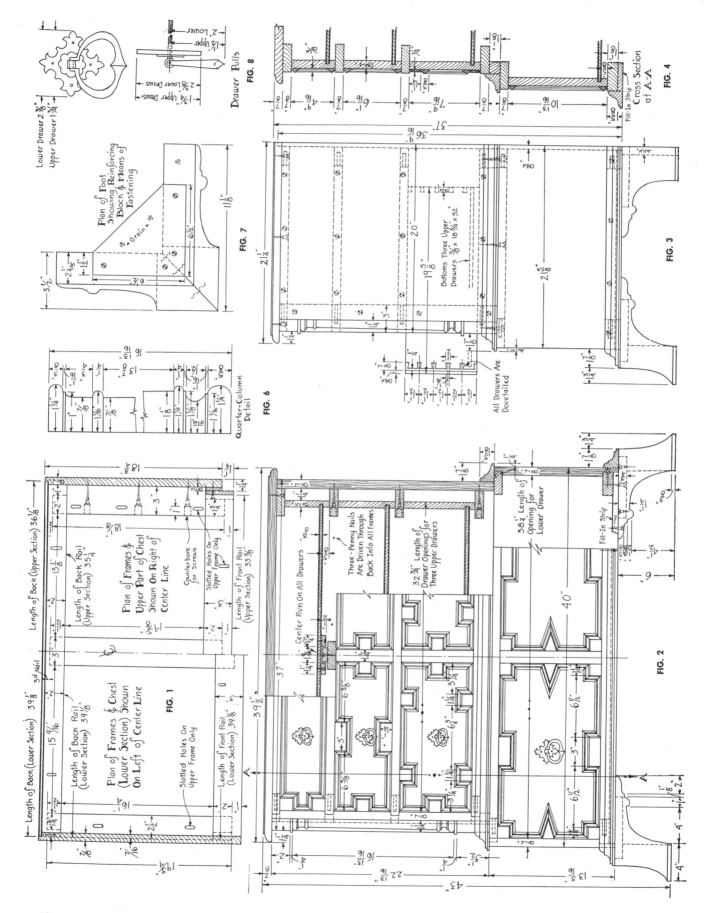

period. The choice is a good one, however, since it carries forward the general widening of the chest at the base.

Drawers on a good chest should do two things: hold a great deal and slide easily. Few things can be more annoying than to have drawers stick.

This piece of furniture should be made of well-seasoned oak, walnut, or maple; the drawer sides should be seasoned white oak or poplar. There should be not less than $\frac{1}{16}$-in. clearance at each end of the drawer and as much at the top. Most important, drawers as long as these should have center runs (Figs. 2 and 5). If properly made and properly aligned, center runs insure drawers which slide easily. Even the largest drawer in this chest, when fully loaded, yields readily to a light pull on either handle.

These drawers are supported by the end rails of the frames, as shown in the cross-section (Fig. 2), and guided in the center by center runs.

A distinct feature of the chest is the interesting pattern formed by the molding applied to the drawer fronts. The small blocks are glued to the face of the drawer fronts, but the molding is nailed on with $\frac{3}{4}$-in. No. 18 brads. To anyone who fears that the molding might loosen, the author wishes to state that this has never once happened since this chest was built in 1928.

BILL OF MATERIAL

DESCRIPTION	PIECES	DIMENSIONS
Ends, upper part of chest	2	$\frac{7}{8}$ x $18\frac{3}{4}$ x $22\frac{13}{16}$
Ends, lower part of chest	2	$\frac{7}{8}$ x $21\frac{5}{8}$ x $13\frac{5}{16}$ or
	1	$\frac{7}{8}$ x $21\frac{5}{8}$ x 27
Top	1	$\frac{7}{8}$ x $21\frac{1}{4}$ x $39\frac{1}{2}$
Stiles to support front of frames, upper chest	2	$\frac{7}{8}$ x 3 x $22\frac{13}{16}$
Battens between stiles and sides, upper chest	2	$\frac{3}{8}$ x $1\frac{3}{4}$ x $22\frac{13}{16}$
Upper drawer front	1	$\frac{7}{8}$ x $4\frac{1}{2}$ x $32\frac{5}{8}$
Second drawer front	1	$\frac{7}{8}$ x 6 x $32\frac{5}{8}$
Third drawer front	1	$\frac{7}{8}$ x $7\frac{1}{2}$ x $32\frac{5}{8}$
Lower drawer front	1	$\frac{7}{8}$ x $10\frac{3}{4}$ x $38\frac{1}{8}$
Upper drawer sides	2	$\frac{5}{8}$ x $4\frac{1}{2}$ x 19
Second drawer sides	2	$\frac{5}{8}$ x 6 x 19
Third drawer sides	2	$\frac{5}{8}$ x $7\frac{1}{2}$ x 19
Lower drawer sides	2	$\frac{5}{8}$ x $10\frac{3}{4}$ x $20\frac{5}{8}$
Upper drawer back	1	$\frac{5}{8}$ x $3\frac{1}{2}$ x $32\frac{5}{8}$
Second drawer back	1	$\frac{5}{8}$ x 5 x $32\frac{5}{8}$
Third drawer back	1	$\frac{5}{8}$ x $6\frac{1}{2}$ x $32\frac{5}{8}$
Lower drawer back	1	$\frac{5}{8}$ x $9\frac{3}{4}$ x $38\frac{1}{8}$
Front rails, four upper frames	4	$\frac{7}{8}$ x 3 x $33\frac{5}{8}$
Back rails, four upper frames	4	$\frac{7}{8}$ x 2 x $35\frac{1}{4}$
End and middle rails, upper frames	12	$\frac{7}{8}$ x 3 x $18\frac{1}{8}$
Front rail, frame above lower drawer	1	$\frac{7}{8}$ x 3 x $39\frac{1}{8}$
Back rail, frame above lower drawer	1	$\frac{7}{8}$ x 2 x $39\frac{1}{8}$
End rails, frame above lower drawer	2	$\frac{7}{8}$ x $2\frac{1}{2}$ x $19\frac{3}{4}$
Middle rail, frame above lower drawer	1	$\frac{7}{8}$ x 3 x $19\frac{3}{4}$
Front rail, frame below lower drawer	1	$1\frac{1}{8}$ x 3 x $39\frac{1}{8}$
Back rail, frame below lower drawer	1	$1\frac{1}{8}$ x 2 x $39\frac{1}{8}$
End rails, frame below lower drawer	2	$1\frac{1}{8}$ x $2\frac{1}{2}$ x $19\frac{3}{4}$

DESCRIPTION	PIECES	DIMENSIONS
Middle rail, frame below lower drawer	1	$1\frac{1}{8}$ x 3 x $19\frac{3}{4}$
Fill-in strip or batten under lower frame in upper section	1	$1\frac{1}{8}$ x $1\frac{3}{8}$ x $32\frac{3}{4}$
Fill-in strip or batten under lower frame below bottom drawer	1	$\frac{1}{2}$ x 3 x $39\frac{1}{8}$
Front feet	4	$3\frac{1}{2}$ x 6 x $11\frac{1}{8}$[1]
Back feet	2	$3\frac{1}{2}$ x 6 x $9\frac{3}{4}$[1]
Board joined to two back feet under chest	1	$\frac{3}{4}$ x 6 x 43
Brace blocks on all feet	4	$\frac{3}{4}$ x $5\frac{3}{4}$ x $10\frac{1}{4}$
Drawer bottoms, three upper drawers (plywood)	3	$\frac{3}{8}$ x $18\frac{3}{4}$ x 32
Drawer bottom, lower drawer (plywood)	1	$\frac{3}{8}$ x $20\frac{1}{4}$ x $37\frac{1}{2}$
Back of chest (plywood)	1	$\frac{3}{8}$ x $36\frac{9}{16}$ x $39\frac{1}{8}$
Center runs, upper drawers	3	$\frac{1}{2}$ x $1\frac{1}{2}$ x $18\frac{3}{8}$
	6	$\frac{1}{2}$ x $1\frac{1}{4}$ x $18\frac{3}{8}$
Center runs, lower drawer	1	$\frac{1}{2}$ x $1\frac{1}{2}$ x 20
	2	$\frac{1}{2}$ x $1\frac{1}{4}$ x 20
Two quarter columns	1	$2\frac{3}{4}$ x $2\frac{3}{4}$ x 18[2]
Small blocks above quarter columns	2	$1\frac{1}{4}$ x $1\frac{1}{4}$ x 2
Small blocks below quarter columns	2	$1\frac{1}{4}$ x $1\frac{1}{4}$ x $3\frac{1}{2}$
Small thin blocks above and below quarter columns	4	$\frac{1}{4}$ x $1\frac{3}{8}$ x $1\frac{3}{8}$
Molding		$1\frac{7}{8}$ x $1\frac{5}{8}$ x 180
Panel molding		$\frac{5}{8}$ x $\frac{3}{8}$ x 550
Thin blocks for decoration of drawers		$\frac{1}{4}$ x $1\frac{1}{4}$ x 108
Hardware:		
8 brass drawer pulls	6	$1\frac{3}{4}$ in. wide
	2	$2\frac{3}{8}$ in. wide
Wood screws, sizes as needed		

[1] All feet may be cut from 1 piece $3\frac{1}{2}$ x 6 x 64.
[2] Glued-up size before turning.

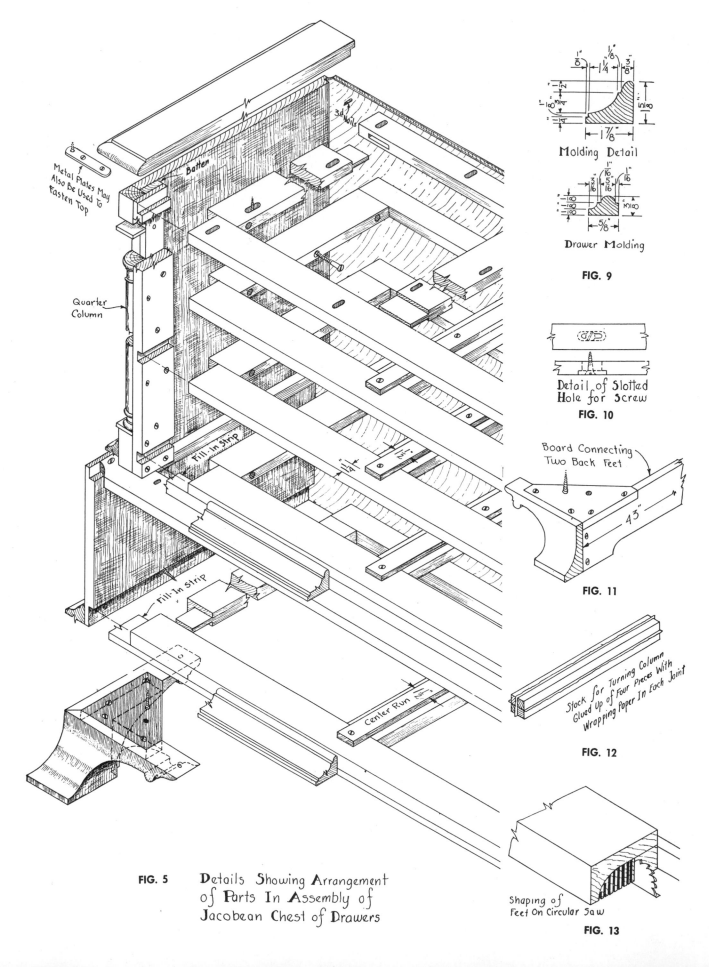

Metal Plates May Also Be Used To Fasten Top

Batten

3d Nails

Quarter Column

Fill-In Strip

Fill-In Strip

Center Run

Molding Detail

Drawer Molding

FIG. 9

Detail of Slotted Hole for Screw

FIG. 10

Board Connecting Two Back Feet

43"

FIG. 11

Stock for Turning Column Glued Up of Four Pieces With Wrapping Paper In Each Joint

FIG. 12

Shaping of Feet On Circular Saw

FIG. 13

FIG. 5   Details Showing Arrangement of Parts In Assembly of Jacobean Chest of Drawers

PROCEDURE

To build the chest of drawers, first glue up the ends of both the upper and lower sections. Since the ends of the lower section are not long, it is better to glue them up in a single piece and later saw the piece in half to make the two ends.

After the ends have been glued up, squared, and dressed to the correct size, make the dadoed stiles which support the fronts of the drawer frames and fasten them to the ends of the upper chest. Place thin battens between the stiles and the ends to make room for the quarter columns (Figs. 1 and 5).

To make quarter columns that will be true quarter columns after they have been split, glue four strips of wood together, each 1⅜ in. square and a little longer than the column. Glue pieces of heavy wrapping paper between these four strips. This will form a piece of stock, 2¾ in. square, which is strong enough to hold the pieces together until they have been turned. After the turning, the column can be split easily into four sections with a chisel, if the split is started correctly in the proper joint. By eliminating the necessity of splitting the column on a band saw and cutting a wide kerf, a true quarter of the turning remains.

Next, make the frames which support and separate the drawers. Join the rails of the frames with mortise-and-tenon joints (Fig. 5). If short screws, like those shown, are used to fasten the frames to the ends, counterbore the rails for the heads and then drill for the screws. The drilling should be done before the frames are assembled.

After the frames have been made and joined and the center runs screwed fast to them, assemble the upper and the lower chests. Rabbet the back edges of the ends to fasten the back to the chest. Rabbet both ends of the lower chest at the top and bottom, as shown in Figures 2 and 5. The slotted holes on the upper frames allow those members which are fastened to them to contract and expand, during different seasons of the year, without splitting. Glue the ends of the front rails into the dadoed grooves of the stiles when assembling the upper chest. Fasten the upper and lower chests together with wood screws.

Make and assemble the feet. The front feet are made of two blocks of wood, 3½ in. thick, mitered at the corners, and held together with glue, corrugated fasteners, and reinforcing blocks (Fig. 7). Make the back foot from a single block. Rabbet it at the back for the board which is to be fastened to both back feet with glue and wood screws (Fig. 11). The curve at the front of the block from which the feet are made is shaped with gouges after the shaping has first been started with a series of saw cuts (Fig. 13). Saw the curved bracketlike shape, shown in Figures 2 and 3, on a band saw after the miter joint has been made on the front feet, and after the recesses and rabbets have been cut for the brace blocks and backboard.

When the feet have been assembled, fasten them to the chest with heavy wood screws, or ¼-in. carriage bolts. If carriage bolts are used countersink the heads.

Drawers for a large chest of drawers such as this should have dovetailed joints (Fig. 3). To lay out dovetails, first draw center lines to determine the position of each pin member of the joint. Then, after setting up the proper angle on a sliding T bevel, lay out the tails and the pins on the sides of the drawer. Saw the tails and pins on a band saw; then, place them on the ends of the drawer front and drawer back; indicate the outlines with a sharp instrument, such as a knife or scriber. Saw the vertical lines of the tail member, with a dovetail saw, and chop out the remainder with sharp chisels. Make and fit the bottom, and assemble the drawer with glue.

Now, fit each drawer to its respective opening, trimming and making the necessary adjustments for an easy-sliding drawer.

Next, make and glue the small blocks to the faces of the drawer fronts, clean off the glue around the blocks when it has dried, and saw and nail on the molding with ¾-in. brads.

Screw and glue the blocks and quarter columns to their respective corners; make, mold the edges, and fasten the top to the chest. The job is completed, except for hand sanding and finishing.

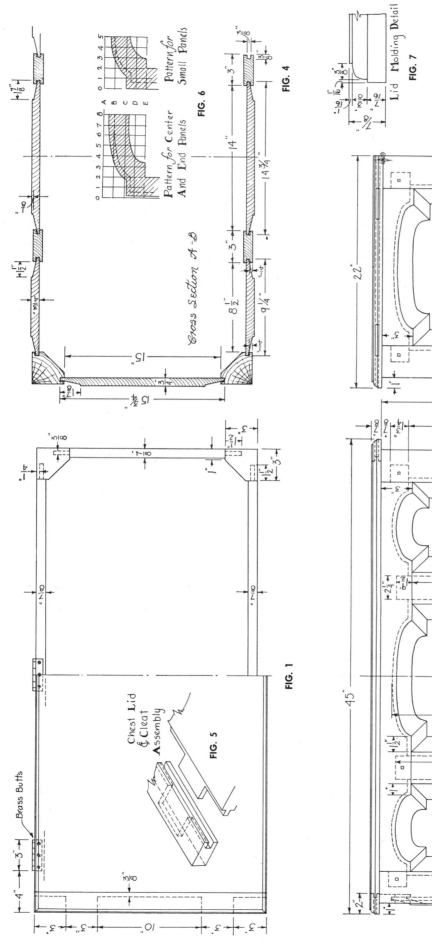

Pattern for Small Panels

FIG. 6

Pattern for Center And End Panels

Cross Section A-B

FIG. 4

Brass Butts

FIG. 1

Chest Lid & Cleat Assembly

FIG. 5

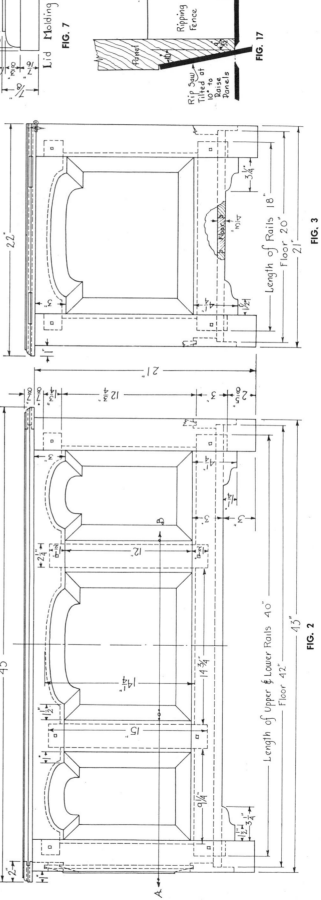

Lid Molding Detail

FIG. 7

Ripping Fence

Rip Saw Tilted at 10° to Raise Panels

Panel

FIG. 17

Length of Rails 18"
Floor 20"
21"

FIG. 3

Length of Upper & Lower Rails 40"
Floor 42"
45"

FIG. 2

26.

PANELED   CEDAR   CHESTS

Chests were used universally in early times to store clothing, bedding, and household gear of every description. They often were prized highly and many fine pieces, excellently preserved, have been handed down through the generations. In the author's family there are three very fine heirloom chests, one of which has been inherited by the author. Many of these fine pieces were dower chests, made expressly to the order of clients who wished to provide daughters of marriageable age with what is now called a hope chest.

Early chests, especially in New England usually were made of oak or pine. The oak chests frequently were ornately decorated with carvings, heavy moldings, or applied ornaments such as bosses, split turnings, and the like. Pine chests were often plain and unadorned, having possibly been made for people in the lower classes.

In Pennsylvania, chests frequently were made of yellow poplar or black walnut. Those made of poplar often were painted with distinctive and brightly colored designs which set them apart from other early American chests. Black walnut chests were seldom painted but were beautifully made, with well-executed, corner dovetail joints.

Many chests had handsome bracket feet and two or three drawers below the chest proper with handsome brass drawer pulls. A fine heirloom chest such as this now belongs to the author's sister. The author's chest, originally hand-painted poplar, had been covered with red paint by his maternal grandfather while in his possession. Many similar, fine old chests have been spoiled. When the author finds sufficient time, he plans to restore the original design, traces of which are still discernible through the offending rusty red.

In recent years, cedar chests have been preferred, although with cedar has come a decline in beauty of design. It is difficult to understand why this should be, unless it reflects the lack of taste, generally, in furniture of this particular era. There is no excuse for ugly cedar chests. Knotty wood has great natural beauty, as the photograph below clearly shows. If unmarked cedar is preferred, wider boards from large trees are almost devoid of knots. In addition to cedar the two chests presented here can be made of any good cabinet wood, for the beauty of the paneling is decoration enough.

PROCEDURE

Since these chests are alike in size and their construction is essentially the same, one set of directions will be given for both, with any exceptions being noted.

Because of the knotty structure of aromatic red cedar, the material from which both chests are made, it is far easier to select good stock from comparatively small pieces than from a large flat piece the size of a whole front and back. This is one advantage of this type of construction. By breaking up the front and back into small, well-proportioned panels, stiles, and rails, it is possible to achieve very interesting effects, as can be seen in the photographs.

Cedar Chest with arched panels

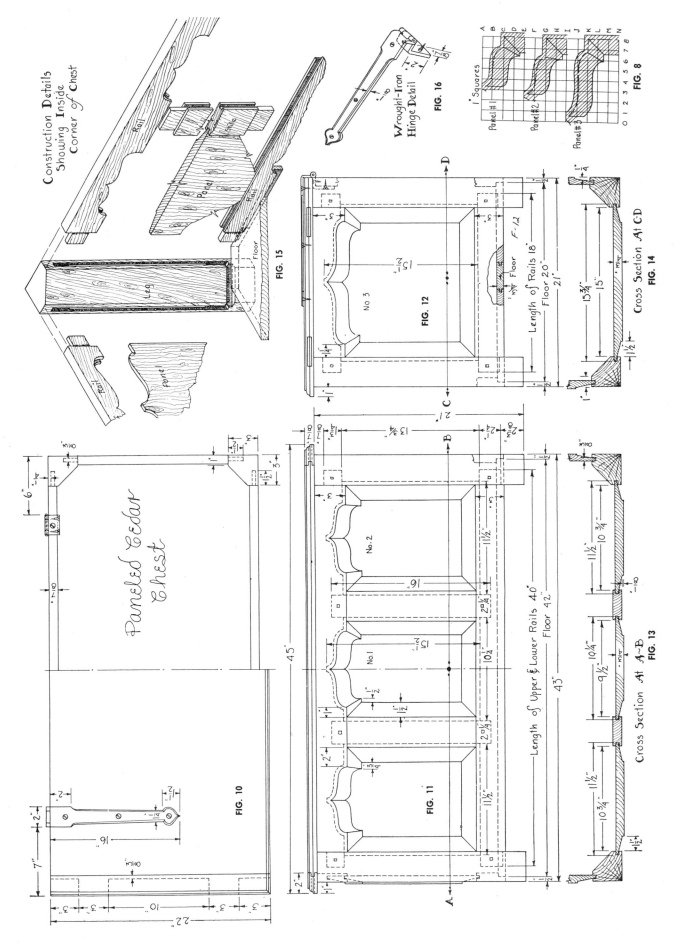

Construction Details
Showing Inside
Corner of Chest

FIG. 15

Wrought-Iron
Hinge Detail
FIG. 16

FIG. 8

FIG. 12

Cross Section At CD
FIG. 14

Paneled Cedar
Chest

FIG. 10

FIG. 11

Cross Section At A-B
FIG. 13

To build either one of the chests, first plane and square the legs to the correct size. Then bevel the inside corner of each leg on a jointer (Fig. 9) by tilting the jointer fence to an angle of 45-deg.

Lay out and cut the mortises on the legs as indicated in Figures 1, 2, and 3 *or* 10, 11, and 12. Groove the legs for the panels with a ⅜-in. dado head on a variety saw. Since the grooves are not cut the entire length of the legs, take care to start and end them at the bottom of the upper mortise and at the top of the lower mortise (Fig. 15). Some consider it safer to do the grooving before the mortising. Complete the legs by cutting grooves, ⅜ in. deep and ¾ in. wide, across the legs where the splayed corners of the floor will be fitted into them. The lower edge of this groove is 3 in. from the floor on the chest with the arched panels, and 2 in. from the floor on the chest with the pointed panels.

Next, make the rails and stiles. Cut the tenons on these pieces with a dado head on a variety saw. Do not cut arches on the upper rails or brackets on the lower rails until all mortises, tenons, and grooves have been cut.

Cut grooves on all rails and stiles with a ⅜-in. dado head on a variety saw. Run full-length grooves on one edge of each upper and lower

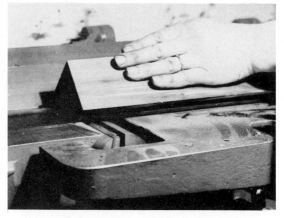

Fig. 9. Bevel the inside corner of each leg on a jointer.

rail and the full length on both edges of the stiles. Now, lay out and cut the mortises on the rails. Then lay out and saw the arches on the bottom edges of the upper rails on a band saw, and file and sand these edges smooth. Groove the arched parts of these rails on a mortising machine. Also cut the rabbets for the floor on the bottom edges of the lower rails. In the chest with the arched panels, the groove will run the full length of the lower rail. When the waste is cut off to form the brackets, part of this groove will serve as a rabbet.

BILL OF MATERIAL

DESCRIPTION	PIECES	DIMENSIONS
CHEST WITH ARCHED TOPS ON PANELS		
Legs	4	3 x 3 x 21
Upper rails, front and back	2	⅞ x 3 x 40
Lower rails, front and back	2	⅞ x 4¼ x 40
Upper rails, ends	2	⅞ x 3 x 18
Lower rails, ends	2	⅞ x 4¼ x 18
Stiles, front and back	4	⅞ x 3 x 15
Floor (glued up from narrow boards with tongued-and-grooved edges)	1	¾ x 20 x 42
Large panels, front and back[1]	2	¾ x 14¾ x 14¼
Small panels, front and back[1]	4	¾ x 9¼ x 14¼
Panels for ends	2	¾ x 15¾ x 14¼
Lid (glued up)	1	⅞ x 22 x 45
Hardware:		
Cleats for ends of lid	2	⅞ x 2 x 22
Three 3 in. heavy brass butt hinges		

DESCRIPTION	PIECES	DIMENSIONS
CHEST WITH POINTED TOPS ON PANELS		
Legs	4	3 x 3 x 21
Top and bottom rails, front and back	4	⅞ x 3 x 40
Top and bottom rails, ends	4	⅞ x 3 x 18
Stiles, front and back	4	⅞ x 3 x 16
Middle panels (No. 1), front and back[2]	2	¾ x 10¼ x 15½
End panels (No. 2), front and back[2]	4	¾ x 11½ x 15½
Panel for ends of chest (No. 3)	2	¾ x 15¾ x 15½
Bottom of chest[3]	1	¾ x 20 x 42
Lid[3]	1	⅞ x 22 x 45
Hardware:		
Cleats for ends of lid	2	⅞ x 2 x 22
2 wrought-iron chest hinges		

---

[1] It is not necessary to arch the panels at the back of the chest. If these are left straight, make them only 12¾ in. long.

[2] The panels at the back of the chest can be made **straight** on top instead of shaped. If this is done, make them only 13¾ in. long.

[3] Glued up of narrow boards with tongued-and-grooved edges.

Cedar Chest with pointed panels

Make a trial assembly of the frame, fitting all joints together properly.

Next, glue up the panels. Scrape and sandpaper both sides until smooth. Raise these panels by tilting the circular saw to an angle of 10 deg., and cutting the beveled molding around the edges of the panels. Hold the panel upright when pushing it across the saw (Fig. 8). Hand-carve the shaped tops of the panels, using a full-sized pattern made from Figure 6 or 17.

After sawing the molding of the panels, scrape and sand where necessary to make the panels smooth. Assemble and glue the sides. Do not glue the panels to the frames. Only the mortises and tenons are glued. The panels, though snugly fitted, remain loose in their grooves to permit swelling and shrinking during different seasons of the year. Aside from the beauty provided by paneling, this construction is the principal reason for paneled construction.

To assemble the chest, glue up the floor, properly fitting it to the grooves of every bracket and every leg. Then glue up the two ends. Each end includes two legs, the upper and lower rail, and the panel. While the clamps are still in place, drill holes through every mortise-and-tenon joint, driving roughly octagoned pegs into the holes to strengthen the joints. Next, glue up the front and back frames; each frame consists of upper and lower rails, two stiles, and three panels. Slip the panels into their respective places just before the upper rail, the last piece to be attached, is put in place. Place one of the assembled ends face down on a clean floor. Apply glue to the mortises and tenons on the front and join it to the end lying on the floor. Then join the floor board to the assembled front and one end, the back to these assembled parts, and, finally, the second end to this assembled portion. This completes the chest proper.

Glue up the boards to make the lid. Cut grooves, ⅜ by ⅜ in., into one edge of each cleat, and then two grooves through the mortises of each cleat (see the top views of Fig. 1 and 10). Another detail of this joint is shown in Figure 5. Cut tongues and tenons on the ends of the main section of the lid and glue these three parts together. Scrape and sandpaper the lid on both sides; then cut a molding on three sides. The top of the chest must be made level so that the top will fit on it perfectly flat.

Attach the hinges. Either the beautiful wrought-iron strap hinges (Fig. 16) or the more common butt hinges (Fig. 1) can be used.

The finish on a cedar chest should be applied to the outside of the chest only, otherwise the aromatic quality of the wood will be lost. Often nothing more than a number of coats of shellac or varnish will be applied, with the proper steel-wooling between coats and a pumice-stone rub for the final coat. A good color can be obtained by applying a transparent oil stain of burnt sienna and turpentine. This gives a deep orange hue to the cedar. Follow with the usual finishing coats.

27.

FURNITURE FINISHING

A book on furniture making is not complete unless it treats the important step of applying the finish, especially since the quality of the finish is as important in determining the worth of the finished product as the quality of its design and construction.

The type of finish to be put on a piece of furniture depends to some extent upon the kind of wood which has been used. Generally speaking, wood used for furniture falls into two classifications. These are hardwoods, which come from broad-leaf trees, including oak, maple, walnut, and mahogany, and softwoods, which come from the cone-bearing trees such as pine and cedar.

The softwoods, and some of the semihardwoods such as birch and gum are nonporous or so slightly porous that they need no filling during the process of finishing.

Many of the hardwoods, however, are decidedly porous. Into this group fall oak, walnut, and mahogany; and these require a filler. Others, slightly less porous, such as birch, maple, poplar, or gum, may or may not require filler, depending upon the judgment of the finisher and the quality of the finish wanted.

Regardless of the type of wood used, the completed piece must be inspected carefully for blemishes, such as file marks, dents, plane or machine marks, and scratches. The finest piece of furniture in this book will look no better than its finish, and the beauty and quality of the finish depend largely upon how thoroughly the blemishes are removed. A very thorough job of sanding and preparing the surface is required to make it smooth and get a high-quality finish. While many of these blemishes can be removed by hand-planing, scraping, and machine-sanding, hand-sanding is still the best way to prepare a surface that is smooth enough to achieve a fine finish.

Hand-sanding can be done with ordinary flint papers, but a much finer job is accomplished with garnet papers, since the abrasive material is much sharper. If flint papers are used, start the sanding with a No. 1 paper, except where thin veneers or carvings are to be sanded. Finer papers will have to be used on the latter. The grit of a No. 1 flint paper about matches that of a No. 2/0 garnet paper so far as roughness of the abrasive surface is concerned, but No. 2/0 garnet paper will do a much faster and better smoothing job. Use finer papers as the surface becomes smoother, ending with No. 4/0 flint paper, or No. 6/0 and even No. 8/0 garnet papers.

In sanding a piece of furniture, it is sometimes necessary to sand parts of a joint across the grain. All final sanding operations should be done parallel to the grain, for, as the saying goes: "Sand it twenty times with the grain to remove a scratch made by sanding once across the grain."

It is often difficult to detect minor blemishes or scratches on an unfinished surface but these markings will show up very distinctly after the stain has been applied. Look closely to detect the faulty parts of a surface, viewing it from various angles by tilting or turning the piece being examined so the light hits it at different angles. Only in this way can all blemishes be detected.

After the surface has been thoroughly prepared, choose one of the methods of furniture finishing appropriate for the piece made. A really fine finish requires a large number of operations; there are a number of shorter methods which will reduce the time, cost, and work involved, but also, of course, the quality of the finished product.

A few notes on finishing have been included in several of the chapters, for example, the method suggested for getting a most interesting color on the mahogany of the Hepplewhite dining-room suite. A method of finishing used in Colonial days, which has not been greatly improved upon even to this day, will now be described briefly.

To do it well will involve a great deal of time and hard work, and therefore, it should not be attempted without a willingness to spend hours of time and effort. A full description of this process was given to the author by Mr. William Moeller of Gilbertsville, Pa. Mr. Moeller has had great success in refinishing a number of his fine antiques with this process, which has been called an oil finish, a hard oil finish or an oil and wax finish. The process consists of applying a considerable number of applications of boiled linseed oil, and then rubbing vigorously to build up a rich glossy surface. This type of finish is not recommended for softwoods, on which the more conventional modern finishes will give better results. It is, however, an excellent finish for mahogany, walnut, cherry, or oak. It will darken the wood on which it is used. Stains to color the wood are seldom used or needed when this method of finishing is employed.

After the wood has been prepared for finishing, mix boiled linseed oil with an equal amount of turpentine and warm the mixture in a double boiler or over steampipes to a temperature of about 80-deg. Warm oil will soak into the wood much more readily than cold. The work also should be done in a warm room. Apply this mixture often, two or three times a day, until, after a twenty-four-hour period the wood will absorb no more of it. Do no rubbing until this point has been reached; then sprinkle fine pumice powder over the surface to be rubbed and, using a burlap pad,[1] rub the surface vigorously. A burlap pad is recommended since it does not form ridges as a soft cloth would. Repeat the application of pumice and oil and the rubbing for four to five days. Be sure to clean off *all* residue after each rubbing, or what is left will cause scoring of the wood when the next rubbing is begun. At about the third application of pumice with the oil, use clear linseed oil without adding any turpentine. The final rubbing should be done with rottenstone and oil to get a higher gloss. Finally, finish the job with an application of a prepared carnauba wax polish, which can be purchased from a paint supply house. To keep the surface in good condition, renew it once every two years with an application of oil, well rubbed in, and wax polish.

The conventional methods of finishing usually begin with staining to get the desired color and to bring out the full, rich beauty of the grain. Two types of stain are recommended: water stain and oil stain.

Water stains are cheaper, are quite transparent, and permit a wide choice of colors. These stains can be bought in powder form and are usually soluble in hot water. Sometimes they are reduced first with a little hot water, and then special solvents supplied by the manufacturer are added to make them "non-grain-raising." Water stains dry very slowly and raise the grain considerably during the process, so that resanding after staining is always required. This does not alter the color of the surface since deep penetration is one of the prime qualities of a good water stain. Sometimes the surface is simply wet down with a sponge before staining and sanded before the stain is applied. This reduces the amount of sanding required after staining, but does not eliminate the necessity for resanding after the piece has been stained and thoroughly dried. Some manufacturers of finishing materials offer concentrated liquid water stains which must be greatly diluted before they can be used. Water stains can be brushed or sprayed on, and sometimes the wood is dipped into large vats containing the proper staining solution. Another important advantage of water stain is that almost any color can be mixed or matched easily by properly combining the three primary colors. The colors may also be tinted or shaded with white or black.

Oil stains, unlike water stains, do not raise the grain of the wood and offer an equally wide range of colors. They are somewhat less troublesome for the amateur to use, but are more expensive. Oil stains also are not as transparent as water stains, and the pigments in them will leave a slightly opaque film upon the surface.

Oil stains can be brushed on in any direction. After the stain has soaked well into the wood, the wood is wiped clean with soft cotton rags.

Sometimes a very thin sealer is applied to the wood before it is stained to prevent the wood from absorbing too much stain, or to get a more uniform color over the entire surface. This is a good procedure for some hardwoods such as maple, which has a texture which makes it difficult to get color uniformity without using a sealer first. Sealers are made of shellac or varnish and thinned with the proper thinning agents: for shellac, alcohol; and for varnish, turpentine or

---

[1] Dispose immediately of all rags soaked with finishing materials, since spontaneous-combustion fires start easily.

mineral spirits. These sealers should be very greatly reduced before application. Generally speaking, there should be several times as much reducing agent as there is sealer, since too heavy a coat of sealer will prevent the wood from absorbing any stain at all. Experiment with scraps of wood first to get the desired results.

On softwoods or woods with a nonporous surface, staining can be followed with a coat of sealer. In addition to the sealers mentioned above, lacquer sealers also are used. Because lacquer is quick drying, it should be sprayed on the surface, since it dries so rapidly that application with a brush is difficult. The purpose of using a sealer over stain or filler is to tie them down and give good adhesion to subsequent finishing applications.

Where porous woods, such as mahogany, walnut, or oak, are to be finished, follow the staining with an application of filler. Sometimes a wash of greatly reduced sealer is applied over the stain before the filler coating, for example, in the case of chestnut wood or oak which have coarse, open pores. Usually, however, it is recommended that the filler be applied directly over the stain.[2]

In filling, the most satisfactory results are obtained if the filler is the exact color of the stain. Fillers can be sprayed or brushed on. The better ones come in a semipaste form and usually are thinned with turpentine or some other reducing agent recommended by the manufacturer. An average mixture consists of a gallon of semipaste to a gallon of the reducing agent, but this mixture varies considerably to suit the requirements of the job. After application, allow the filler to "set up" for a short period of time; usually 15 to 20 minutes, until it begins to lose its wet appearance. Then rub the filler well into the open pores of the wood first across the grain and then with the grain, to remove any streaks resulting from the cross-grain rubbing. Rub the filler into the wood with the hand and with pads made of burlap.

Exercise great care in putting on fillers, for once they begin to harden they will do so very rapidly. If every last vestige of surface filler is not quickly

and thoroughly removed, it will harden like a coat of paint, and can only be removed by re-sanding the surface back down to the bare wood. For this reason, it is essential to fill only small areas at a time; or if a large area is to be treated, several people will have to help. Always follow the filler with a coat of sealer.

Allow the sealer coat to dry overnight or longer, and then sand or rub it down. Sand with very fine grit papers and rub with steel wool parallel to the grain whenever possible. There will be places where cross-grain sanding will be unavoidable. When this operation has been completed satisfactorily and the whole surface is smooth, remove every particle of dust with a soft bristle brush or cloth. The cloth may have to be dampened with a small amount of very thin sealer to remove the last traces of lint or dust from the surface.

The sealer is followed with two or more finishing coats, depending upon the type of finish being applied and the quality of finish desired. Lacquer should never be used over a varnish sealer, though sometimes it is applied over a shellac sealer. Varnish can be used over a shellac sealer, though some wood-finishing authorities frown upon it. The author, over a period of many years, has obtained good and long-lasting results by using tough floor varnishes over sealing coats of thin shellac, and he has yet to experience a failure as a result of this practice.

In recent years many new finishing products have appeared on the market. A very good one is a type of varnish known as floor sealer. Floor sealer is almost water thin compared to regular varnish but it is exceedingly tough and durable both as a sealer and a surface finish. Since it is slow drying, it has exceptional penetrating qualities. The author has found it superior to most varnishes when properly used.

If lacquer sealers are used under a varnish finish, spray on two coats of lacquer. Two great advantages of a lacquer finish are: (1) it dries quickly and is, therefore, more dust-free than a varnish finish, and (2) it is available in dry glossy, semiglossy, and dull or flat finishes. Because of the second advantage, the final operation of costly and time consuming hand-rubbing often may be eliminated entirely. Hand-rubbing is desirable, however, to get a higher-grade finish, even when lacquer is used.

Varnish and shellac give excellent results when properly used as finishing coats, and are desirable

---

[2] These methods, recommended and used by the author, digress somewhat from general practice employed in many furniture factory finishing rooms. General practice in these factories uses a sealer under the filler, but the author found that in most instances the sealer obscures rather than accentuates the grain and natural beauty of the wood. It would be wise for the craftsman to experiment and select the method he prefers.

if the application is to be done with a brush. Additional coats of shellac will be needed to build up the proper surface for a good hand-rubbed job if shellac alone is used for surface coats. Many coats of thin shellac are preferable to a few heavier coats, because a heavy coat of shellac seldom gives smooth, uniform coverage. Varnish dries much more slowly, therefore uniform coverage is possible, especially if the room temperature is 75 deg. or warmer during the brushing and drying.

Every coat of finish — lacquer, varnish, or shellac — must be sanded or rubbed down with fine steel wool (No. 2/0, 4/0, or finer), and then dusted off before the next coat is applied. Only on the last coat is the procedure different; the last coat should be rubbed instead with powdered pumice stone and rubbing oil — a thin paraffin oil especially manufactured for the purpose. If a shellac or lacquer finish is used, overnight drying is sufficient before the next coat is applied; but most high-grade varnishes require a much longer drying time, often as much as 48 hours before.

A good job of hand-rubbing is achieved by first sanding the surface with a No. 360 or No. 320 wet-or-dry sandpaper, lubricated either with rubbing oil alone or with rubbing oil mixed with other thinners to allow faster cutting. The surface is then rubbed with a felt block which is kept well soaked in a mixture of XXX powdered pumice stone and rubbing oil until a perfectly level, glossy surface has been produced. For a high polish, follow this step with a rubbing of rottenstone and oil. The surface is then thoroughly wiped off until clean with soft cotton cloths. Polish the surface from time to time with wax to preserve the finish.

The foregoing covers most of the operations followed in producing a high-grade finish on a piece of furniture. Many other phases of furniture finishing, such as glazing, shading, bleaching, and preparation for refinishing, have not been discussed, while some essentials have been described very briefly, since only the minimum essentials could be treated in one short chapter.

Another phase of finishing should be discussed briefly and that is bleaching. For a bleaching process which is practical for the amateur to employ, the Sherwin-Williams Brochure, F-501, recommends the following procedure:

"Based upon experiments, an ideal bleaching system would be as follows: hydrogen peroxide is applied to the wood first and the piece is then placed in a closet or confined space in the presence of ammonia vapors. This bleaches deeply, and the wood can be sanded well without danger of cutting through to the unbleached wood.

"Wood bleached by this method has a natural appearance. The grain stands out and is clear . . . there are no salts or residual bleaching materials remaining on the wood to affect further finishing. This method is economical since only a double coat of hydrogen peroxide is applied and no caustic is needed. Also, no neutralizer is needed after bleaching. The closet or confined space should be air-tight, and the size would depend upon the size and number of pieces to be bleached at one time. This system may be used on unassembled wood or on the completed piece.

"The enclosed area confines the ammonia vapors, preventing their escape because of the very volatile nature of ammonia. The vapors then remain longer in contact with the wood and do a more complete job of bleaching. A pan partially filled with household ammonia is placed somewhere in the confined room. The wood is given a coat of the hydrogen peroxide by applying either with a rag or sponge. A few minutes should be allowed for the solution to soak into the wood. Another coat is then applied and the pieces immediately placed in the presence of the ammonia fumes.

"Several hours may be required for the bleaching operation to become complete. As soon as the panel or piece of furniture is dry, it can be sanded and finished. No neutralizer or cleaning agent is necessary."

INDEX

(Wherever practical, the page reference is to the drawing rather than the text since the drawing is of greater importance to the experienced craftsman.)

Photo:Christopher Dow/View-1

After an antique of Portuguese design, ca.1680. Solid aged English oak.
Crafted in our East Anglia workshop. Each piece signed and dated.

ELIJAH SLOCUM

FINE HANDMADE ENGLISH FURNITURE

LOS ANGELES   DALLAS   WASHINGTON, D.C.   HOUSTON   NEW YORK
Tel: 800.310.8011   www.elijahslocum.com

Jacques Lamy

JACQUES LAMY DESIGNS

CUSTOM FINE ART: CLASSICAL · CUSTOM · ABSTRACT

1607 DRAGON STREET   DALLAS, TEXAS 75207   PHONE 214-747-7611   FAX 214-747-7611

BROCHURE AVAILABLE: $10